Jermaine E. Martin

American Mindset

Unstuck & Unstoppable

AMERICAN MINDSET

UNSTUCK & UNSTOPPABLE

By Jermaine E. Martin

Copyright © 2019 by Jermaine E. Martin

All rights reserved. No part of this book may be reproduced or transmitted in any form or by any means, electronic or mechanical, including photocopying, recording or by any information storage and retrieval system, without the written permission of the author, Jermaine E. Martin.

Cover design and layout by Jermaine E. Martin.
Buck Commander™ Logo is a registered trademark of Under Armour®.

Pre-First Edition: May 2019

DEDICATION

This book is dedicated to my grandparents, Ethel Lee Martin and George Howard Martin who taught me that seeing the beauty in all things is a mindset.

ACKNOWLEDGEMENTS

First and foremost, thank you to my Lord and Savior Jesus Christ for his continuous Grace. Any great achievement in life is only possible through the Grace of GOD. Without Him and the encouragement, love, and support of my loving bride and soulmate, the journey to create this project and follow my dreams would never have been possible. I am also forever grateful to be blessed with a strong and loving mother that provides me with the foundation to live life with courage and love. Much gratitude and love also goes out to my best friend Shane, who has been by my side through every great battle, victory, and achievement. I love you like a brother. Also, a strong thank you goes out to my friend Glastinne, who saw the success of this book before I typed the first word. Your belief and support in the vision will always be appreciated.

For my unwavering desire to fight for truth and do right by my country, I am forever thankful to those who have served or currently serve in our great armed forces. Last but not least, I would like to thank all of my relentless teachers and professors who pushed me when I needed to be pushed. Out of this tough love, my American Mindset was born.

> "To tell you my story is to tell of Him."
>
> -Big Daddy Weave, "My Story"

"The righteous will flourish like a palm tree." —Psalm 92:12-14

CONTENTS

INTRODUCTION 1

1. VALENTINE'S DAY 5

2. A CUP OF COFFEE IN BRUSSELS 7

3. PLAYING THE CARDS DEALT 15

4. THE PROJECTS 25

5. ELEMENTARY SCHOOL 75

6. MOVING TO THE SUBURBS 99

7. FAST TIMES AT SURRATTSVILLE HIGH 127

8. THE DIVORCE 155

9. A FOOL'S GOLD 175

10. BEAUTY FOR ASHES 193

11. IN THE CLOSET	**221**
12. TAKING NEW TERRITORY	**235**
13. MUSIC	**245**
14. NOT WITHOUT "HIS" APPROVAL	**259**
15. A GOOD GUY WITH A GUN	**273**
16. AWAKENING THE PATRIOT	**283**
17. THE POWER OF MOMENTUM	**293**
18. STUCK: THE COMFORT ZONE	**301**
19. UNSTUCK: TIME TO MAKE THE DONUTS	**345**
20. AWAKENING THE ENTREPRENEUR	**351**
21. ASKING THE RIGHT QUESTIONS: CRITICAL THINKING	**383**
22. UNSTOPPABLE	**397**

AMERICAN MINDSET

UNSTUCK & UNSTOPPABLE

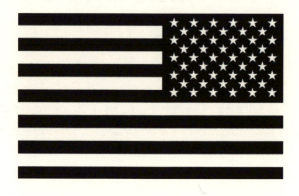

THIS FLAG IS STRONG

INTRODUCTION

"After all these years, I finally realized that sometimes the greatest gift that GOD gives us is OUR STORY. It is through His grace and our perseverance through the toughest of times that we are awakened to our true gifts." - Jermaine Martin, Author

This book was written from my complete heart and soul. Through it, I open myself up to reveal personal challenges and failures and my journey to overcome them. It is an American journey. One that is shared with the hope and purpose of inspiring and empowering others to step into their own personal greatness —to become the "you" that GOD intended you to be.

Throughout this journey of remaining "Unstuck & Unstoppable," there are, like all journeys, inevitable ups and downs. The challenge to keep moving forward has always been allowing faith to overpower fear. "Not feeling ready" or "not being enough" is typically at the heart of most of our fears that will keep us stuck. In the Bible, GOD tells Moses to use what's in his hand when he questions how to lead his people across the Red Sea. With only a rod in his hand, that proved to be enough to divide the sea and lead his people to freedom. What do you have in your hand? What abilities and talents do you have immediately at your disposal that can get you closer to your dreams? These are questions we should all ask ourselves when we think that the "things" that we carry with us every day aren't enough to get us where we need to go.

Growing and moving forward in life starts first with acknowledging and overcoming our challenges. It is then that we can take responsibility for our own personal success and happiness. Facing life's temptations and challenges, we all have the ability to set our own course, not succumbing to the unproductive forces and distractions of our past experiences or our current situations. Our ability to resist the destructive influences of our emotions on our decision making process is key. It's all about our mindset and our willingness to train and discipline our thoughts in ways that will propel us forward instead of holding us back. As a result we can begin to make informed decisions and choices in our life that are grounded in truth and reason as opposed to emotion.

As we consider the many possible journeys in life, there is no place on Earth that allows us to spread our wings further and step into our own personal greatness more so than in the United States of America —if you are willing to work for it. This great country was founded on timeless principles of freedom that protect individual rights, encourage personal responsibility, and cultivate personal achievement. The journey to understanding this great country and its ability to empower each and every one of us begins with sharing and analyzing my own personal American journey. Coming from the streets of a public housing project in Washington, D.C., the odds of achieving the American Dream appeared not to be on my side. Developing a mindset early on that refused to play victim was key to opening doors and developing the confidence needed to achieve and grow. No journey is without pain of course and my life has been no different.

In life, true greatness cannot be achieved without faith and sacrifice. There are no free rides or free lunches in this world. The character that results from individual effort and hard work is at the heart of greatness. As a nation, these are ideals that "We the People" of the United States of America have traditionally lived by. The greatest nation on earth has undoubtedly achieved much following these sound principles. GOD's grace and the tremendous sacrifice of those that came before us have forever blessed this nation. The very birth of the nation itself and the freedoms that we enjoy today were paid for with a heavy price. As written by the Founders, the last line in the Declaration of Independence sums up this price so powerfully:

"And for the support of this Declaration, with a firm reliance on the protection of divine Providence, we mutually pledge to each other our Lives, our Fortunes and our sacred Honor."

Through GOD's grace, focus, and commitment, I push to remain on a forward path in life. As I travel this path, my mission is to awaken passion for this great country and discover the secrets and principles behind America's true greatness. Join me on this American journey of self-discovery and achieving true greatness for ourselves and our country. No other country has done more to uplift the human spirit more so than the United States of America. As individuals and as a country, we always have to be willing to grow through our challenges and put truth above all else. It is only then that we can become, as people and a nation, truly Unstuck and Unstoppable.

- Chapter 1 -

Valentine's Day

It was a day to celebrate love. The year was 2007 and it was Valentine's Day. My fiancé and I celebrated the special day by breaking out one of those "cheesy" romantic card games where we got to ask each other random questions on topics we had never discussed or opened up to each other about. One of the first questions was —"What is something that is very special to you that you haven't shared with me or anyone else?" At first, it seemed like a "gotcha" question that could get you into trouble if you didn't give the right answer. After all, the whole point of this couples game was to heat things up. For some reason, this particular question made both of us pause and really think about what we were going to say. Of course, my fiancé had already made up her mind that I had to go first. After hesitating for a few seconds, all of a sudden I became slightly emotional and said —"My Country."

Before that day, I had never talked about or expressed so poignantly to anyone, the love that I have for this country. I always felt proud to be an American and knew that I was blessed to be born here, but I never felt the level of emotion and appreciation for this country as I felt the moment I answered that question. It was as if a spark went off inside of me. By speaking my feelings, I gave life to my feelings. From this random Valentine's Day card game, came an awakening in my life —a sense of purpose. From that day on, my mind and heart began to open up to what it truly means to be an American. My desire to learn about the things that make this country great grew stronger from that day forward. The journey to follow my passion of promoting love for this great country had begun.

    We are truly blessed to live in a country where we are free to be all that GOD made us to be. Using our GOD given gifts and abilities, the sky is the limit on how far we can go. Taking a look at the often dark history of humankind, you can easily see that there is something truly special about America. What is it that makes this country unique? Why do people come from all over the world to pursue their dreams here? Why is America considered the land of opportunity? What are the conditions in this country that allow us to excel in sports, innovation, and entrepreneurship? Throughout my life, I always knew America was special. As I got older, it wasn't enough to just know. I wanted to know why —in practical, common sense terms! One of the first things I was taught during my studies as an engineering student in college was that to understand the complex, you must first break things down to their simplest parts and components. Could I apply these same principles to figuring out what makes America so successful as a country? Could I also discover a success formula for those who want to achieve their dreams and live life to the fullest? The following chapters of this book reveal my journey to do just that.

- Chapter 2 -

A Cup of Cofee in Brussels

Traveling was something that I always watched other people do. Growing up as a kid in a public housing project in Washington, D.C., I would watch television shows that depicted traveling and vacation life as something that only the well-to-do took part in. In our home, the words "Remember that trip to…" were never uttered. There were no photo albums with vacation photos on our coffee table. In fact, it was very rare for anyone in my family to even fly, let alone take a vacation. One of the only childhood memories I have of anyone in my family actually flying on a plane was of my aunt, who had to take a flight to St. Louis from D.C. for work. It was a big deal. Her trip was such a big deal that my entire family piled in two cars to take her to the airport. It's amazing how the significance of something is so much related to where we are in life. Because my family struggled financially, we weren't exposed to a life of vacationing and air travel. Something as simple as catching a flight out of town for work was just as exciting as if someone in the family had hit the lottery.

At the time, being black and living in low-income public housing, there were just certain things that we considered outside of our perceived reality. As a result, the desire for vacation and travel, which should have been a part of our lives, tended to get dismissed or ignored. In the case of traveling, the idea or even suggestion of taking a flight out of town for a vacation was never even brought up in a conversation. Unfortunately, such perceived limited realities can be passed down from one generation to the next, as was the case for me. My lack of exposure to traveling early on in life eventually evolved into fear —a fear of flying and a penchant for fear of the unknown and unfamiliar.

As someone who had a "fear of flying" throughout his entire childhood and most of his early adult life, it wasn't until I turned thirty before I finally got the nerve to get on a plane. My battle to overcome the debilitating fear of flying began the day I was invited on a trip with some friends to South Beach Miami. For the very first time in my life, I was determined to overcome the fear of flying. It started by first convincing myself that no person in their right mind would pass on the opportunity to go to South Beach. Of all reasons to hop on a plane, South Beach is definitely a place worth "flying" for. With some clever persuasion from my friends and some personal push back against my fears, I was successfully convinced that the trip would be too much of a good time to pass up. To make sure that I didn't chicken-out, one of my friends even called me up and made me buy plane tickets online while we were on the phone. A few weeks passed and the next thing I knew is that I was borrowing a suitcase from a friend to pack for the trip.

The morning of the flight, I remember riding in the back cab of my friend's Toyota Tacoma pickup truck on the way to

Dulles Airport and thinking to myself that I had lost my mind going forward with this trip. There was no way I could back out at this point. It was a forty minute ride to airport, so I pounded Bud Lights as fast as I could in order to relax and keep my nerve up. By the time we arrived at the ticket counter, checked in, boarded the plane, and Lord knows how many beers later, I felt like I was relaxed enough to fly the plane myself. Before I could even take it all in, we were buckled in, up in the air and on our way to Miami. To my surprise, my first flight ended up being an awesome experience. Most of the fears I had carried around in my head for years about flying ended up being baseless. Maybe it was seeing the Earth from the air for the first time or maybe it was the Bud Lights that I slammed that overshadowed my fears, either way, my first flight was a great time. After being stuck for all those years, the fear of flying was finally behind me. I was now able to fly to see other places, which was something completely new to my world.

It was a few years after taking that first flight to Miami before I eventually got the chance to travel overseas. During my first trip to Europe, it didn't take long before I realized the many benefits to traveling abroad and having the opportunity to experience other places and cultures. It was both, an educational and eye-opening experience to say the least. As someone who spent the first thirty years of his life basically seeing only the cities and towns in and around Washington, D.C., traveling outside of the country was a big deal. Up until this point, my perspective of life outside of the U.S. didn't exist. Traveling to Europe not only gave me a larger world view, but it also allowed me to develop a better perspective of my own life in America. Seeing America from outside of America gave me a renewed sense of appreciation for my country. Even with all of its imperfections now and throughout our history, there are just so many things that are special about America that should never be taken for granted. Unfortunately, sometimes we have to leave America in order to truly appreciate America.

My first two trips outside of the U.S. were to Spain and then several years later to Belgium. Both were amazing countries to visit, especially for a new traveler such as myself. Even with so many sights to see and so much to take in, I couldn't help but to notice some of the cultural differences in comparison to life here in the United States. For example, it blew my mind that in Spain, cities shutdown in the middle of the afternoon for "siesta." This is a period of time when businesses temporarily close for an afternoon rest or nap. Something like this is unheard of in the States. During my trip to Belgium, the cultural contrast didn't come in the form of a city shutting down, but in the form of a random conversation with a Belgium hotel bartender. I was staying in Brussels, Belgium as part of a graduate school class trip to Europe. We were only two days into our trip and I managed to screw up the experience by drinking too much wine with my classmates on the second night. Too hungover to tour Brussels with my class that next morning, I ended up spending the day at the hotel bar, chatting it up with the daytime bartender. He did his best in trying to take care of me by feeding me food to absorb the remnants of the wine. I was in Brussels, so there was no pizza, sliders, or wings on the bar menu. One of the good things about greasy, unhealthy American food is that it's perfect for hangovers. Instead, I had to settle for a paper-thin, white bread ham and cheese sandwich and a cup of coffee. Now I knew what Dorothy must have felt like in the Wizard of OZ. I was a long way away from Kansas!

With no greasy food to the rescue, I threw back my ham and cheese sandwich, sipped my cup of coffee and struck up a conversation with the hotel bartender. Right away, he assumed that I was American and preceded to ask me which state I was from. I told him Washington, D.C. and to my surprise, he said that he had been to the U.S. a few times for vacation, once to Florida and a couple of times to New York City. I told him that I was in Brussels for my graduate school international business trip. He smiled, letting me know that my current hangover predicament was all starting to make sense to him. From what I could tell, it appeared that we were close in age. He asked me what I was studying and what my career plans were. I told him that I was getting my MBA so that I could learn more about business and hopefully get into a career where I can make some good money. Surprisingly, he smirked and laughed at my answer. I asked him why he laughed. Trying his best not to be offensive, he replied, "I don't understand Americans. You guys work too much, missing out on the beauty of life. And for what?" This was the first time in my life that I had actual heard someone so confidently devalue the benefits of hard-work. For a few moments, I have to admit, this bartender had me thinking about my perspective on life and work. I couldn't help but to ask myself, "Did he have a point?" After all, it's a common perception throughout the world and even amongst some within our own country, that America is a society that functions on money and greed. I asked myself, "Was I actually attending graduate school to get an MBA because I was greedy or was it because I wanted a better life for myself and my family?" Right away, the answer to my question became strikingly obvious and my reasons had nothing to do with greed.

Up to this point in my life, everything that I had invested in my education and career was done for the purpose of getting to a better place in life. As a result of trying to get "me" to a better place, I have hopefully helped the people around me get to a better place. I believe in the old adage, "A rising tide lifts all boats." What better way to lift up ourselves and others than through the empowering benefits of hard work? Unlike the mindset of my bartender buddy, I would never consider working hard to be for nothing. In my own life, I have seen the benefits of hard work and where it can take you. In fact, if it wasn't for hard work, I wouldn't have even had the opportunity to be in Brussels at that very moment, carrying on that spirited conversation. It was only through working hard for an education that I got the opportunity to enjoy a cup of coffee in Brussels. Considering the poor environment I was born into, I could have easily been in jail or even dead like some of my friends who I grew up with in the projects. It was at this point in our conversation, that I truly realized how important it was for me to grow up in a country that reveres hard work. If it wasn't for me being pushed to work hard by family, teachers, friends, and American society itself, I doubt if I would be where I am today. In life, strength and character is built by doing the hard work, not avoiding it. This is the American mindset. No matter where you come from or your current circumstances, if you are willing to put in the work, it is in America that you will find your place to grow.

As the bartender and I continued our very spirited conversation, we both started to really enjoy the different perspectives on life we each brought to the table. I was now the "crazy-hardworking American" and he was the "chill-no-worries European." He told me that he loved his bartender gig and made just enough money to afford a small apartment and a moped to get around town. We were both similar in the fact that neither one of us flew very often. He mentioned that he did most of his traveling by train, which is common throughout Europe. It's fair to say that my Belgian friend lived a pretty laidback lifestyle. If I had been twenty-one at the time we met, I would have thought this guy was living the dream! But I wasn't twenty-one and neither was he. We were both just in two different places in our lives with regards to our goals and ambitions. Judging my new bartender friend for his relaxed views on life was the last thing I should have been doing at this point. After all, I was the one who couldn't join the rest of my class that morning because I was too hungover from the night before. The fact of the matter was that we were from different cultural backgrounds. Passing judgement either way would have been pointless.

Looking back, I would like to think that we both learned something that day from both sides of the bar. The big take away for me was an appreciation for the value of different perspectives. I've learned over the years that our perspectives on life can be influenced by our circumstances and the environments in which they are formed. Maybe if my Belgian friend on the other side of the bar had seen how hard-work had given me the discipline and mindset to get out of the projects, escaping the perils of poverty, then maybe he would have a different perspective on hard work. Maybe if he knew how much my grandparents struggled and sacrificed so that I could have a better life than they did, he could understand why I worked so hard and why I wanted more out of life than just to be comfortable. This is not to assume that my Belgian bartender friend didn't have aspirations, but only to draw a distinction between our two mindsets at this particular stage of our lives. For all I know, he could have grown up in a low-income neighborhood just like me, but was choosing a humble life of comfort at this point in his life. Financial security and making money may not have been his goal at the time. Either way, our different views on "what's important in life?" made for an interesting and educational conversation. There was no doubt that we had very different views on what it means to live comfortably, but that didn't keep us from having a great conversation none the less.

My enlightening experience at the Brussels' coffee bar taught me that there is so much to learn about yourself and the world when you travel. For me, getting a taste of how some people from other countries view the traditional American work ethic, at first, gave me a shock. I was truly surprised that not everyone believes in the value of hard work. Life teaches us that hard work, grit, and determination aren't just about making money. These are values that build character, strength, and momentum that uplifts society as a whole. Of course, comfort is a necessary part of life, but never should the value of hard work be dismissed. The natural desire to achieve your dreams not only results in personal benefit, but plays a positive role in society as a whole. Consider the work ethic of people like Bill Gates or Steve Jobs. Sure they made lots of money, but look at the millions of lives that have benefitted from their hard work and the technology that resulted. Don't get me wrong, it's nice to take life easy and enjoy the moments, as my bartender friend so convincingly explained to me. But it's also nice to create a life that is better than it was yesterday and the surest way to make that happen is through hard work. Somehow, I am pretty sure that millions of people, just like me, are sure glad that Bill Gates or Steve Jobs didn't settle for a moped and an apartment.

- CHAPTER 3 -

PLAYING THE CARDS DEALT

Like so many black children born in the inner cities of America, my life began without the fundamental underpinnings of a married mother and father. A stable, two-parent household was just not in the cards for me. Unfortunately, by the time I was born, black communities were starting to look less and less down on couples having children out of wedlock. The importance of two-parent households was starting to take a backseat to individuality and independence. One week, daddy would be around and the next, it was only mommy. With fathers, sadly, missing in action, mothers and grandmothers typically held down the fort. Sadly, this trend continues today and the consequences inflicted upon America's inner city black communities speak for themselves.

Of course, not all cards dealt in my deck were bad ones. I have many cherished memories of my parents operating together as a cohesive couple. When the three of us spent time together as a family, my parents did everything they could to portray the stability of a married couple. They even lived together at one point, with probably the best intentions of building a life together. At the time I was born, my mother and father lived together in a two-bedroom apartment building in Northeast, Washington, D.C., not too far from the public housing projects in which my grandparents lived and both of my parents grew up. My earliest memories go back to probably the age of three or four. From what I remember, the apartment they rented was really decked out. It had an upstairs and downstairs and was furnished with "70's Soul" décor from top to bottom. There were leather bean bag chairs, hanging bead curtains, African velvet paintings, and incense burners everywhere! This place was a "Disco-Soul" castle!

During the time that I lived with my parents in their apartment, I was a pretty spoiled kid. My father spoiled me with the latest toys and my mom with the latest clothes. Life was good. One of my best memories in that apartment was Christmas morning, 1975. Even though I was only four years old, I remember every toy Santa Clause left under our tree. One toy in particular that I still think of today is my "bearded" 12-inch tall G.I. Joe action figure with the backpack that talked when you pulled the string. Santa even brought me the G.I. Joe Adventure Team accessory pack to go with it! Even today, I consider this one of my best Christmases ever.

Both of my parents were quick to express their love for me, but also were quick to discipline. They believed that it was very important to discourage bad behavior, but even more important to recognize good behavior. I recognized early on that the benefits of behaving far outweighed the benefits of misbehaving —and was less painful if I may add. Some may disagree in today's over sensitive world, but a slight slap on the butt carries a lot of weight when you are a kid.

Maintaining the "Soul Train" apartment and buying me G.I. Joe toys meant that both of my parents had to work. This meant that they needed someone to babysit me. My grandparents, of course, were always available to help out, but my mom didn't feel right putting that responsibility on them. No matter how much they liked having me around during the week, my mom knew that a four year old was a lot of work. I knew that once my mom found a babysitter, the good times with grandma and granddad would have to end. Even though I was only four years old at the time, the thought of being left at a stranger's house all day was frightening. I could tell that my mom wasn't too comfortable about it either, but she probably felt like she had no choice. This was all just part of her attempting to be a responsible adult. In her mind, she thought that if she could find a babysitter that was "nice," things would work out. I would be happy and she would be happy. At least that's what she thought. Any parent who has gone through the babysitter choosing experience will tell you that "nice" doesn't' tell you a whole lot about a person. My mom and I had to find this out the hard way.

    The babysitter that my mom ended up choosing was a master at the art of "nice." She did everything that she could at drop-off in the mornings to make my mom feel that she was leaving me in good hands. But after the warm and cheerful sendoffs, her true colors would appear. She put on her "nice show" just long enough to get my mom out the door so that she could go back to being her selfish self. Within five minutes of my mom jumping into her car to head to work, me and the other kids that this lady was supposed to be taking care of, were all left alone in the middle of the living room floor. This is where we would stay all day while she sat her lazy ass on the couch watching game shows and soap operas as if we weren't even there. She would angrily scream at us if we cried or did anything that would require her to get up. We were not allowed to leave the center of the living room floor for any reason. For a child, who was used to love and attention, this was very traumatic. Still practically babies, we had no choice but to endure the loveless, dark, television-lit living room. All we could do to pass the time was play with the dirty toys that she spread out on the floor to occupy us.

At the young age of four, life was already giving me a tough lesson in what it feels like not to be loved. Contrast had been introduced into my happy world. Fortunately, the hurtful experience only lasted a few months, thanks to an observant aunt. One day my Aunt Niecy wanted to ride with my mother to pick me up from the babysitter. They had both left work early that day to go shopping and decided to pick me up a little early. It was one of the happiest moments in my life when I saw both of their faces. From the moment I climbed into the backseat of my mom's car, my aunt knew right away that something was not right with me. My level of excitement was that of a child being rescued, not of a child who was just happy to see their family. Not having a child herself, my aunt was able to observe my emotions with clear eyes. My mother, unlike my aunt, thought I was just acting like any other child who was excited to see their parent after spending all day at a babysitter. Working parents go through this every day, she thought. Thank GOD my aunt sensed something more. Her unbiased instincts were telling her that something was hurting her nephew.

As my mom began to drive away, my aunt turned around to ask me if I had a good day. Immediately, I started to cry. This was the moment that they both knew something was wrong. My mother immediately pulled the car over to ask me why I was crying. I told them that the babysitter lady was mean and we cried all day long on the floor. This was all my aunt needed to hear to confirm what she was feeling in her gut. I wasn't being picked up from a loving environment. This babysitter was all about making money, not caring for children. It was obvious in my tears that I was being emotionally abused. Trusting her instincts, my aunt told my mom to never take me back there again. My mom agreed.

Knowing how much my mom loves me, there isn't a doubt in my mind that she would have found a different babysitter if she would have known how I was being treated. She might have even kicked that babysitter's ass if they had ever crossed paths again. Looking back, I know that my mom always did the best she could with the choices she had. Blaming her for a horrible babysitter experience would be pointless. I'm just thankful that my aunt rode with my mom that day to pick me up. For a child to have to experience neglect at such a young age typically leaves a scar. It can lower expectations of what it means to be loved, even carrying over into adulthood. The only positive thing that came out of this painful experience, was developing the strength to deal with it. It's a basic human instinct to grow strong in order to handle pain. Unfortunately, our emotional strengths can sometimes turn into emotional walls. The problem with walls is that they don't just protect, but they block things out. Thankfully, I left that horrible babysitter without building a wall. A wall that could have blocked any future expectations of being loved by anyone other than your family. Instead, I escaped growing in strength.

As we drove away from that shitty babysitter's house for the last time, my mom and aunt told me that I never had to go back there again. I cried with happiness, making my mom and aunt cry too. They ended up taking the happiest kid in the world straight to the happiest place in the world, McDonald's. It looked like grandma and granddad would be coming to the rescue once again.

MY FATHER

"The best social program is a job."
- Ronald Reagan, 40th President of the United States

Some may disagree with the simplistic statement from our 40th President, but there sure is a lot of evidence to support his argument. Both of my parents were raised under the shadows of social programs. Once they became adults, they realized that hard work is the only way to escape those shadows. For my mother, work provided independence and for my father, it was more about escape. Escape from the temptations of street life. My father, like many fathers born in the projects, struggled to resist the full-time professions of hanging out on the corner or getting drunk in front of liquor stores. All too familiar with that life, my father realized that the only chance he had to resist that life was to maintain a job.

With barely a high school education, the first job I remember my father having was working full-time as a trash truck driver. I remember waking up in my parents' apartment, hearing my father getting ready for work and seeing that it was still dark outside. My mother would wake up with him to cook breakfast and pack his lunch. The smell of bacon coming into my room at 4:00am would wake me up every time. Getting up this early every day had to be a tough routine for my father. The good thing is that it made it tough for him to stay out in the streets —tough, but not impossible. His job may have brought him out of the projects, but leaving behind that life was an entirely different story. The temptations of street life would inevitably prove to be too strong to resist. The destructive habits of the old neighborhood gradually took a toll on my parents' relationship. They would eventually go their separate ways. At the impressionable age of five, I witnessed the closest thing to a family that I had ever known fall apart. From that moment on and for many years to come, life would be mom and me.

 Looking back on life with my real father, I am thankful that I at least got to experience his love. Even with his weaknesses, his love for me stood out. Whether he was buying me the latest toy or letting me ride on the handle bars of his ten-speed bike as we sped through the neighborhood, he always treated me like his pride and joy. Everyone who ever saw us together, knew how proud he was that I was his son. My father showed me love the best way he knew how. The short, but special times that I did get to spend with my dad were good times. Unfortunately, as I grew older, it seemed like those good times turned into last times. Our occasional, special encounters that I looked forward to during my childhood eventually ended as I became a young man. Life had moved on. Before I even had a chance to miss my father, elementary school, middle school, and high school had all passed by in the blink of an eye. During those years, sadly, I could probably count on one hand the number of times we saw each other. By the time I started college, the only chance I really had at seeing my father was when I would take a trip to the projects to see my grandparents. Just like me, he had family and friends who still lived in the old neighborhood.

Surprisingly, one of the last times my father and I saw each other was outside of the projects. I was on summer break from college and working part-time for a moving company to make some money before school started back up. One evening after work, my crew and I were riding in our moving van back to the warehouse after a long day. As we were driving back, we just so happened to pull up to a traffic light next to a huge moving truck from another company. I was sitting in the front passenger seat of the van, so I naturally checked out which moving company the other truck was from. As my eyes glazed over the company name and logo on the driver's side door, I suddenly looked up at the driver and it was my father! Without hesitation, I yelled "dad!" He instantly turned his head to look down at our van next to him. It was as if he recognized my voice right away. It seemed like years since I had seen or talked to him, so it was shocking that he recognized my voice so quickly. I felt so proud to just utter the word "dad" in front of someone. Right away, my father got a big smile on his face when he saw that it was me. He yelled, "Walkman!" This was his nickname for me ever since I was able to walk by his side. We both really didn't know what to say before the light turned green, so we both just said "I love you" as we drove off from the light. Before that day, I never realized how saying one simple word like "dad" can provoke so many feelings. This becomes obviously true, especially if you are unfortunate enough to never have a reason to use it, like me.

Sadly, this special encounter with my father would be the last time I would see him before learning that he had contracted AIDS. I heard from those who were close to him that he possibly contracted the disease by shooting up on heroin using a dirty needle. It was hard for me to believe that the man who gave me life could potentially be losing his. The next time I saw my father, it appeared that the bad news that I had been hearing about was indeed true. Of all places, it was at my grandfather's funeral that I got to see with my own eyes the toll that the disease had taken on his body. The body that used to lift me proudly up on his shoulders.

I knew that my father was going to be at my grandfather's funeral because everyone who grew up in the East Capitol Dwellings was going to be there. My grandfather was loved and respected throughout the projects. For the service, I chose to sit in the back of the church with most of my cousins. None of us wanted to see granddad in that casket. We all sat in the back, right next to the church entrance doors. From our seats, we could see almost every single person who came in through those doors for the service.

As I nervously remained on the lookout for my father, I suddenly got a tap on the shoulder from my uncle telling me that my dad just walked in. My chest tightened right away because I didn't know what he was going to look like. AIDS was a viscous disease, especially during that time when treatments where mostly still in their testing phases. I kept turning around in my seat, waiting to see my dad and his frightening condition. Suddenly through the crowd, my dad appeared and was surrounded by a group of people I didn't recognize. Right away, I stood up from my seat and turned towards him so that he could see me. Immediately, he saw me. Slowly, he walked over to me and shook my hand. My father then leaned in towards me and in a very raspy voice, he quietly whispered, "hey son." He was very frail and his face was dry as sand. The shine that we both always had on our noses was now gone from his.

I fought hard to hold back my tears because I could sense that he was struggling emotionally at this point. He stared at me with a look that I will never forget. Without saying another word, the emotions written on my dad's face seemed to say it all. He was obviously in physical pain, but emotionally he seemed to be dying. I sensed that he was hurting because of the thought of causing me pain. Also, I sensed anger and regret for doing this to himself and letting the people who loved him the most down. With a gently smile, I tried to let him know that I loved him and that I was okay. Based on how he smiled back at me, it seemed as if he read his son's thoughts perfectly. That was the last time I saw my dad alive.

- Chapter 4 -

The Projects

LIGHT AMONG THE DARKNESS

My mother was one of seven kids born and raised during the 1950's in a low-income public housing project in the Nation's Capital of Washington, D.C. For those living outside of these government planned and funded housing projects, they were referred to as the East Capitol Dwellings. Those who lived there called them "The Projects." The government owned housing units were not even fifteen minutes away from the U.S. Capitol Building, this nation's shining symbol of democracy. Since its founding, even the most powerful nation on the earth has had to fight against racial and economic barriers that have attempted to keep this great nation from moving forward. During the 1950's and 60's, racial discrimination and inequality casted a huge shadow over the entire country, but the black community in particular. Growing up, my mom would tell me stories of how times were different in the 1960's for black people. Opportunities were slim to none and racial tensions were high. The fight for civil rights was at its peak, as riots and protests raged across the nation. Amongst the chaos, a sign of hope managed to come forward in the form of a young civil rights leader by the name of Dr. Martin Luther King, Jr. He would turn out to be one of the most revered and respected leaders in our lifetime. For the disenfranchised black community, he was a shining symbol of hope.

That hope all but diminished on April 4th, 1968, the day Dr. Martin Luther King, Jr. was struck down by an assassin's bullet. It was a day that will forever leave a scare on our nation. The loss of this great civil rights leader sparked riots in urban communities all across America. My grandparents' community was no exception. Stores in their neighborhood were set on fire and storefront windows were smashed. Sadly, some saw the rage, violence, and destruction as justified. Fortunately, these were not the values shared by my grandparents. No matter how much the anger at Dr. King's death may have tempted them, they refused to give in to the destruction of hate. Being the GOD-fearing souls that they were, my grandparents would not allow themselves or their children to take part in any of the violence that was taking place in the projects. Their Christian values forbid it.

The first time I really got a true appreciation of these values is when my mother told me about a frightening situation that took place in the projects during the riots. It involved a helpless man who ended up making a wrong turn into the wrong place at the wrong time. The wrong place was the projects and the helpless man was white. Somehow the man had gotten lost driving and mistakenly ending up in the all black projects. This all taking place while angry black people filled the streets of the neighborhood, still raging from Dr. King's assassination. In a strange twist of fate, my grandparents noticed the lost man driving through the neighborhood. They were in shock by what they saw. Either he was lost or crazy. Nothing else made any sense. It didn't take long before others in the neighborhood noticed the lost white man. My grandparents knew that they had to do something to keep this man from being killed. Undoubtedly, there would have been some in the neighborhood who would have seized on the opportunity to take out their anger on this man. Risking the wrath of the angry rioters, my grandparents waved down the lost man, who obviously feared for his life, and took him into their home. They allowed him to stay inside their home until they were sure he could safely get on his way. When I heard this story for the first time as a teenager, it didn't surprise me one bit. This is who my grandparents were as people. They embodied light in a sometimes dark America.

Mark 12:31 (KJV) And the second is like, namely this, Thou shalt love thy neighbor as thyself. There is none other commandment greater than these.

Considering the discrimination and racism that my grandparents must have gone through in the early part of their lives —years before any civil rights marches, you would have expected them to harbor at least some level of racial animosity. Born at a time in America when blacks were not afforded equal rights and protections under the law, a certain amount of racial bitterness could have been fathomable. Fortunately, they never allowed the pains of their past to hold hostage of their future.

116 57TH STREET

The beauty of a child's mind is its ability to find the joy in all things. For me, growing up with my grandparents in the projects was nothing but joy. If it wasn't for the fact that our neighborhood was referred to by a unique name, I would have thought that "the projects" was just like any other fun neighborhood. As a child, I always thought it was strange when my mother would tell me to never say "the projects" when talking about where we lived, especially in front of my grandparents. For them, it was considered a derogatory term. It was probably also a constant reminder that they were not the ones in charge of the roof over their heads. The place that they called home was owned by the government. Even though they didn't live life feeling ashamed of where they lived, they still maintained a certain level of pride. For any material wealth my grandparents may have lacked, they made up for it a million times over with the wealth of love they shared with their family. Not owning their home never stopped them from keeping their doors open to the people they loved. Whether it was a cooked meal, a kind voice, or just a little change for the ice cream truck, their home was your home.

If you were one of the lucky grandkids, like me, and got the chance to spend the night at grandma's house on the weekends, waking up on a Saturday morning was like waking up in heaven. The smell of bacon and sausage coming from the kitchen would put a smile on your face even before you stepped one foot out of the bed. If that didn't wake you up, it would be the smell of Maxwell House coffee brewing in her old-fashioned metal percolator pot with the little glass bulb handle on top. No matter how good it all smelled, I couldn't step one foot in that kitchen until I brushed my teeth and washed my face. As soon as I would walk into the kitchen and say, "Good morning grandma!" she would turn around and ask me, "Did you wash your face?" It was like a secret password question that I had to answer correctly before I could sit down at the kitchen table.

    For breakfast, grandma usually cooked grits, eggs, and toast to go along with the meat. Every couple of weeks or so she would switch it up and fry salted fish instead of bacon or sausage. It was never a surprise when she cooked salted fish because she would soak the fish the night before in a big white plastic bowl that would sit on the kitchen counter. I never really understood why she bothered soaking the fish because even after it was fried, it still tasted like pure salt. It's scary to imagine what that fish would have tasted like if she hadn't soaked it. To spread out the saltiness, most of my family would chop up a piece of fish and mix it with their grits. For me, I never really liked the idea of mixing up my food, so I would just bear the saltiness. Even as a kid, I wanted my syrup to stay on the pancakes and my sausage to stay away from the grits. None of it really mattered though because grandma's food was delicious anyway you liked it. Born and raised in the south, my grandmother brought that good "southern cooking" up north with her. In fact, most of the grandparents in the projects migrated from the south, so this explains why the grandmothers of the projects were known for their good cooking.

    Aside from the cooking, strangely one of the things I remember most about my grandparents' house is my grandfather's bedroom furniture. Just like it was yesterday, I can still remember the details of the furniture pieces. Intricate paisley patterns covered the cherry-stained headboard, dressers, and nightstands. Even the distinctive smell of the antique wood resides freshly in my mind. Before I was born, the timeless antique furniture wasn't just a part of granddad's room, but grandma's room as well. Sadly, years before I was born, my grandparents decided to sleep in separate bedrooms. Grandma moved upstairs and granddad stayed downstairs. My grandfather ended up staying in the bedroom that they once shared. The beautiful furniture that this once young, black couple from the south scrimped and saved to get, was now only a symbol of the early romance that they once had as a couple.

As a child, I was too clueless to ask questions or wonder why granddad had his own room. Even to this day, I don't know the whole story. My guess is that it probably had something to do with the bottles of VAT 69® whiskey that forever resided under his bed. Grandma wasn't a drinker, so I'm sure this took a toll on the relationship. Whatever it was that got my grandfather the "single suite," my guess is that the need for separate space was something that built up over time. Eventually, it just became normal that grandma and granddad slept in separate bedrooms. This was the way it was ever since I was born. No one in the family ever brought it up, at least in front the grandkids. It appeared that my grandparents made a decision at some point in their relationship that for the sake of holding the family together, they needed their own space. As a family that depended on their love, we will be forever indebted to their sacrifice.

Whether it was the smell of a good breakfast cooking or the smell of antique furniture, there are so many special memories from my grandparents' house. There were also many life lessons learned. Through their continuous selflessness, my grandparents taught us that one of the most important things about being a parent is your ability to put the interest of the family above your own. Even with their less than perfect relationship, my grandmother found it within herself to make sure my grandfather had a hot breakfast and dinner every day. In turn, my grandfather respected my grandmother's wisdom in running the house. She was the strict boss that he couldn't help but love. They had decided long before I was born, that no matter what problems they faced, their children and grandchildren would always come first.

THE NEIGHBORHOOD

For someone who has never stepped foot in the projects, it's hard to imagine using words like "good times," "fun," and "educational" to describe it. This is not to minimize the obvious struggles that come along with that life, but to appreciate the many positives that are sometimes overlooked when you are living that life. If I didn't know any better today, I would consider growing up in the projects a privilege. Every day provided a free education on survival. You could be playing catch in the street with your friends one minute and the next, you are jumping out of the way of a speeding police car chasing someone. This was just a normal part of life in the East Capitol Dwellings —"the projects," the place we called home.

The government built housing development was divided into numbered streets and cul-de-sacs. My grandparents lived on 57th Street, which cut through the heart of the maze of red brick housing units. It was a winding street with a slightly sloping hill. The slope was absolutely perfect for coasting downhill on a bike. You could start at the top of the street and barely have to pedal, as the hill gave you just enough momentum to speed through the neighborhood. Kids from other blocks would come over to our street just to take a bike ride down the 57th Street hill. Bikes weren't the only things kids rode for fun in the neighborhood. Sometimes groups of kids would take to the streets on Big-Wheels or Green-Machines. For anyone who grew up in the seventies, the Green-Machine was the super advanced version of the Big-Wheel. Similarly, it had three wheels, but it also featured rear-wheel steering, which you could control using the dual front levers mounted in front. The Green-Machine was one of the hottest toys at the time. In my old neighborhood, if you were lucky enough to get one, you best be watching your back and your Green-Machine at all times.

It should be no surprise that living in a poor environment, such as the projects, can inspire a great level of ingenuity. Whenever my friends and I would get bored with bikes and Big-Wheels, we would build what could be called "ghetto go-karts." Using 2x4 pieces of wood, seats from broken Big-Wheels, and wheels from grocery carts, we would build the closest thing we could to a go-cart. Usually, the toughest parts to get were the grocery cart wheels. Safeway was the closest place in our neighborhood to "pick up" a set of wheels. Usually, the oldest one in our "go-cart crew" would take the hike down to the Safeway to permanently "borrow" one of their grocery carts. Even after successfully "borrowing" a cart, it was extremely difficult to remove the wheels. We didn't have any tools, so we had to use anything that we could get our hands on to bang the shit out of those wheels until they came off. A metal pipe would usually do the trick. Once we got the wheels off, we used large nails to attach them to the ends of two short 2x4's that would serve as the front and rear axles. The wooden axles would then be nailed to longer center pieces to form an "H-shaped" go-cart design. Whatever old seat we could find would then get nailed to the center 2x4's and we were done! Our "ghetto go-cart" was ready for the 57th Street hill!

Taking a ride through the projects did not offer much in terms of landscaping and scenery. All of the streets were lined with identical red brick housing units that matched in every detail except for the graffiti on the walls. Each of the units were spaced roughly twenty-feet apart. With three separate residences per unit, the families lucky enough to live on the ends of a unit benefited by having side yard space. My grandparents just so happened to be one of those lucky families. My grandmother loved yardwork, so she really appreciated having the extra yard space on the side of the house. She and my grandfather took pride in keeping a good lawn. They did their best to bring beauty to the projects, something that was often in short supply. Sadly, there were those in the neighborhood who didn't give two cents about the place they called home. Instead of planting flowers, they used their extra side yard space for dumping garbage or emptying cans of dirty cooking grease. Sometimes they wouldn't even empty the grease on the ground, but pour it down the brick on the side of their house. You couldn't help but notice the old cooking grease that stained the walls. It looked like dirty wax dripping down the bricks. As kids, we always had to be careful when playing in some of those side yards because you never knew what you could step or fall into.

    Being from the south, the only thing my grandmother may have loved more than cooking was gardening. Living in the projects, she may not have had the garden she dreamed of, but she made the tiny patches of dirt that surrounded the house her own. A few feet here and a few inches there, she manage to find enough room to put rose bushes in front of the house, and a few African Violets in the back. Mums were usually planted on the side. The front yard was only about fifty square feet and the back yard was only a strip of dirt two feet wide and five feet long. For her, the size was irrelevant. Nothing stopped her from taking pride in every single inch of that yard. That was just who she was as a person. As the head of a family, it was important to her to be able to teach her family the value of taking pride in the things that are left in your care. As a young child, seeing my grandmother espouse these values helped me realize early on the importance of individual responsibility. It doesn't matter what your circumstance are or where you live, you owe it to yourself to have a certain amount of self-respect. Examples set by adults, such as my grandmother, allowed me to realize sooner, rather than later, the importance of knowing right from wrong. It all comes down to dignity and self-respect. None of these lessons, of course, would translate to me being a perfect kid growing up. It just provided me with a positive approach to life. Instead of me growing up continuously thinking that it was okay to permanently "borrow" grocery cart wheels from Safeway, I learned before it was too late that it was safer just to ask my mother for a new Big-Wheel.

Most of the friends I grew up with in the projects were children of single, working parents. This meant that grandma and granddad typically had to step in. Any single parent will tell you that there is no role model more important than a loving grandparent who can instill core values that otherwise would be expected from a parent. For the grandparents who took care of these kids while their parents worked, it was not an easy job. In some cases, the grandparents would find themselves caring for three or more kids at a time. To make matters worse, a lot of these kids, which were my friends, were out of control. They knew that as long as grandma couldn't grab a hold of them, they could pretty much do what they wanted. Quite naturally, it's tough for a grandmother or grandfather to catch a hold of a six or seven-year-old.

Comparing speed and maneuverability it's a no brainer. Even with the obvious disadvantage in speed, a grandmother would make up for it in brains. Just when that six-year-old thought that enough time had passed for grandma to forget his shenanigans, that's when grandma would strike. Without warning, she would use her quickest hand to implement the inescapable hold and the other hand to provide the lesson.

Being a fairly quick learner, I realized early on that acting a fool and thinking that I could out-run grandma was not in my best interest. For some of friends, they insisted on being slow learners. They seemed not to mind getting hit with the backhand or the freshly pulled tree switch. In their minds, it was just the price of acting out. Today, I still wonder why I chose to be a fast learner. There were a few times that I was slow to get the lesson, but for the most part, I got on board with grandma's program. I'm sure that my friends didn't like getting hit either, so I never understood why some of them would just keep acting up. Why was I so quick to conform? Was it the way my grandparents disciplined me? These were questions that would swirl around in my head for years to come. As I grew older and looked back on the way I was raised, two distinct parenting characteristics would stick out: *consistency* and *enforcement*.

BB-GUN PREACHER

My mom, dad, and grandparents were always *consistent* when it came to disciplining for bad behavior. Even though my dad was only around sporadically for a short period in my life, he always took a consistent approach to disciplining. In fact, one of my most memorable disciplinary moments involved my father. At the age of nine, my father decided to give me a BB-gun rifle as a present. It was one of the coolest gifts my father had ever given me. None of my friends had BB-guns at the time. Rightfully so, most parents wouldn't trust their nine-year-old with a BB-gun, but for some reason my dad trusted me.

For a kid growing up in the projects during those years, sling-shots were the closest thing to a gun. Sadly, a lot has changed since the 70's. My father surprised me with my new BB-gun one day when he came to visit me at my grandparents' house. From the moment he handed me the gun, I was both, nervous and excited at the same time. He knew that he was assigning me a great responsibility and seemed a bit nervous himself. In a very stern voice, he told me that I was never allowed to shoot the gun without him around. . His reason was that I could accidentally shoot someone's eye out, including my own. Overwhelmed with excitement for my new gift, I immediately said "okay." At this point, I would have said anything if it meant the difference between keeping that BB-gun and giving it back. After feeling assured that I would not play with the gun without him around, he hugged me tightly, knowing that he had just made his son the happiest kid in the world.

The excitement of owning a BB-gun would soon be overshadowed by my impatience. With my father rarely coming around, the opportunity to shoot my new gun seemed to almost be never, once a month if I was lucky. The urge to disobey my father's wishes continued to grow. "He ain't going to catch you!" is all I kept hearing my friends say. Peer pressure combined with the small chance of him actually catching me, eventually was enough for me to convince myself that I wasn't going to get caught. Besides, I was only going to shoot a few soda cans in the back of grandma's house. "How mad could he get?" I asked myself. Bowing to my own pressure, I decided to take a chance. In fact, I ended up taking many chances. At least twice a week, my friends and I would line up soda cans on the edge of the curb in the back of my grandparents' house. It was always a fun time, but I couldn't stop looking over my shoulders for any sight of my father.

My grandparents knew that my father had told me not to play with that BB-gun without him. Because he was rarely around, I guess that's why they didn't make a big deal out of me shooting it without him. Unfortunately, my grandparents' tacit approval did not translate to my father's approval. After two months of not getting caught, my luck finally ran out. It happened during a typical after school session of shooting soda cans with my friend Robbie. He had just handed me the gun so that I could take my shots, when all of a sudden, I saw my father walking up the alley. Instantly, my heart stopped. My only hope was that he saw how much fun we were having and would somehow overlook my disobedience —wishful thinking.

As my father approached us, seeing me holding the BB-gun, he gave me a look that I will never forget. It was a combined look of utter disappointment and fierce anger. "Didn't I tell you not to play with that gun without me!" he said in a stern voice. Before I could say anything, he snatched the BB-gun out of my hand, walked up to side of a brick wall in the back of my grandmother's house and smashed the BB-gun into a thousand pieces. I began crying hysterically. Not so much because he was smashing my gun, but because I thought I was next. Lucky for me, he thought that destroying the BB-gun right in front of me would teach me a big enough lesson.

After my father completely destroyed my BB-gun, he told me to stop crying and to look him in the eyes. In his firmest voice, he said, "When your father tells you to do something, you better do it!" You best believe I got his message loud and clear. With all of his faults, my father was a master at *consistency* and *enforcement* when it came to disciplining his son. He knew that I stood to lose a lot more than just a gun if my disobedience would have been allowed to go unchecked. Of course, I missed having that BB-gun around, but life has taught me that I could have missed even more if I would have ignored the lessons from that experience.

TOUGH LOVE – UNCLE TOOTSIE

As crazy as it sounds, sometimes I consider myself lucky not having a dad around every day. Any smart kid will tell you that it's better not having a dad around all the time, especially when you get into trouble. I had cousins with full-time dads, and they would tell me scary stories about their dads and leather belts. There were times when I would see my cousins cry at the very thought of their mom telling their father on them. "I'm going to tell your daddy" is sometimes the scariest thing a mom can say to a kid. Don't be mistaken, moms back in those days could definitely hold their own, but it was nothing compared to daddy's wrath. As life teaches us, the strictest discipline and toughest lessons often come from the ones who love us the most. In those painful moments, it sure doesn't feel like it. I've never known a kid to get a spanking from his father, then walk away to tell his friends how much his father loves him. I guess discipline is a lot like fine wine, it requires time to pass in order for it to be truly appreciated.

Unlike my sometimes unlucky cousins, I didn't have a full-time father around with a collection of leather belts. But, I did have a full-time uncle around, who used a different tool for disciplining. Rather than using a leather belt to enforce a lesson, he believed strongly in "tough love." My uncle Tootsie was my youngest uncle, who still lived at home with my grandparents. To say that he played a very important role my life growing up would be a vast understatement. My uncle Tootsie loved and cared for me just as much as any father ever could. His perspective on life was above his circumstances and above where he lived. He envisioned instilling that same perspective in me. Learning how to ride a bike without training wheels, flying a kite, roller skating, catching a football, putting up a Christmas tree, and knowing when and how to fight —I owe it all to him.

Being a young man in a tough neighborhood, who constantly had to fight to stay on the right path, my uncle Tootsie still found the time to make sure I was on the right path. In order to keep me on this path, there were times that it seemed that he was being unreasonably hard on me. He was the master of implementing "tough love." My mom and grandparents would often argue with him for being too hard on me or being too critical of something I did or didn't do. In his mind, he was trying to make me into a man. A man who doesn't make excuses and admits when his wrong. To my uncle, life was all about learning your lessons in order to move forward. As a kid, sometimes those lessons were extremely painful, but I was always comforted in knowing that I had a loving uncle that would be there for me at the end of those lessons.

THE LAWNMOWER

As human beings we have a propensity for learning things the hard way. How many times are we told or warned not to do something and it goes right in one ear and out the other? For the most part, this behavioral pattern doesn't change, even when we become adults. In the school of life, pain is often the only teacher that doesn't get ignored.

One of the most memorable and painful lessons I learned growing up in the projects with my uncle Tootsie was an incident involving a lawn mower. No, I still have all ten fingers for those who might be jumping ahead in this story. As one could probably guess, grass fields were in short supply in the projects. Asphalt and concrete were the surface coverings of choice. As a result, scraped and scabbed knees ran rampant in the streets. Lucky for me, one of the few grass covered areas we did have in the projects happened to be located directly behind my grandparent's house. If it wasn't for it being slightly sloped, the random garbage, and dog poop, it would have been the perfect football field. This cherished grass field, like the few others, was typically mowed by the facilities maintenance workers, which were employed by the D.C. government. The problem with this system of maintenance was that in the summer months, the grass would sometimes grow over a foot or taller before someone would show up to cut it. Not only was this an ugly sight to see, but the kids in the neighborhood couldn't use the field. The only choices we had were to either wait for the maintenance guys to show up or find a way to cut the grass ourselves. In the projects, pretty much no one owned a gas lawn mower. This made cutting the tall grass ourselves nearly impossible. Most families, including my grandparents, owned non-powered, push lawn mowers. These were the old school mowers in which you had to push in order to get the blade to spin. Needless to say, no one was crazy enough to attempt to cut a large overgrown field with a manual push mower. For small areas of grass, such as my grandmother's front yard, I must say, that old push mower did just as well as any power mower.

With nearly no options available for cutting the large grass field themselves, residents increasingly started to complain to the facilities management office. Eventually a solution was worked out whereas residents could borrow gas mowers from the community facilities center on a first come, first serve basis. The community facilities center was located in the center of the East Capitol Dwellings Housing Project. The facilities building housed both, a supplies-repair warehouse and a recreational center. Everyone in the neighborhood referred to this place as "the Center." You could go there to get supplies to fix a broken screen door or meet up with your boys to play a game of basketball. Now, thanks to complaining neighbors, it was also a place to borrow a gas lawn mower.

One summer morning, instead of walking down to the Center for a game of basketball, my uncle Tootsie decided to walk down there to take them up on their offer. He and a few guys from the neighborhood wanted to borrow a couple of gas lawn mowers to cut the tall grass field behind my grandparents' house. They had all grown impatient waiting around for the facilities maintenance guys. During a football game on the field the day before, they all decided enough was enough. All of the guys met that morning in the back of my grandparents' house. When I saw them meeting through the kitchen window, I ran outside to ask if I could come along. As a young kid, the idea of watching my uncle cut grass using a gas lawn mower for the first time sounded exciting. Seeing how badly I wanted to go, my uncle agreed to let me come along.

That morning, we all headed down to the Center with our fingers crossed, hoping that they had mowers that we could borrow. As soon as we walked into the supplies building, there were three mowers staring right at us. My uncle filled out whatever paperwork that was required and we were on our way. As we pushed the gas mowers through the neighborhood, heading towards the grass field, I could sense the pride in the group. By deciding to take personal responsibility for something as simple as a field of grass created a sense of empowerment. An occurrence that was, unfortunately, rare in the projects.

As soon as we got to the overgrown field, my uncle and two other guys started up the three gas mowers. My uncle told me right away that it was okay to watch, but to stay off the field while they were cutting. Easy enough, I thought. I sat in my grandfather's old lawn chair on the back porch as I watched the guys go back and forth across the field. About halfway through mowing the field, my uncle's mower ran out of gas. Fortunately, the Center had given them a full can of extra gas just in case one of the mowers ran out. My uncle pushed his mower off the field to refill the tank. Being a typical inquisitive kid, I took this as an opportunity to run over to ask questions. This was also my chance to see the lawn mower's levers, cables, and engine parts up close. Predictably, instead of asking anything, I immediately reached out to touch some of the parts. Thankfully, before I could touch any of the engine parts, my uncle quickly snatched my hand away. Not knowing at the time, my inquisitiveness almost caused me a lot of pain. In a stern voice, my uncle said to me, "This is very,

very hot. Don't touch nothin' on here!" He was pointing at the engine, but he specifically singled out the exhaust muffler. Being a typical kid, his warning didn't scare me, but only made me more curious. It all went in one ear and out the other. Suddenly, my urge to find out more about that engine overshadowed any remaining interest I had in my uncle cutting grass.

With my uncle back on the field with a full tank of gas, it didn't take long for the guys to finish up. Finally, our cherished neighborhood field no longer looked like a small jungle. More importantly, it was all accomplished by doing it ourselves. Filled with pride for a job well done, my uncle and the other guys all high-fived one another before parking the mowers on the edge of the field. Afterwards, they all sat down on the concrete curb on the edge of the field for a much deserved rest. Instead of running over to my uncle to thank him for a job well done, I immediately ran over to the parked, burning hot lawn mowers. I knew that my uncle was distracted and not paying attention to me as he was talking it up with his friends on the curb. This was my perfect opportunity to get up close and personal with those gas lawn mowers. As my uncle sat there distracted, for some uncontrollable reason, I decided to touch one of the mufflers to see if it was still hot. Out of all the parts that I could have touched, it figures that I wanted to start off with the one part that my uncle specifically told me not to touch.

I can still remember the piercing pain. It was nothing like I had ever felt before. Hearing my screams, everyone came to a halt and ran towards me to see what happened. My uncle somehow was able to jump up from the curb and get to me first. It was tough for him to immediately figure out exactly what happened because I was crying hysterically. Once he noticed that I was holding my right hand, it was a matter of seconds before he saw my badly burned, blistered fingertip. The tip of my right hand index finger had swollen up to the size of a grape. For an adult finger, this may not seem large, but for a kid finger, this was huge. As I stood there crying in pain, waiting for my uncle to do something to take away the pain, no relief came. For as painful as it was for him to see me cry, once my uncle Tootsie realized it was only a bad finger burn, he let me experience the pain in full before providing any comfort. No ice, no water, no cold towel —nothing. After making sure that the seriousness of the situation sunk in, my uncle placed his hand under my chin, forcing me to look him in the eyes. In a "told you so" voice he said to me, "Didn't I tell you not to touch nothin'?" Still crying hysterically, I was able to squeeze out a "yes" somehow.

After sensing that I learned my lesson, my "tough love" uncle picked me up and took me inside to run cold water on my burn. Once he got the pain to go away, he wrapped my finger in a big Band-Aid. Now that my tears were gone, my uncle finally asked me if I was okay. I told him "yeah," then he kissed me on the side of my face and told me to go outside and play. At that moment, nothing else needed to be said. The lesson had been taught, loud and clear. Pain once again had been proven to be the teacher that can never be ignored.

THE SNOW SHOVEL

There are many ways to grow in life and not all of them require us to endure physical pain. Education, experience, and overcoming fear also contribute to personal growth. Life's "teachers" can come in many different forms and at any given time. As I get older, I realize more and more that one of the most important things for personal growth is our ability to overcome fear. Growing by overcoming our fears is something that every child and adult will continuously grapple with. From the moment we are born, we learn the concept of fear. Being afraid is a natural reaction that is born out of the human instinct for survival. Fear can be a useful in the presence of real danger, but it can also be a hindrance if that danger isn't real. In order to move forward in life, we must learn to control our fears. This starts first by facing them. As fears are confronted, this forces us to make rational choices that will either substantiate or eliminate those fears.

My uncle Tootsie was very hard on me when it came to getting me to face my fears. As a kid, one of the things I struggled with the most was my fear of thunderstorms. As much as I would look forward to summertime, I lived in fear knowing that summertime also meant thunderstorm time. I would often close my eyes and sit on my grandmothers lap until a storm would pass. This was something that really bothered my uncle because he knew that it wasn't healthy. Living in fear never is. I knew that I would eventually have to face my fear of thunderstorms, but I just didn't know how or when it would happen. The simple fact was that thunderstorms were always going to be a part of life, at least as long as I lived on the planet Earth. There was no way I could continue to hide from them forever. It was unrealistic to think that I could jump into grandma's lap every time I heard the sound of thunder. None of these rational points mattered at the time though. As long as I remained fearful of thunderstorms and as long as I could fit on grandma's lap, nothing was going to change. It was becoming more and more obvious, that something was going to have to happen to cause me to face this fear.

That something eventually did happen. The push that I needed to conquer my fear of thunderstorms finally came. I was eight years old and the year was 1979. The D.C. metropolitan area had just been hit with one of its biggest snow storms in history. With almost two feet of snow on the ground and still falling, schools were closed all over the D.C. metro area. My friends and I couldn't have been happier. For a schoolkid, nothing is better than waking up, turning on the TV, and hearing that schools are closed because of snow. For my friends and me, this meant a day of nonstop sledding and snowball fights. Most of time when it snowed, we played in the back area of the housing units that ran along 57th street. This allowed us to play in the snow without worrying about cars driving by. Also, there was a continuous hill in the back area that ran parallel to the alleyway behind the housing units. We called it the "alley hill." It was perfect for sledding.

Besides being a dream hill for sledding, the alley hill also served as somewhat of a buffer, separating the 57th street housing units from the 58th street housing units. Even though both streets were part of the same East Capitol Dwellings Housing Project, they were considered by those of us who lived there, two different neighborhoods. There was somewhat of a "gang" mentality that shadowed over the two streets, especially with the young people. It was not unusual for fights to break out between the two neighborhoods or for someone from 57th street to get jumped for walking through 58th street or vice versa. Sometimes the two streets would even have rock fights. Rocks would fly up to 58th and rain down on 57th until a window got broken or somebody got badly hurt. During one of these rock fights, I ended up being the one badly hurt. With my grandparents and uncle out of sight, I figured I could join my buddies from 57th and throw a few up at the boys on 58th. This ended up being a painful mistake. As I was taking aim to throw a rock towards one of the 58th street kids, I was hit directly in the side of my head with a large rock. It almost knocked me to the ground. I ran off the battle field crying my eyes out. With blood coming out of my ear, I ran as fast as I could into my grandmother's house. Once I got inside, my uncle, "Mr. toughlove," checked to see how badly I was hurt. He looked at my ear and the side of my head and made his professional diagnosis that it was nothing a little bit of ice couldn't fix. Instead of consoling me, he told me "That's what you get for throwing rocks!" He sure did get me there. After hearing that, I had to suck it up. I had no reason left to cry.

    Getting hit in the head by a big rock, usually was something you didn't have to worry too much about when there was snow on the ground. Snow days meant that it was nearly a zero chance that a rock fight would break out. Neighborhood rivalries took a backseat to playing in the snow. The older kids had snowball fights and the young kids went sledding. As you can imagine, going sledding in the projects was a creative sport. There weren't too many real snow sleds around in our neighborhood. We would use trash can tops, plastic trash bags, plywood, old tires, shovels or anything else that we could get our hands on to sled down a hill. It's always amazing how resourceful kids can be when they have to be. Just like most of my friends, I didn't have a real snow sled. I would always use my grandparents' snow shovel, which worked just as good if you knew what you were doing. I would sit inside the shovel scoop, with my legs and the shovel handle facing forward. While holding onto the handle with one hand and pushing off with the other, that shovel instantly became my ghetto snow sled. If you were a kid lucky enough to get his hands on a metal shovel, that was even better. The plastic shovels, usually, would get scratches on the bottom and not slide as fast as the metal ones in the snow. Lucky for me, my grandparents had a metal shovel. It would have been unlucky me, if I let something happen to it. Back then, metal shovels were a lot more expensive than the plastic ones.

When the crazy snow storm of 1979 hit D.C., it was the perfect opportunity to put grandma and granddad's coveted metal snow shovel to the test. With schools shutdown, my friends and I couldn't wait to hit the alley hill. There was at least a foot of snow on the ground and the storm was showing no signs of letting up. We started sledding around 9:30 am and never stopped. The only thing that could stop us was a wet pair of socks. Being the professional snow "sledders" that we were, we had that covered. We would put plastic bags over our socks before putting on our boots. This worked like a charm. So far, we had been out sledding for almost three hours and no one had yet complained about having cold feet. This was a perfect snow day on the alley hill.

Just when we thought things couldn't get any better for our sledding crew, around 1:00 pm, the snow fall started picking up. The way things were looking, it was a good chance that schools would be closed again tomorrow. With no end in sight to the fun, I started making my millionth climb up alley hill. Halfway up, with shovel in hand and socks still dry, I was suddenly blinded by a bright light that lit up everything around me. A few seconds later, before anyone could figure out what was going on, we all heard a loud, crackling boom. It sounded like a bomb went off right next to us. It was the second loudest sound I had ever heard in my life. The loudest sound being a thunder boom, which I heard the very summer before. This was wintertime. It was impossible for that flash of light to be lightning and that loud boom to be thunder. Not knowing what to do and scared out of my mind, I dropped my shovel and ran as fast as I could to my grandparents' house. As soon as I ran in the backdoor, my grandparents knew what happened. The saw the flash and heard the thunder. I could tell that they were just as confused by what they saw and heard as I was. Again, this was wintertime.

The loudness of the boom shook me up so badly that my grandparents thought I might have been actually struck. They realized I wasn't hurt, but just scared out of my mind. After calming me down, they explained that it was just a random wintertime flash of lightning and thunder. I was already terrified of thunderstorms, but I was usually able to cope with this fear when those storms were predictable. Lighting and thunder is expected in the summertime, but this random occurrence happened in the middle of a snow storm. I didn't understand how that could happen. There were no lightning flashes or sounds of thunder off in the distance to provide any type of warning. Not even the slightest increase in wind speed was noticed. It was complete calmness before the flash.

After finally getting control of my emotions, suddenly my uncle Tootsie —"Mr. tough-love" came walking in from the store. Before saying anything, strangely, he walked over to the pantry looking for the snow shovel. Right away, he noticed that it was missing. "Where's the snow shovel?" he asked my grandma while looking at me. Of all the times in the world, why would my uncle be looking for the snow shovel at this very moment? It made no sense that he walked in the house and the first thing he thought of was shoveling snow. I knew right away that this had everything to do with me.

Earlier that morning, my uncle knew that I took the snow shovel with me to go sledding with my friends. Knowing my uncle, he probably saw me running scared from the alley hill without a snow shovel in my hand. With an opportunity to teach me one of his life lessons staring him clearly in the face, he seized on this moment. He started by asking me a rhetorical question —"Where's the shovel?" I had already told my grandmother that I left it on the hill and that I would get it, but first I wanted to make sure that the thunder and lightning were gone. This was not going to fly with my uncle. He told my grandma and granddad that I needed to go back to the alley hill to get that shovel right away before someone steals it. Convincing my grandparents that someone might steal the shovel was key to getting them to take his side. Even though they felt bad for me being afraid to go outside, they were very worried about their metal shovel getting stolen.

    I cried and begged my uncle Tootsie not to make me go outside, but he insisted. He made me put my coat on and then led me out the back door towards the alley hill. Keeping my head down, afraid to look up for fear of seeing lightning or hearing thunder, I walked as fast as I could with my uncle. He told me to stop crying, to stop being scared, and to hold my head up. He said to me, "Nothing is going to happen to you when I am with you. I am not going to let anything happen to you." When I heard those words, my anger towards him quickly turned into love. He was teaching me courage and to face my fears head on. When we got to the alley hill, I grabbed the shovel and wiped away my tears. My uncle put his hand on my shoulder as a sign of his approval. We walked back towards the house, but this time I walked slowly. It was as if I wanted to put my new found courage to the test. I almost wanted to see another flash of light or hear another loud boom.

The fear was now gone. My uncle Tootsie filled the shoes of a father on that snowy day. He saw an opportunity to walk with me in my battle to overcome a debilitating fear.

PROJECT LIFE

For a black family growing up in the projects during the 1970's, it was almost mandatory to watch reruns of "Good Times" every evening. Even though I was very young during those years, I took notice of the issues of race and poverty being played out on the show. The "Evans family," which were the main characters, were considered the quintessential black family at that time. Facing what was referred to as the "black struggle" in 1970's America, they relentlessly chose to live life to the fullest, making the best out of what they had. Faith and family were the only things they could count on when all else failed. Humor was often a source of happiness when their world seemed to be falling apart. Remembering most, if not all of the amazing "Good Times" episodes, I realize more and more that the "Evans family" wasn't just a black family, they were an American family. Their faith and grit transcended all races.

Just like the "Evans family," there were real-life families of faith living in the projects where I grew up, that were committed to finding good, solid sources of happiness. Unfortunately, there were also those who lost hope, seeing happiness as being only attainable through bad means. It was usually obvious in our neighborhood who was involved in shady activities. Walking around the projects, selling new clothes, still on the hanger and with the tags, was a clear sign that you were doing something you had no business doing.

Driving around the projects on a brand new Honda dirt bike and trying to sell it for $200 dollars the first day you got it, was a clear sign that you were doing something you had no business doing. This quick dollar lifestyle, unfortunately, was seen by some as the only way. In our neighborhood, those that lived this lifestyle were called "hustlers." Whether it was selling stolen suits, shirts, or steaks, it was seen as a legitimate way to make a living. Ironically, they lived and operated amongst their honest, hard-working neighbors. This mixture of values in such a small, close-knit community ensured that there was never a dull moment in the projects.

The East Capitol Dwellings Housing Units may have been an all-black community, but that didn't mean that it wasn't diverse. One of your neighbors could be a "church-going-ask your grandmother if she needs milk from the store" kind of neighbor and the other could be an "in and out of jail" kind of neighbor, who robs and steals for a living. Good or bad, this is why living in the projects can produce a variety of character traits as well as teach a variety of skills. Most of the things picked up in a low income environment, such as the projects, are geared towards survival. This type of education is often referred to as "street smarts." For the parents and grandparents raising kids in this environment, they hope and pray that these "street smarts" don't convert over to "criminal smarts." Unfortunately, for too many of those who I grew up with, the criminal influence won out far too often. Some would get on a criminal path that would eventually become inescapable and their lives would forever be destroyed. Stealing would typically be followed up with robbing. This was usually a sign that the end of the road was right around the corner.

Most of the guys I knew who would steal and rob, did it outside of the projects, in the suburbs. It was foolish to try to steal from someone in your own neighborhood and expect to get away with it. The biggest risk wasn't so much about getting caught by the police, but retribution by someone within your own neighborhood. In the projects, everyone talked because everyone knew each other. Fellow neighbors did not take kindly to preying on people in your own community. This was an unspoken, but very enforced rule. If you were looking to steal, going out to the suburbs to do your dirt just made a lot more sense. Also, the chances of actually stealing something of significant value was greater in middle class neighborhoods. Occasionally, lazy thieves who didn't want to make a trip out to the suburbs would hit a cash register at one of the neighborhood liquor stores or carry-outs. This was very rare though, because even the dumbest criminals knew how much the people in our neighborhood talked. The word would spread around the projects in no time about Mrs. Brown's grandson "Tony" robbing the chicken wing carry-out. It was just a fact, people talked in our neighborhood. It didn't make any sense to think that you could steal from the mini-mart where grandma always sent you to pick up milk and bread or that you could rob the carry-out that you just bought chicken wings from yesterday.

MURDER ON "THE CORNER"

As a low income community, we depended on the handful of shops and stores that were in walking distance from our homes. They were all located in the same area that those of us from the East Capitol Street projects referred to as "the corner." This small group of stores was located at the intersection of Central Avenue and Southern Avenue. Southern Avenue was a busy street that divided D.C. and Maryland. "The corner" had stores on the D.C. side of the border, as well as the Maryland side. On the D.C. side, you had a barbershop, mini-mart, cleaners, carry-out, and liquor store. Surprisingly, the stores on the Maryland side almost mirrored the stores on the D.C. side. There was a liquor store, a carry-out, a record store, and a small hardware store. At any time, on any day you could always count on running into someone you knew being down on "the corner." It was just the place to be. Those stores and the people who worked there were just as much a part of our community as anything or anyone else.

Throughout the years, several of the stores had switched owners, but usually every attempt was made to keep things the same. People in the community had been coming to these stores for years and were not very fond of change. By the time the 1980's rolled around, a shift began to take place on "the corner." The first sign that change was coming was when the old neighborhood dry cleaners went out of business and was replaced by a Chinese owned carryout. For the young people in the neighborhood and the drunks who hung out on "the corner," this was seen as a good thing. This was another tasty, cheap carry-out for the neighborhood. For the older working people, losing the dry cleaners was considered a huge loss for the community. Instead of having a dry cleaners within walking distance, now folks had to drive to get their good clothes cleaned.

Not too long after the dry cleaners went out of business, the neighborhood was soon shocked to find out that the mini-mart right next door had been sold to a Korean family. Prior to this, the store had been black or white owned since its opening. This was a shock to some in the community, but didn't come as a surprise to others. A national trend in America's poorest communities was suggesting that American's were less likely to open and operate businesses in inner cities because of the escalation of crime in those areas. It seemed that with every passing year, crime was not only increasing, but becoming more and more violent. This pattern seemed to be spreading across the country. Our neighborhood was no different. It appeared that Koreans and other immigrants looking for a shot at the American dream were more willing to take the risks associated with owning businesses in low income, minority communities.

    There were those in our neighborhood who never became comfortable with the fact that the only convenience store in the neighborhood was now owned by people who had no ties to the community whatsoever. From the moment a Korean family began running the mini-mart, there was an instant clash of language and culture. Because of the language barrier, it was tough to build any type of relationship between the Korean employees and their customers. To add to the contention, the Korean owners did not hide the fact that they were keeping an eye on every customer. Employees would sometimes follow, who they thought were, suspicious looking customers through the aisles. Also, there were security cameras installed above every store aisle, in every corner, and at every entrance and exit. In all honesty, I understood their reasoning behind installing the cameras. There were a lot of kids with sticky fingers in my neighborhood and I knew plenty of them. If it wasn't for the fear of being seen on one of those security cameras, it was really tempting to stuff a free pack of Now & Laters.

    Because of the language barrier and the feeling of always being watched, some customers no longer felt welcome in their own neighborhood mini-mart. As animosity increased over time, the community itself seemed to lose respect for the store that once proudly served the community. Unfortunately, this lack of respect evolved into a wrongful justification for evildoers in our own neighborhood to carry out a shocking crime against the Korean owned market. This unforgettable crime would not only shock our community, but the entire city of Washington, D.C. itself.

    The tragedy took place one evening during a typical school week for me. School had let out and some of my friends and I were riding bikes through the streets and alleys of the neighborhood. As we were riding, we saw a group of our friends running up the hill from the stores on "the corner." We all hit our brakes because they looked like they were running from someone chasing them. We asked them what happened, but they were so out of breath that they could barely speak. They told us that someone robbed the mini-mart and that there were police down on "the corner" everywhere. All of us split up on our bikes and went in different directions. Some of my friends took off towards "the corner" and some went home. I decided to go home because I was concerned about my grandfather, who might have still been down on "the corner."

    As soon as I walked in the backdoor, I put away my bike in the pantry and ran upstairs as fast as I could to tell my grandmother what happened. She told me to go downstairs and turn on the TV in the kitchen so that we could see if anything about robbery was on the 6 o'clock news. We had a little RCA black and white TV that sat on the far back corner of the kitchen table that we used mostly for watching the 6 o'clock news, Good Times, and late night episodes of Sanford & Son. As soon as I turned on the TV, thank GOD, my grandfather walked in the backdoor. He told us that the mini-mart had been held up and two of the workers had been shot and killed. By this time, the 6 o'clock news came on with the breaking news that there had been a robbery and murder at a convenience store in southeast Washington, D.C. We stared at the TV in shock and disbelief that all of this was happening only a few blocks from our house. The news reporter confirmed what my grandfather had already told us, that two of the Korean workers were killed during an armed robbery. My grandmother was really upset by the horrible news. The fact that this happened to people from outside of our community attempting to serve our community was saddening. These were immigrants to America who chose our neighborhood as a place to build a business, provide for their families, and have a better life in America. Unfortunately, this painful event would only increase the size of the broad brush that was often used to paint poor communities such as ours.

As all of us stayed glued to the TV that evening, we noticed that they didn't mention anything about possible suspects. Quite naturally, we couldn't help but wonder if someone from the neighborhood committed this unspeakable crime. After the news finished with the story, I went back outside to find my friends. Of course, everyone on the block was talking about what happened down on "the corner." This is why I knew that if it was someone from the neighborhood who did it, their secret couldn't stay secret for long —people talked.

The next day I went to school like any other school day, but I knew that it was going to be nothing like any other school day. Out on the playground, before the 9 o'clock bell rang for class, the only thing anyone talked about was the robbery down on "the corner." During all of the excitement, I noticed that my friend Antonio was surrounded by a bunch of kids asking him questions. Before I could walk over to find out why, I suddenly overheard one of my other friends say that Antonio was in the store during the robbery! I ran up to Antonio right away to ask him if it was true. Still looking a little scared, he shook his head up and down and said, "Yep." He said that he would tell me all about it at lunch time. A few seconds later, the 9 o'clock bell rang, clearing the playground.

When lunch time rolled around, you best believe that I was right up in Antonio's face asking him what he saw. He told me that he was in the store picking up something for his mom and all of a sudden he heard loud bangs coming from the front of the store. "They sounded like ash-cans!" he said. "Ash-cans" were quarter sticks of dynamite, which were very popular in the projects around the 4th of July. My friends and I would use them to blow up stuff in the name of fun. After Antonio heard the loud bangs, he said that he saw two guys running out of the store. The people standing at the register were all screaming as they stared at the floor behind the counter. Assuming that is was now safe to run out, this is when Antonio made his way towards the front exit. It was at this moment that he realized that the loud bangs that he heard came from something much scarier than an ash-can. The loud bangs were shotgun blasts that left two Korean store workers lying dead on the floor. Antonio described what he saw as the "nastiest" thing he had ever seen. "Guts, skin, and blood were sprayed all over the check-out counter," he said. One of the workers had been shot in the stomach and chest. The blasts ripped his upper body with holes, leaving his body lying in a pool of thick blood mixed with pieces skin. This was something that no one should ever have to see in their lifetime, especially a kid in the fourth grade, like my friend Antonio.

A few days had passed since the deadly robbery, but of course it was still fresh in everyone's mind. From kids on the playground, to adults standing on the corner waiting on the bus, it was all anyone talked about. As long as that market remained closed, it was a constant reminder to every one of the evil that took place there. As far as who did it, no suspects had been named on the news, but rumors started to spread that it was someone from the neighborhood. The news was only reporting that the police were looking for two armed and dangerous suspects. There was no mention of where they might be from or where they might be hiding. Quite naturally, when the gossip started circulating, fingers started pointing towards the roughest dudes in the neighborhood. I knew them all, but I couldn't imagine any of them doing something this vicious.

No one in my house seemed to have a clue as to who might have committed this deadly robbery. At least, that was until the day my uncle heard some solid rumors down on the neighborhood basketball court. During a game, he heard a group of guys saying that "Fat" Will and Tony did it. As soon as my uncle shared this news with me, I immediately thought, "No way!" Not only were they from our neighborhood, they both lived on our street. Having known both of them my whole life, I knew that they weren't angels, but I could never imagine them doing something like this.

Up until this point, all of the rumors and everything that my uncle told us was just hearsay. At least that's what we thought until one morning, when over a dozen police cars and SWAT showed up in front of "Fat" Will's house. It was around 8:00am when my grandmother and I heard the sounds of car doors slamming and police radios coming from the front of the house. We both ran into my grandfather's bedroom to look out of his window, which faced the front of the house. That's when we saw the swarm of police cars in front of "Fat" Will's house. Before any of the police officers approached his front door, we noticed several groups of heavily armed officers running towards the back and side of the housing unit to stake out positons. At first my grandmother and I were confused about why some of the officers ran to the back, but we quickly realized they were preparing to take "Fat" Will down if he attempted to run out the backdoor. The officers taking up positions in the back of the housing unit hid behind a group of bushes directly in front of my grandmother's kitchen window. It was a frightening sight to see. All of the officers had their guns drawn, ready to shoot in the event "Fat" Will attempted to run or come out armed. My grandmother started praying right away. "GOD, please don't let 'Fat' Will come running out of that backdoor!" she prayed over and over again. At this moment, I thought to myself, "If he had something to do with killing those Korean workers, why is my grandmother so concerned about what those officers are going to do to him?" The answer to that question became more and more obvious as I grew older.

    Praying for "Fat" Will wasn't about whether or not he was a good person or deserved what he had coming to him. My grandmother praying for "Fat" Will during that scary moment was about showing respect for life and placing a value on that life. It was also about demonstrating to me the importance of strength of character. It would have been easy for my grandmother to express anger for what "Fat" Will may have done or to justify any harm that would come upon him, but instead she showed remarkable strength by withholding judgement. She refused to allow someone else's actions to impact her character and the person she strived to be. I asked myself, "What example would she have set for her young grandson if she would have allowed her emotions to justify anger or revenge for the Korean store clerks who were murdered?" It probably wouldn't have been a good one.

Instead, she chose to pray to GOD for the strength not to allow her judgement to cloud her respect for life.

On that very frightening morning, my grandmother's prayers were ultimately answered. "Fat" Will never came running out of that back door. He came to the front door, surrendering peacefully without incident. Those police officers who waited anxiously outside our kitchen window, with guns drawn, fortunately, never had to fire their weapon. As far as Tony, the other suspect, we eventually heard that he was taken into custody without incident as well.

After all of these years, I'm not sure what ever happened to "Fat" Will and Tony. As far as I know, neither one of them was ever seen again in the neighborhood. The few worthless dollars they may have gotten during this senseless crime couldn't have been worth the taking of a life, the destruction of their own life, and the heavy pain inflicted upon the families involved. The senselessness of the entire ordeal taught me just how cruel life can be when life isn't valued. By not valuing their own lives, "Fat" Will and Tony failed to value the lives of others. Life and experience has taught me that valuing life first starts with respecting life. As with anything, where there is no respect, there is no value. "Fat" Will and Tony allowed their lack of respect for themselves and the Korean workers to ultimately destroy the value of their own lives.

THE CORNER HUSTLERS

During the 1970's, running a drug operation in the projects seemed just as easy as running a corner lemonade stand. All you had to do was stand on the corner and the customers would just show up. The fact that you could make quick, easy cash without leaving your block was quite appealing. Those willing to take the risks associated with that lifestyle were often close friends, neighbors, and even a family members. It was no big deal to see people exchanging cash for drugs on the corner or random cars driving through the neighborhood to buy "dime bags" of "weed." As a child walking through the projects, I would hear guys standing on the corner yelling, "Got that lovely! Got that love boat!" or "Got that wack!" It wasn't until high school that I would find out that "lovely" or "love boat" and "wack" are the street names for marijuana dipped in PCP. At the time, I didn't know exactly what they were selling, but I knew it wasn't lemonade and I knew it wasn't legal. No one runs at the speed of light at the sight of a police car for selling something legal. The drug dealers had lookouts that would yell, "Jump-out! Jump-out!" whenever a police car would come around the corner. It was an everyday street game of cat and mouse.

Selling drugs on a street corner in an American inner city public housing project today is a completely different ballgame than when I was growing up in the 1970's. The shootings and killings tied to drug dealing today are a plague upon this nation of the likes never seen before. During my childhood, the guys I knew who sold drugs didn't even carry a knife, let alone a gun. For the smalltime, dime-bag dealers on my street, any score that had to be settled was typically handled with fists.

Most fights that broke out involved buyers who tried to get over on the dealers. Buyers from outside the neighborhood would sometimes pull up in a car to buy drugs and then speed off without handing over the money to the dealer. This usually ended badly for everyone in that car that tried to speed away. Cars attempting to flee without paying would often fail to recognize one very crucial factor. The people that they would have to get pass in order to get out of the neighborhood, were neighbors of the dealer they were attempting to rip off. Even if they weren't friendly neighbors, they would always take the side of the neighborhood dealer over the outside-of-the-neighborhood buyer.

    In order to catch a car trying to get away without paying, a dealer would yell, "jack! jack!" Anyone that heard that would immediately look for a speeding car that was unfamiliar to the neighborhood. If spotted, people would run into the street to attempt to get the driver to stop. If the crowd sensed that the driver wasn't going to stop, they would wisely jump out of the way. It was written off as just a bad deal for the dealer, but a good deal for the people in the car —they just made off with some free weed. More significantly, they also made off with their life. If they would have been caught, they would have been pulled out of the car and beaten by, not only the dealer they attempted to rip off, but everyone else surrounding the car. Also, the drugs, cash, and anything else of value in the car would be taken. The beaten-up fools that thought they could get away were warned to never step foot back in the projects ever again. Considering how retribution in the drug game is carried out today's inner cities, getting beaten-up could be considered getting off easy. Black eyes and bruises have been replaced by bullet holes.

    Without a doubt, my understanding of the true costs associated with dabbling in the drug game has grown a lot since my youthful days of watching petty, smalltime drug dealers sell dime-bags of weed on the street corner or my grandmother catching my mom and aunt smoking a joint with friends. Once I hit high school, I would see the ugly side of drugs and the destruction that it leaves behind. Over the years,

I have come to see firsthand the real consequences of not only selling drugs, but using drugs as well. I have had close family members that have been shot in the face and neck and some even killed as a result of their involvement with drugs. Also, I have personally witnessed lives destroyed because of incessant drug use. Something that starts out as a quick way to make some cash or a quick puff for a few laughs, can quickly become the reason you are buried in the ground.

THE BARBERSHOP

There is nothing like the feeling you get after getting up from a barber's leather chair after a fresh cut. It's a feeling that says, "I'm ready to take on the world!" Whether it's for a job interview, a date, class pictures, or just a Friday night out, it all starts with a fresh haircut. A new you emerges the moment the barber hands you the mirror, brushes off the hairs from your face, and pops the towel from around your neck. This is especially true for black men. Just the smell of that mysterious spray in the black and gold can that the barber sprays all over your head when he's done is enough to make you go out and make something happen.

    Barbershops have always played a unique role in American culture, especially in the black community. The reason being, they are not just places to get a haircut, but gathering places to socialize. In fact, if you walk into any black barbershop in this country, you will find more people hanging out talking politics and sports, rather than actually getting a haircut. I saw this first hand in my old barbershop growing up. When my mom first started taking me to the barbershop, one of the first things I noticed was that there were a lot of guys sitting around who never got called up to the chair for a haircut. This didn't make any sense to me until the next few times I went to the barbershop and noticed that it was the same guys sitting around. They weren't there for haircuts, but there to hang out and talk trash. The barbershop was the neighborhood hub for current events and conversation. If you wanted to talk about who won the fight or game, or grab a peek at last month's issue of Penthouse magazine, the barbershop was the place to be. Because kids were usually in the barbershop, the older guys would hide their dirty magazines by placing them inside of an Ebony, People, or some other kid friendly magazine. I may have been young back then, but I wasn't stupid. There was no way Mr. Johnson, one of the neighborhood drunks, could possibly sit in the barbershop for two hours every day and be that interested in reading People magazine.

 In the projects where I grew up, there were no bars for men to hang out, so the barbershop filled that void. If only the guys who owned the barbershop had found a way to legally sell alcohol and cut hair, they would have made a fortune. My grandfather, just like a lot of the other older men in the projects, treated the barbershop like his second home. If it wasn't dinner time, there was probably a good chance that you could find him there. It was quite easy to understand the social attraction to the barbershop. For men, it was a place were friends could sit around in torn, but comfortable leather chairs and be themselves without the wives in sight. Also, to add to the seduction, there were liquor stores and carry-outs only a few doors down. The guys hanging out at the shop could step out for a minute to grab a few chicken wings or even sneak a taste of whiskey or two. Life couldn't be any better. Drinking was not allowed in the barbershop, at least not in view of the customers. The regulars, including my grandfather, were allowed to go in the back room of the barbershop and take a few swigs. Sometimes, I would go back there with him to use the restroom. While back there, I would always pretend not to notice the Jet magazine and naked Penthouse centerfolds taped to the walls. Whenever I got caught looking, my grandfather would say, "Boy, what you lookin' at!" I would just smile and say, "Nothing granddaddy!"

In addition to good talk and dirty magazines, the barbershop was also known as the place to go for a good game of checkers. The young guys in the shop would always try to go up against the old-timers. It was something truly fascinating to watch. My grandfather was one of those old-timers. He developed a reputation in the barbershop for being one of the best at the game of checkers. One part of his strategy was to pretend not to take the game too seriously. He would smile or laugh after each move, regardless of who the move appeared to benefit. Another part of his strategy was to let his opponent think that they were winning and then come from behind to crush them with his well thought out moves at the end. The guys in the barbershop loved watching my grandfather's last few lethal jumps. He would go in for the kill with such grace. It was a thing of beauty to watch.

My grandfather, who went by the nickname "T," was treated like a rock star at the barbershop. Hanging out with him there made me feel like a rock star. I think he got the nickname "T" because he was a very tall and slim man. All of his friends, even my grandmother, called him "T." The regulars in the barbershop knew me as "T" Martin's grandson. Every time I got the chance, I would tag along with my grandfather to the barbershop. So much so, that the two owners eventually asked me if I was interested in making a few dollars working part-time at the shop. They said that they needed someone to sweep the hair off the floor and clean up around the shop. The owners not only took pride in cutting hair, but also the appearance of the barbershop itself. They knew that customers didn't want to step over clumps of hair, especially well-dressed customers, who would often pop in the shop during work hours for a quick cut. This was the early 80's, so there were still lots of guys sporting Afros, which meant that after a few haircuts, the floor would be covered with hair. Sweeping up discarded Afros sounded like a job I could easily handle. With a big smile on my face, I immediately looked at my grandfather for his approval. He said that he had to check with my mother first to see if it was alright. I couldn't imagine her saying no to my very first job offer. It would be a chance for me to learn my very first lessons about the value of work. Also, school was out for the summer and what better time to have my own spending money. All I could think about from the time I left the barbershop that day was having my own cash to buy Atari cartridges. For a ten-year-old during the 1980's, this would be a dream come true. All I needed was my mom's approval.

  That evening, I could barely sit still waiting for my mom to get home from work. Every five minutes, I looked out my grandmother's kitchen window for her car to pull up. When she did finally pull up, I was so excited that I nearly knocked her down before she could walk in the kitchen door. She didn't even have a chance to set her purse down before I started talking her ear off about the good news. My grandfather came into the kitchen as soon as he heard me talking to my mom about the part-time job down at barbershop. Not really knowing for sure what the job entailed, my mother asked my grandfather for his thoughts. He told her that the job would be good for me and that it would teach me the responsibilities that go along with work. Once my mom heard that, she seemed to be onboard.

Lucky for me, the next day was a Saturday, so my mom didn't have to work. She agreed to walk down to the barbershop with my grandfather to talk to George and James, the owners, about the part-time job. My mom had known George and James for years, way before I started coming in their shop for haircuts. They told her how much they admired me, "T" Martin's little grandson, and would love for me to help out around the barbershop. My job would be to come by the shop three times a day to sweep the floors and clean whatever needed cleaning. Even for a ten-year-old who had never had a real job, this sounded like a piece of cake. I guess I owed that to my mom and uncle Tootsie, who taught me early on to never shy away from the duties of work. The difference this time was that I was going to get paid. Up to this point, the only incentive I ever had for saying yes to work was to avoid the painful consequences of saying no.

It only took a few minutes of talking with George and James before my mom gave me the final green light. I was so excited that I almost started crying. Right away, I ran over to my mom and grandfather to give them a hug. The owner George, with a big smile on his face, stepped from behind his barber's chair to show me around the shop, while James continued to cut hair. George pointed out the areas that I would be responsible for sweeping and cleaning. Next, he showed me the broom closet where all of the brooms, mops, and cleaning products were kept. George, who was the head barber and owner, instructed me on the proper brooms to use and the order in which I was to use them to sweep up the hair. Admittedly, I was confused as to why it even mattered which broom I used first and why sweeping up hair had to be a multi-step process. George told me to use the large, wide broom first. He explained that the large, wide broom should be used first because it would allow me to quickly sweep the large clumps of hair with minimum interruptions to the barbers working. The smaller broom was only to be used afterwards to sweep the fine, loose hair, but only when the barbers weren't busy with customers. George knew in his gut, that there was a ten-year-old's way of doing things and a proper way of doing things.

    With a little guidance, I quickly learned how to properly sweep barbershop floors. My commitment to doing a good job grew as my new bosses praised my work. The regulars in the shop began to talk about how much nicer the barbershop was looking since George and James hired me. My very short time on the job so far had already begun to enlighten me to the benefits of having a good, solid work ethic. No matter how small or insignificant your job may appear to be, hard work is always valued. Taking pride in what you do is the surest way to open doors of opportunity that otherwise may be closed. People notice a hard worker. Just like my bosses George and James who saw the value that I brought to their shop, other shop owners could have seen that value as well. At any moment, another business owner could have walked into the barbershop and offered to pay me twice as much for the quality of my work. I learned early on in life that people appreciate and reward those who take pride in their work. Doing a good job isn't just about getting nice compliments. Sometimes those compliments are accompanied by opportunities. As a ten-year-old, I wasn't just sweeping hair off the floor in a barbershop, I was learning how to sow seeds of opportunity. Working at the barbershop was a life enriching experience and one that I will never forget. From building a positive work ethic, to learning the fundamental responsibilities associated with employment, the experience was priceless.

Out of all of the valuable lessons that I learned during my brief childhood days of sweeping hair at the barbershop, one that sticks with me the most involves a lesson in self-worth. After a month of working at the barbershop, it became obvious to George and James that I had mastered my routine and technique for sweeping and cleaning. I began finishing my tasks in half the time that it took me when I first started out. Realizing that they could take advantage of how quickly I worked, little by little, my bosses started piling more and more job responsibilities on my plate. All the while, keeping my pay the same. Things began to hit the fan one afternoon after I popped into the shop to do my typical second round of sweeping. As always, once I was done sweeping up the hair, I bought a coke from the old coke machine in the back of the barbershop. While relaxing and sipping my coke, George randomly walked over to me and told me to clean and dust all of the pictures and trophies in the shop by the end of the day. I knew that he was serious because right next to him was a bucket filled up with hot water and something that smelled like Pine-Sol. I thought to myself, there is no way I can clean all of those picture frames and trophies by the end of the day. Regardless of what I thought, it became obvious to me that this new task wasn't up for negotiation. Suddenly, my job description expanded from sweeping and mopping floors to include dusting and polishing picture frames and trophies.

This might not have been a big deal if there were only a few pictures and trophies in the shop, but there were a whole lot more than a few. For black barbershops, it is traditional to display pictures and trophies that represent the people of the community in which it serves. Martin Luther King, Jr., JFK, RFK, and nearly every black kid in the projects had their picture hanging in that barbershop. In fact, I personally added to the picture count myself. My favorite barber James, hung class pictures of me on his mirror from kindergarten to 5th grade. Photos of my friends were right beside mine. For the regular customers, the barbershop mirrors were a beautiful montage of memories. In addition to the many photos that were hung throughout the shop, countless trophies lined the shelves. Any kid or team from the projects that ever won a championship, had their trophy displayed on one of the barbershop's shelves. It was considered a privilege to earn a spot on one of those coveted shelves. Surprisingly, it wasn't until I started working at the barbershop that I realized that a lot of the trophies on display were from one of my uncles. Uncle "Itch" was a black belt Karate champion throughout the 1970's. He was not only well known in the projects, but throughout Washington, D.C.

As special and as delicate as the barbershop pictures and trophies were, I knew that they would be a pain in the butt to clean and dust. Never the less, I put on my "good-work-ethic hat" and started the task set before me. It was a tough and tedious job for a ten-year-old. All of that "taking pride in your work stuff" was definitely being put to the test. Just like I did with sweeping up hair, I developed an efficient routine that would allow me to clean and dust the fastest. Unfortunately, the faster I worked, the more things they told me to clean and dust. George and James started bringing out old, dusty junk from the back storage closet that looked like it had been stored away for years. This was the point at which I drew my line in the sand. My attitude went from feeling valued to feeling used.

The guys who gave me my first part-time job opportunity, unfortunately, started to take my personal kindness for professional weakness. In their defense, this wasn't personal, it was just business. Why would you pay someone more if they didn't expect to be paid more? It was time for a ten-year-old boy to put on his business hat. Deciding enough was enough, I put down my cleaning rags and asked George and James if they were going to pay me more for doing more. Shocked by my confidence, they looked at me and laughed. It was obvious that the level of appreciation and respect in this employer-employee relationship wasn't mutual. I couldn't help but to feel hurt and angry about the way I was being treated. With no gesture of a possible negotiation coming from George or James, I put away my brooms and rags and walked away. Not knowing what else to do, I headed towards the front of the shop and sat down in one of the old green leather waiting chairs until my grandfather showed up.

It was tough sitting there knowing that my name wasn't ever going to be called for a haircut. Time seemed to drag on longer than ever before in that old green leather chair that evening. By the time my grandfather showed up, I could no longer hide my anger. As soon as he stepped into the barbershop, he could see that something was really wrong with me. In a nervous voice, George told him that I got upset because I didn't want to work anymore. My grandfather knew me better than that, so George's story wasn't making any sense. Deciding not to make matters worse, my grandfather wished everyone a good evening, as we both headed towards the door. Once we got outside, my grandfather asked me what happened. I immediately started crying and told him that George and James were making me clean the whole barbershop. Then I told him that George and James laughed at me when I asked them to pay me more money. Even though I was only ten-years-old, my grandfather could tell that his grandson was no fool.

    My experience that day at the barbershop was very emotional. Feeling like people, that I almost considered family, were taking advantage of me was one of the worst feelings I had ever experienced. By the time my grandfather and I got home from the barbershop, I pretty much made up my mind that my part-time gig of sweeping hair was over. Once my mom heard about what happened, she pretty much made up my mind for me. She decided that it was time for me to get back to being a ten-year-old and let George and James get back to cutting hair. Besides, she didn't want me to harbor any hard feelings towards George, James, or the barbershop moving forward. This was the place where I got my first haircut and every haircut after that. This was the place where my grandfather was revered. This was the place that my family often called my grandfather's second home. The barbershop was too special of a place to let a misunderstanding change that.

    As my mom and I talked about what happened on that last day of sweeping hair at the barbershop, she reminded me of why she agreed to let me take on a summer job in the first place. The new experience was supposed to be fun, educational, and rewarding. Working for the guys that ran the most popular hangout place in the projects was never supposed to be a negative experience. It took me a few years, but I eventually realized that it was far from negative. A simple job like sweeping hair gave me confidence, self-respect, and a sense of self-worth that would remain priceless for years to come. As I grew older, I also became wiser when it comes to the risks associated with working for or with close friends.

Even as a young boy, I learned that mixing personal and business relationships can sometimes cloud professional expectations. This often leads to negative consequences due to the fact that business and personal relationships operate under a totally different set of rules.

Today, it's easy for me to give George and James the benefit of the doubt that they acted with good intentions. Maybe they thought that it was important to push me hard at a very young age so that I could know what to expect in the real world. Maybe they were right, but respecting my awareness of my own self-worth at such a young age was also important. If they were going to work me more, they shouldn't have been surprised when I asked to get paid more. As a ten-year-old, I called it commonsense. Today, I call it Capitalism.

- Chapter 5 -

Elementary School

Marion P. Shadd was a lady who I knew nothing about until I "Googled" her name while writing this book. But somehow, I managed to walk through the doors of an old red brick building in the projects with her name on it nearly every single day for seven years of my life without questioning who she was. Within the walls of that old red brick building is where I received a public elementary school education that was supposed to lay the foundation for living out my dreams. Located on East Capitol Street in SE, Washington, D.C., Shadd Elementary School was named after Marion P. Shadd, a teacher and administrator in the D.C. public schools from 1877 to 1926. She was the first woman in the Washington school system to be appointed assistant superintendent in charge of elementary education and a leader in educational and civic affairs. Marion P. Shadd was born in 1856 in Chatham, Canada and died in 1943. Her contributions to the city of Washington, D.C. and the nation earned her a spot on the list of names of D.C. schools that reflect the rich heritage of black leadership in the educational system of this country (Washingtonpost.com,

1980, Article: Names of D.C. Schools Reflect Heritage of Black Leadership).

    Marion P. Shadd would have been proud of the D.C. public school that took on her name. For me, Shadd Elementary wasn't just the place where I learned how to recite the alphabet, read, and do math, but it was also the place where I learned how to dream —dream of a life outside of the projects. That old red brick building with the sun-stained frosted windows, wasn't just an invaluable resource of hope for me, but for a community where there was often none. In addition to hope, Shadd Elementary also provided something else that was much needed by the kids of the projects —discipline. Strict discipline was absolutely necessary if the teachers were going to have any shot at maintaining a stable educational environment. The disintegration of the two-parent household presented a two-front battle in the education process. Instead of being able to solely focus on academics, strict discipline had to be a part of the educational package. Back then, there was no such thing as "timeout." Teachers were allowed to spank, pop, snatch, grab, and do whatever else they needed to do to control a misbehaving child. The parents actually expected the teachers to do what they had to do to keep their child in line. Back then, teachers didn't operate under the fear of being sued or arrested for spanking a child in class. Pain was distributed freely and unimpeded. Things have surely changed a lot since those days.

    Other than a few smacks on the butt and hands, I managed to stay on the good, less painful side of most of my elementary school teachers. It was never fun getting laughed at by your classmates for getting spanked in front of the class. There were other benefits as well, that came along with staying on a teacher's good side. Some teachers would allow their best behaved students to pass out class assignments or even give them hall passes to run an errand. Nothing made a student kiss the teacher's butt more than the opportunity to get a hall pass. How else could you run the halls to kill time or peep in on your friends in other classes without getting into trouble? The priceless hall pass was more than enough to convince me to strive for the coveted positon of teacher's pet. Soon I would learn that there were far more important reasons to stay in good graces with my teachers. Reasons that would have far reaching implications on more than just my elementary school educational.

By all accounts, the teachers at Shadd were masters in the education arena. They had to be. Getting a bunch of hard-headed kids from the projects to stay focused on a chalkboard was no easy task. The most effective teachers at my school were the ones who could covertly get a student to focus without them even noticing. My sixth grade teacher, Mrs. Pettifer, was a master at this. Always with a calm smile on her face, she was a chess player when it came to implementing strategies to push her students to a higher level. She would often push us to what seemed like a breaking point, only to reveal abilities that my classmates and I didn't realize we had. As an incentive for students to push harder, Mrs. Pettifer would often hand out candy bars to her best students. The so called "cool" kids in class would try to pretend not to care that they didn't get a candy bar. I thought to myself, "Who are they kidding?" Everybody likes candy. I have come to realize that sometimes acting "cool" will not only keep you dumb, but it can also keep you hungry.

I HAVE A DREAM

On top of handing out candy bars, another way Mrs. Pettifer would reward her brightest students would be by choosing them for lead roles in her school plays. Mrs. Pettifer was Shadd's own Steven Spielberg when it came to topnotch production. Sure, other teachers put on school plays, but none at a professional production level as Mrs. Pettifer. She took her plays very seriously and therefore, expected a lot from the students who were fortunate enough to participate in them. Being one of those lucky kids who landed a few roles in some of Mrs. Pettifer's plays, I can attest to her dedication to her craft.

One of the most memorable school plays that Mrs. Pettifer ever produced was a play entitled "I Have a Dream." It was an educational drama she put together to celebrate the life of Dr. Martin Luther King, Jr. This was a very special production appropriately scheduled for the month of January to commemorate the civil rights leader's birthday, January 15th. This particular play was a very big deal not only to the school, but to the community as well. Two months before the play was scheduled to hit the stage, Mrs. Pettifer began putting together the script and assigning roles to her students. She shared the script only with her students, which seemed to be made up mostly of famous civil rights speeches and songs. So far, I had not been picked for any of the roles. I pretended not to notice and was somewhat relieved. Being chosen for a part in a Mrs. Pettifer play was cool, but it also came with a lot of pressure. A good performance meant a lot of practice. No kid wanted to screw up his or her lines on stage in front of their parents, teachers, and friends.

Mrs. Pettifer set aside a week to make her final list of who would be standing on stage during the much anticipated "I Have a Dream" play. Based on the casting sheet taped to the side of her desk, it appeared that all of the character slots had been filled. It was looking more and more like I would be enjoying this play from a seat in the audience. At least that's what I thought until Mrs. Pettifer randomly called me up to her desk one afternoon. A bit caught off guard, I quickly jumped up from my desk chair and walked towards her desk. Even though I had done nothing wrong, at least nothing I could think of, it was typically never a good sign to get called up to the teacher's desk. Surprisingly, when I got to the side of her desk, she had a big smile on her face. "Please sit," she said in her typical calm voice. Unsure of what was coming next, I stared nervously at the cup of pencils and pens on her desk. Suddenly, Mrs. Pettifer says, "I want you to play Dr. Martin Luther King, Jr. in our upcoming play in January." Completely in shock, all I could say was "Ok Mrs. Pettifer." She smiled and then hit me with the real scary part of the whole conversation —"I want you to recite his entire 'I Have a Dream' speech on stage!" Just like that, my hopes of sitting this one out disappeared like a puff of smoke.

Being only eleven years old, I thought to myself —"That's impossible. No eleven year old can memorize something that long." I tried to remain calm and think carefully before I responded. Unfortunately, my mouth wasn't on the same page. "I can't memorize all of that Mrs. Pettifer!" suddenly rolled out of my mouth. That was a big mistake. Just like at home, the words "I can't" where not permitted in Mrs. Pettifer's classroom. She told me to never say "I can't" about anything else again in her classroom. With an unforgettable sternness in her eyes, she promised me that with practice and hard work, I could do anything. The way that Mrs. Pettifer spoke those words to me that day at her desk, was nothing short of pure empowerment. There was no doubt in her voice, there was no trying, only doing. It was as if she wanted to prove, not only to me, but to herself, just how far a child can go with someone in their corner to push them.

My big assignment of memorizing one of the most, if not the most, powerful and famous speeches of all times began after Thanksgiving break, roughly a month and a half before Dr. King's birthday. A month and a half might seem like a long time to memorize and prepare for a speech, but it didn't seem like it for me. I didn't even know how to begin preparing. Instead of allowing myself to get overwhelmed with fear, I decided to put all of my trust in the "master strategist." Mrs. Pettifer gave me a book of famous Dr. King speeches and told me to take it home and write down the words of the entire "I Have a Dream" speech for homework, in cursive, three times. "Why three times?" I thought, but wouldn't dare ask why. That night I sat at my grandmother's kitchen table with my pen and mint-green colored cursive notepad and like a good student, got cracking on my assignment. Thinking that I would be graded on my cursive, I wrote every letter of the speech exactly as it appeared on the alphabet banner that wrapped the top edge of my classroom. I'm not sure what time I ended up finishing my strange homework assignment, but I know it was late because my grandfather was up watching Sanford & Son on TV.

The next morning when I turned in the three handwritten copies of the speech to Mrs. Pettifer, she thanked me and smiled. "Good job Jermaine!" she said as she stood up from behind her desk. Nervously, I said "thank you" and returned to my desk for the Pledge of Allegiance. I tried everything I could to start the morning like any other morning, but I couldn't stop looking towards Mrs. Pettifer's desk to see if she was looking over my homework. After about thirty minutes of constantly turning my head around to check, I noticed her comparing one of my copies to the speech in the book. It didn't take long before I got the scary call to come up to her desk. The first thing I noticed when I walked up was the word "PERFECT" written and circled in bright red on one of my copies. Before I could even crack a smile, she immediately took my other two copies, folded them in half, and tossed them in the trash basket on the side of her desk. I thought to myself, "What! After all of that hard work and time, how could she do this?" Immediately, I asked her, "What's wrong with the other copies Mrs. Pettifer?" "Nothing!" she replied. She explained that the reason she had me write out three copies was my very first step in memorizing the speech. All I could do was stand there, scratching my head. None of it was making any sense at this point.

    My cluelessness regarding the point of this tedious homework assignment all goes back to an earlier point I made at the beginning of this chapter: the most effective teachers are typically the ones who can covertly get a student to focus without them even noticing. To make my point, by the time I had gotten halfway into my second copy of the "I Have a Dream" speech, unknowingly, I began to look over less and less at the first copy. I naturally started to rely more and more on memory in order to finish the assignment faster. At first, what seemed to be a somewhat useless homework assignment turned out to be an extremely effective way to memorize the speech. Mrs. Pettifer knew something about the human brain that I didn't know at the time. Our brains tend to naturally seek out sources of efficiency in repetitive processes. In this case, my brain determined that memory was a source of efficiency. It was a natural reaction of my brain to evaluate my initial approach to completing the assignment and determine if there were internal or external tools at my disposal that would help with completing that same task more efficient the next time. In a nutshell, it's fair to say that our brains don't like to waste as much time as we do. Thankfully, Mrs. Pettifer was hip to this little known fact. Her simple assignment of having me write out a speech three times was key to helping me realize that I was indeed capable of more than I was willing to give myself credit for. This experience left me with the question, "What other tricks could I play on my brain to reveal my potential or accomplish my goals?"

With more work to do still, my next step in preparing for the speech would require help from my mom. She was so proud and honored that her son was chosen to play the role of Dr. Martin Luther King, Jr. in a school play. From the moment I told her what Mrs. Pettifer had asked of me, she promised to help me out in any way that she could to nail the speech. Now it was time to take her up on her offer. First, I had to write out another copy of the speech for my mom. Mrs. Pettifer told me that this new copy didn't have to be in perfect cursive…yeah, right. Either she was testing me or tricking me. Things wouldn't have gone over well, to say the least, if I would have handed over to my mom a junk copy. Once I was done with the new copy, I was instructed to keep both copies at home and start practicing the speech with my mom. We started practicing the speech in my grandfather's bedroom nearly every night after my mom got home from work. His bedroom was far enough from the kitchen to have a sense of peace and quiet, but close enough to grab something to eat. The kitchen was always loud because that's where everyone typically hung out. At my grandparents' house, the kitchen was the "living room," but with a stove.

Just like it was yesterday, I remember the very first night that I practiced Dr. King's historic speech with my mom. Standing in the middle of my grandfather's bedroom, I attempted to recite each line by memory, as my mother sat on the edge of my grandfather's bed, following along with her copy of the speech that she held in her hand. Her goal each time we practiced was to get me to memorize one paragraph at a time and keep expanding from there. Every day that we practiced, I was able to memorize more and more of Dr. King's speech. I couldn't believe that I was actually doing it! With every paragraph I was able to recite from memory, my fear shrank and my confidence grew. My mother became so excited with my progress that she decided that it was a good time to show off to my other family members just how far I had come.

One evening she invited my uncle Tootsie into the room to watch us practice. I became a bit shaky and nervous with someone new in the room, but I fought through it. I had to. The date of my first performance was quickly approaching. In a couple weeks, I would be giving this speech on stage in front of an entire auditorium full of people! If I couldn't get control of my nerves in front of my family, how would I be able to handle a packed room full of people? Taking a few deep breaths, I started reciting the speech in front of my uncle for the first time. Right away, within the first few sentences, my uncle's eyes opened wide in disbelief. The look on his face was as if he didn't recognize his eleven year old nephew standing in front of him. Through practice, dedication, and hard work, the person that I had transformed into was unrecognizable to him. My face was the same, but who and what I had become was new. As I watched my uncle Tootsie's reaction and how proud he was of me, this gave me the boost I needed to conquer my fears.

    Those next couple of weeks quickly flew by and it was now only two days before the first performance of the much anticipated school play. During those last two days, my classmates and I relentlessly rehearsed our parts. We had to keep at it until Mrs. Pettifer felt comfortable with our performance. We rehearsed in the classroom and in the school auditorium just to make sure we were indeed ready. Practicing my speech for the first time in the auditorium was very scary. It was a completely different experience than standing in the middle of my grandfather's bedroom. The echo of the auditorium and the height of the stage was intimidating and exciting at the same time. To my surprise, the echo and the height gave me a sense of power and command. For an eleven year old, this was a pretty cool feeling. On the last day of practice before the show, we rehearsed until 4:00pm that evening, an hour after school officially let out. Mrs. Pettifer was beyond confident and happy with how far we had come over those last few months. Tomorrow was the big day —time for me to shine.

    Making me shine on that stage is exactly what my mom set out to do. A week before the big day, my mom had gone out and bought me a pair of shiny new dress shoes, a crisp white dress shirt, and a blue clip-on tie. Of course, she waited until the night before I was set to hit the stage to iron my shirt and pants, just to make sure my clothes were crisp to perfection. On the morning of the performance, my mom made me my favorite breakfast, a sausage sandwich on buttered toast. As boring as it may sound, she knew that it was special to me. My mom would slice two hand cut sausage patties sideways to open them up so that they would cover an entire piece of toast. Next, she would sandwich them between two slices of Wonder bread toast, covered in no less than a quarter stick of butter. This simple little piece of heaven was the perfect way to start my big morning. Right after breakfast, I quickly got cleaned up and dressed. My mom had everything I was wearing for the play laid out on the ironing board in the kitchen. All I had to do was wash up, make sure I didn't forget to put lotion my face, and perfect the "part" in my hair. For little black boys, having a perfectly straight "part" in your hair back then was the shit. It was just a necessary accent on a good haircut. Once I was done perfecting my "part," I headed to the kitchen to put on my clothes. All my mom could do was smile as she watched me get all dressed up for this very special day. With tears in her eyes, she clipped on my tie and told me how proud she was of me. At this moment, I realized that there was no way I could let her down. She was expecting me to "bring it." It was show time.

    The moment of truth had finally arrived. It was time to show my family and Shadd Elementary the fruits of my hard work. My mom insisted on walking me to school that cold January morning. The short, ten-minute walk from my grandparents' house down to my school was just enough time for my mom to fire-off a few words to boost my confidence. Of course, like a typical mom, she told me not worry about anything, to do my best and the rest would take care of itself. More importantly, she also told me that when I stand on stage, to remember why Mrs. Pettifer chose me. This was simple, but powerful advice. When we finally got to the school, my mom and I walked into Mrs. Pettifer's class, greeted by a big smile on her face. She was so proud of all of the obvious parental support that went into bringing this project to the finish line. As Mrs. Pettifer and my mom hugged, I couldn't help but to stare at all of my classmates who were dressed up for the big day. It was strange to see so many of my friends, who typically wore anything they thought was halfway cool, all dressed up in their Sunday best. This indeed was turning out to be a special day. It wasn't long after walking me into class that my mom had to quickly say her goodbyes. Fortunately, she got to hang out with Mrs. Pettifer for a few minutes, before having to rush out the door. Show time was quickly approaching and Mrs. Pettifer had started lining us all up to head down to the auditorium. My mom had to walk back up to my grandparents' house to meet the rest of my family before heading back down to see the show. She told me that she would be back with grandma, granddad, Aunt Niecy, and uncle Tootsie in time for the start of the show. My family wouldn't have missed this day for the world. To them, this was one of the most special events anyone in our family had ever been a part of. I was literally attempting to fill the shoes of a giant that morning. That giant being Dr. Martin Luther King, Jr. There wasn't any doubt, that there was a lot riding on my shoulders that morning, but nothing was more encouraging than having a family in that audience who supported and believed in me one hundred percent.

    Teachers and students began filling up the auditorium at least thirty minutes before the play was scheduled to start. Soon after, family members began trickling in as everyone involved in the play geared up and prepared backstage. Occasionally, one of my fellow cast members or I would peak through the side of the stage curtains to see if we could see our family in the crowd. After looking several times with no luck, I noticed that I was becoming nervous and distracted. This was not good. The show was starting in ten minutes, I needed to be focused. Deciding to look one last time, I spotted them! Mom, grandma, granddad, Aunt Niecy, and uncle Tootsie were just taking their seats in the center, six rows back from the front of the stage. Everything was set. It was now time for me to do my part.

The play began with Mrs. Pettifer thanking everyone for their attendance and support of this huge effort only made possible because of the dedication and hard work of her students. Next, she presented an introduction and outline of the play that she produced to celebrate the legacy, life, and contributions of the late, great Dr. Martin Luther King, Jr. The play began with my classmates reading historical accounts of Dr. King's early life and how he began the journey of dedicating his life to the civil rights movement. Throughout the play, there were musical selections sang by students that captured the essence of the black civil rights movement in American. While I remained backstage throughout the first half of the play, I would occasionally peek out at the audience. It was impossible for me not to notice that were very few dry eyes in that auditorium. The history of the black struggle in America is a very emotional and sometimes painful topic. This was ever so obvious in my school auditorium that day.

It was both a blessing and a curse that my part in the play came towards the end of the second half. The blessing was that I could practice with myself backstage during the first half, but the curse was that my anxiety grew as I waited to take the stage in the second half. It made sense that Mrs. Pettifer purposely chose to put the "I Have a Dream" speech towards the end of the play. Not only was it his most famous speech, but it captured the very essence of what he stood for and desired for America as a nation and as a people. In other words, I couldn't mess this thing up. Judging by her calmness, Mrs. Pettifer appeared pretty sure that I wouldn't.

As the last song of the play was wrapping up and I was just about to walk towards the curtains to step on stage, I looked at Mrs. Pettifer one last time for some sort of blessing. She looked straight into my eyes, remaining silent, as to say, "You got this." I continued towards the curtain, hoping and praying that she was right. Slowly emerging from behind the curtain, clip-on tie and all, I was met by the smiling faces of my family and an audience that seemed so proud. Proud of me even before I spoke a single word of the speech. Seeing this overwhelming support was more encouraging than anything I could have imagined. Throughout all of my practicing and rehearsing, I had never taken into account the power and importance of the audience. With every word I spoke, I became more and more emboldened. The more I was able to tap into the emotions of the audience, the stronger I became in my delivery. I could even sense a change in my voice as I pushed through the speech. It was as if a "Higher Power" had taken over the voice of this little boy wearing a clip-on tie. Up to this point, I didn't' realize that there is a certain synergy that occurs when any performer steps out in front of his or her audience to perform. A synergy that cannot be replicated in a rehearsal environment. As a result of this synergy, I gained a sense of power during the performance. From that power came confidence. The confidence that my words and presence had the potential to empower a group of people.

    Delivering Dr. King's "I Have a Dream" speech was the first time in my life that I had ever experienced a moment that I truly felt was meant for and reserved by GOD just for me. It was also the first time I had ever seen my grandfather cry. From the second I hit the stage, it became obvious that this moment was bigger than me. Going into this whole performance, I was pretty sure that everyone in that audience had heard Dr. King's "I Have a Dream" speech before, just not given by me. In fact, most of the folks in that audience probably never expected to hear that speech given by me. After all, I was just an elementary school kid from the projects. I was one of them —from the same school, same neighborhood, same projects and same city. I was proud to stand alone on that stage representing the community from which I came. The truth of the matter is, I was never really alone on stage. It may have appeared that way, but GOD and my entire community was standing right beside me. Every single person in that audience who yearned for the uplifting power of Dr. King's words had a spot on that stage.

    I will forever be grateful that GOD placed someone like Mrs. Pettifer in my life. It is a true blessing to cross paths with someone who can sometimes believe in you more than you believe in yourself. The fact that Mrs. Pettifer never allowed the pressure of putting on a good performance to dissuade her from believing in me will forever be cherished. Her faith in me thirty plus years ago, serves as a reminder that we all are capable of more than we typically give ourselves credit for. At eleven years old, I would have never dreamed of successfully memorizing a speech as lengthy as Dr. King's "I Have a Dream" speech. That's because I was basing my fears on an anticipated experience. In other words, my fear was based on a predicted reality instead of actual reality.

    It's unfortunate how often we sell ourselves short because of our tendency to base our future capabilities on our past experiences. Having to memorize Dr. King's speech taught me that there are always factors that we don't take into account when it comes to bringing out our true capabilities. When confronted with a new challenge, we naturally fall back on an old mindset. We evaluate our chances of success based on "what we know" and "what we don't know." Rarely do we consider the "don't know what we don't know" factor in assessing our capabilities. Mrs. Pettifer knew that writing out multiple copies of a speech was a crucial part to memorizing a speech. This was unknown to me and therefore not taken into account as I considered whether or not I could memorize the speech. If I would have known about this powerful memorization tool, maybe I would have approached the assignment with more confidence. Another factor that I didn't consider was the role that an audience plays during the delivery of a speech. If I had known that my audience would be a source of confidence and not fear, I would have been less afraid to walk out on stage. These are examples of what I like to call "don't know what you don't know" factors. If we fail to realize that these factors exist, we are more likely to be limited in our confidence in our abilities. As human beings, it is naturally easier to see our environment working against us than for us. Unfortunately, this assumption can come at our own peril.

 Thanks to my sixth grade angel, Mrs. Pettifer, I learned the importance of taking into account "the unknowns" when taking on new challenges. It is often unwise to presume that current knowledge is adequate enough to predict future outcomes. One can't help but wonder: If Dr. King had relied on his current knowledge regarding racial inequality to predict future outcomes, would it have been possible for him to believe so strongly in HIS DREAM? Great leaders often teach us that sometimes the dream itself has to be enough to push us forward.

KARATE

As a kid who loved being outside and running the project streets with my friends, I can tell you that there were only three things that could make my friends and I go inside the house: grandma or mama's voice, rain, and "Kung Fu Theater" on Saturdays on channel 20. Every weekend on channel 20, they would show classic Bruce Lee, Bruce Li, Jim Kelly, and Bolo Kung Fu flicks. At the gullible age of ten, my friends and I believed every flip, kick, and move was real. So much so that we practiced these Kung Fu moves at school during recess as soon as we hit the playground on Monday. My 5th grade friends and I had every fake fighting sound effect, technique, and round-house kick mastered down to an art. We couldn't wait until after lunch recess to bust out our best Bruce Lee moves.

Martial Arts wasn't just popular in my neighborhood during the 70's and 80's, but throughout the country. During those years, there was a very popular "Jhoon Rhee" Karate commercial that aired constantly on TV. There were two kids in the commercial who became famous for saying the phrase— "Nobody bothers me...Nobody bothers me either!" My friends and I had seen that commercial a million times, but as far as I knew, no one had ever taken "Jhoon Rhee" Karate classes. Because of my growing fascination with Kung Fu and Karate, I eventually decided to ask my mom if I could take Karate lessons. She reacted strangely at first, but agreed to look into it. About a week later, she took me to one of the local "Jhoon Rhee" Karate studios at the mall to sign me up for classes. I remember walking into the studio with my mom and seeing all of the kids training in their Karate suits, which I later learned were called "Gis." This was the real deal. Even though I had watched tons of Kung Fu and Karate movies on TV, I was blown away by what I saw. The discipline and focus of the kids in the class was unbelievable. I couldn't help but wonder how the instructors maintained so much control of a class full of ten-year-olds. Were the kids afraid that they might get punched or kicked for acting up? It sure seemed like it. All kinds of thoughts were swirling around in my head at the time. All I knew for certain was that I wanted to be one of those kids in that class.

My mom was also blown away by the command the instructors had over the kids. It was obvious that she was impressed by the discipline being taught, but she remained nervous about the kicking and punching. As my mom talked to the people at the registration desk, I continued to watch the class through the glass wall that surrounding the studio. While I looked on, I couldn't help but hear the studio workers discussing pricing, scheduling, and membership requirements with my mom. Even though my mom was on board for signing me up, I knew cost would be a deciding factor. I was just a kid, but I was still pretty good at interpreting my mom's mood when it came to affordability. As I looked towards the registration desk, I could immediately sense the hesitation in my mom's mood as the guy at the registration desk ran through the list of fees and costs. All I could do was just stand there with my fingers crossed, pretending not to notice the drop in her mood. After a few minutes of going back and forth with questions and concerns, to my surprise, my mom suddenly reached for the purse! For a ten-year-old, a mom reaching for her purse is just as exciting as hearing the bell from an ice cream truck coming around the corner. I couldn't believe it! I was getting signed up for "Jhoon Ree" Karate classes! As excited as I was about taking classes, I was even more excited about getting my white belt and Karate suit.

    My first class was scheduled a week from the day my mom signed me up. The only thing the instructors told me was to wear sweat pants and a t-shirt on my first day. I didn't know it, but my Karate Gi had to be ordered, so I wouldn't have it until my second or third class at the earliest. Wearing sweat pants didn't leave any room for doubt about who was the new fish in class. Just like the first day at a new school, all of the kids stared at me as I walked into the studio. I was really nervous, but my excitement to be in a "Jhoon Rhee" Karate class overshadowed my anxiety. As the class began to start, it only took a few minutes before I realized my ignorance of Karate and Kung Fu. I thought I would be learning how to flip in the air and break bricks on the first day. No one told me about the necessary physical conditioning component of learning Karate. In the movies, the Karate guys didn't do jumping jacks, push-ups or sit-ups. For some crazy reason, I guess I thought that the strength and flexibility required to learn Karate came naturally.

    If there was anything that I took away from my first training class, it was the realization that I was a long way from being able to bust out any Bruce Lee moves. I had to learn to appreciate Karate as an art, and something more than just flipping and fighting. The training is all about building discipline, control, and both, physical and spiritual fitness. My first class began with lots and lots of stretching. The goal was to create flexibility in the body and to lessen the chance of injury. I consider this stage of training "the breakdown" stage. Our bodies were being prepared to take on a whole "new form." This new flexibility would be physical as well as mental. As our bodies were pushed further, our minds opened wider. This was the first time in my life that I realized that mental fitness is directly related to physical fitness. The discipline that it takes to achieve physical fitness becomes the foundation for mental and spiritual fitness. For all the times that my mom had a hard time getting me to focus and listen, I can't help but wonder about the difference it would have made if she had made me start each day with twenty push-ups and fifty jumping-jacks. Of course, she had other ways to get me to listen, but there is something to be said about the ability of a single Karate instructor being able to get a room full of ten-year-olds to remain as still as a rock by giving a single command.

One Karate class in and I was sure hoping the second class was more exciting than the first. Doing a bunch of jumping-jacks in sweat pants was not what I envisioned when I signed up for Karate. I had only been to one class, but I needed some excitement. If I could just punch the air or lift one foot off the floor, I would have been happy. A week later, when I showed up for my second class, the instructor surprised me with my new Gi! My mom was so proud when she saw me come out of the changing area dressed in my first Karate suit. As a new student, I wore a white belt, but you would have thought it was a black belt, judging by the huge smile on my face. There were other white belts in my class, but most of students had either yellow or orange. Being a typical, jealous ten-year-old, that smile on my face eventually faded as I began wishing I had a colored belt. I hadn't even attempted a kick or thrown a punch, but I was already ready for a promotion.

With six training classes in, everything seemed to be going smoothly. I was becoming good friends with some of the other white belt kids in my class. The instructors had even begun teaching us "Chon-Ji," the first Tae Kwon Do form that is taught to a student. Finally, I felt like I was actually learning Karate. We still did a million jumping jacks at the beginning of class, but at least we were getting to the "real deal" basics of Karate. Just when I thought I was on my way to becoming the next Bruce Lee, my happy bubble suddenly popped. It was at the end of my sixth class when I was hit with the bad news. My mom told me that she was going to have to pull me out of Karate because it was too expensive. Needless to say, I was devastated. I did everything I could to hold back my tears until I got into the car. There was no way I could let my Karate classmates see me crying. As soon as we pulled off, the tears started rolling. My mom, attempting to be strong, didn't shed any tears. However, there was a sadness on her face as if she knew that she had let me down. Usually, it was only me that got upset when I didn't get what I wanted. This was different. It was as if my mom was losing out on something too. Signing me up for Karate classes had turned out to be more than just something fun for me to do once a week. As her son, the discipline and training that I received every week, over the course of those six weeks, was a priceless experience. It was only natural that it broke my mom's heart that I could no longer be a part of that experience.

    After a few days of being sad about the hiccup in my Bruce Lee aspirations, I moved on and got back to the reality of playground Kung Fu with my friends. In a weird surprise, my mother had not moved on. Ever since she canceled my Jhoon Rhee classes, she had been asking around about places that might offer cheaper Karate classes. Eventually, her efforts paid off! A friend of a friend told my mom about a Karate instructor who taught classes in the evening at one of the local high schools. Supposedly, this instructor offered classes at very reasonable prices with flexible payment options. Hearing that made it worthwhile to at least go and check out this guy's classes. It spoke volumes about the integrity of an instructor who was willing to sacrifice his time and income in order to expose kids to Martial Arts, who couldn't normally afford it.

When my mom told me about the cheap Karate classes being offered at a nearby high school, I was hesitant to express interest at first. The last thing I wanted to do was to get my hopes up and be let down again. Regardless of my hesitation, I figured it couldn't hurt to at least go and check out the class. After a few minutes of thinking about it, I asked my mom if she would take me to see the class one day that week after she got home from work. Two days later, my mom and I were driving down to the high school, which was located in Seat Pleasant, Maryland. It was about a fifteen minute drive from my grandparents' house in Southeast, D.C. Before we pulled into the parking lot of the school, we both agreed that we were only there to check the class out. She told me, "If you like it great, if you don't, no big deal."

As soon as we walked into the school gym, we were both shocked by what we saw. The old high school gym may not have looked anything like the fancy Jhoon Rhee studio with its Karate posters and weapons on the walls, but the training that was taking place blew Jhoon Rhee out of the water! This was no commercialized or cookie-cutter Karate training franchise. This was a real deal Karate class. The instructor that stood in front of that class in that high school gym was there for one reason and one reason only —to teach Karate. It was as if he was training a unit of soldiers for battle. As a nervous observer considering joining the class, I was just hoping that they knew that I was on their side. All I could think about was that if my old Jhoon Rhee class ever had to go up against this class, team Jhoon Rhee would be in some trouble. To say that my mom and I were impressed by what we saw in that high school gym that evening would be an understatement. We ended up staying until the very end of class to meet the instructor. After he and my mom talked for several minutes, the instructor suddenly looked at me and asked if I was ready to begin training next week. Not knowing what else to say, I said, "Sure!" That was it. All it took was one visit to see this instructor teach and I was now enrolled in my new Karate class.

From the moment I started the class, I was told by my family not to let any of my friends in the neighborhood know about it. They thought that if the word got out in the neighborhood about me taking Karate classes, kids would begin starting fights with me or worst, feel the need to use a weapon if they got into a fight with me. For a kid who was so excited about learning Karate, it was tough for me to keep my mouth shut in the beginning. When I would see my friends on the schoolyard doing pretend Karate or Kung Fu, I no longer joined in. I thought that they might see something different in my moves and I would have no choice but to tell them. Even though I was only a kid, Karate was something that I took very seriously. More than anything, I wanted to be good at it. I didn't want to do anything to jeopardize my classes. The excuse I gave my friends was that "Mr. Roberts," the recess teacher, told us not to play "pretend" Karate anymore. My friends found it suspicious that I was the only one who heard Mr. Roberts say this, but they were too afraid to ask him. It eventually became easier to hide my new found Karate skills once my friends got the hint and stopped asking me to play "pretend" Karate.

Even though my training was supposed to be kept a secret, I would still practice techniques and moves in the back of my grandmother's house, hoping that someone walking by would notice. The few times that I was caught by friends, I just told them that I learned a new move on Saturday Kung Fu Theater. One of the things that I picked up from training that I didn't try to hide was my new found flexibility. Just like a high school cheerleader, I could do a full-blown split, legs completely straight! My friends couldn't believe it! It was fun showing off and seeing the confused looks on my friends' faces. Even I couldn't believe the positions I could place my body. As a kid, this was the first time I realized how truly amazing the human body can be. The product of my commitment and training was taking place right in front of my own eyes. I started asking myself —"What else can I achieve with my body? What else can I be trained to do?"

- Chapter 6 -

Moving to the Suburbs

Before the age of twelve, I had essentially no interaction with white kids. Growing up in an "all black" public housing project gave me a zero chance of having any white friends. The fact that every day everyone around me was black was my reality. It was the only world I had so far ever known. Little did I know, things were about to change for me in a big way. My mom was getting ready to shake up my world. She was getting ready to introduce someone new into our lives that would bring us out of our old neighborhood. Someone that would open my eyes to a whole new world.

    As we all know, change can be very scary. For nearly all of my childhood, life was all about my mom and me. Of course, she had off and on boyfriends since her and my biological father went their separate ways, but nothing super serious. Even though most of those boyfriends didn't stay in the picture long, I inevitably became attached to a few of them. Sometimes it was tough when they would just all of a sudden disappear from the scene. My mom never really explained why "that guy" that she seemed to be having a great time with was no longer around. I guess she thought that I was too young to understand the dynamics of a relationship or that I might become sad knowing that this person would no longer be coming around.

It's always tough for a child of a single parent to accept and get used to sharing their mom or dad with someone else, especially if you are the only child. Speaking from experience as an only child, the idea of some strange dude coming into your life and trying to play dad is just weird. These poor guys, who were probably just looking for a casual, fun date had me to deal with. I didn't hesitate neither, to let them know how protective I was over my mother. Even if I liked the guy, it took me a while to warm up to him. These boyfriends would sometimes try to buy me off with toys and money, but I wasn't cheap. This was my mother after all. As her only son, I wasn't going to make it easy for any of these guys.

By the time I entered the fifth grade, I started to notice that it had been a while since my mom had mentioned anything about any new guys in her life. This was fine with me of course, but it had to be tough on my mom sometimes being alone. Unfortunately, I would selfishly forget that she had feelings too. My mom was still a young woman with dreams of her own. I'm sure she wanted more than anything to meet someone special, to be married, and to have a home. So far, life for her just wasn't' going in that direction.

THE NEW GUY

My mother made the best life she could without a steady man in her life. She had a stable job and her own apartment, which was, conveniently, only a fifteen minute drive from my grandparent's house. I rarely ever stayed with her at the apartment because of school. My elementary school was less than a five minute walk from my grandparents' house, so it didn't make sense for me to stay at the apartment during the week. Besides, all of my friends lived in the projects. I still got to see my mom pretty much every day since she would always stop by grandma's house for dinner after work. She wasn't the only one who couldn't get away from "mama's" cooking. My uncles and aunts would also conveniently show up around dinner time, pretending just to visit. Even though most of them had moved out years ago, "mama's" cooking was obviously something they couldn't outgrow.

    Regardless of the reasons that my family magically showed up at grandma's dinner table every evening, it was our way of staying close as a family. It was also a time to bond and share any new developments in our lives. One evening, my mom decided to share her new development. She would finally end the mystery regarding her relationship status. Up until that moment, no one knew anything or had bothered asking. She told us all in the kitchen that she had met a new "friend" and his name was Kurt. They had met at her job and that she wanted us to meet him. Judging by her mood, I could tell that there was something special about this guy. Her face was filled with pure joy, only to be immediately robbed by a protective son. Predicting my insecure reaction, my mom hugged me right away. She told me that she loved me and that I had nothing to worry about. Trusting her, I quickly wiped away my tears and ran out the backdoor to go play with my friends. They were in the middle of playing hide-and-go-seek, so I found a perfect hiding spot behind the green dumpster in the alley. It was a good spot, but all I kept thinking about was mom's "new friend."

During the time when my mother met Kurt, she was working for the Department of the Navy in Arlington, Virginia. He was in the Navy, but taking a break from ship duty for a desk job. The first thing she told me about him was that he was a really nice guy and wanted to meet me right away. Also she mentioned that he was from Florida, which caused all kinds of questions to popup in my head. I had never met anyone from Florida, let alone a black person. A black guy from Florida? That was unheard of in my small little world of South East, D.C. As millions of questions swirled around in my head, I started to actually look forward to meeting Kurt. Who was this out-of-towner that my mom was so excited for the family to meet?

Two weeks had passed since my mom first told me about the "new guy." For the first time, I would get a chance to finally meet him that upcoming weekend. My mom was bringing Kurt over to my grandparents' house for the first time. She told me that they were coming by on Saturday afternoon and to make sure that I was presentable by 3 o'clock. You bet I was going to be looking sharp to meet this guy. He had to know right away that I meant business. I had my grandfather take me down to the barbershop right after breakfast that Saturday morning to get a fresh shape-up. My mom had already picked out and ironed the outfit she wanted me to wear the night before. Mom was counting on me to represent her and our family well.

Just like clockwork, Kurt and my mom pulled up in front of my grandparents' house at 3 o'clock sharp. He was driving a 1980 black Ford Granada with raised white letter sport tires. The same car my mother drove, except hers was a different year and dark green. If compatibility was based on their car choices, they were sure off to a great start. Staring out the front screen door, one of the things that caught my eyes the most was his Florida license plate that stood out from the other D.C. license plates that lined the street. If I noticed that happy Floridian license plate, I'm sure someone else in the neighborhood did as well.

When Kurt finally stepped out of his shiny black Granada and started walking towards my grandparents' house, it was hard not to notice the kind, gentle smile he had on his face. It was also hard not to notice the fancy leather sandals he was wearing. This was a guy who had clearly experienced life outside of city life. If the sandals didn't make that obvious, his walk surely did. Kurt walked with his back straight and shoulders back. He projected a level of confidence and seriousness in his walk that I wasn't used to seeing from men. Most of the guys his age from my neighborhood walked with a carefree "swagger" that was typical of black men from the projects. We often referred to this carefree "swagger" as "walking with a pimp" or "pimping." It's when you walk and slightly swing your arms and shoulders forward and backward while delaying bending one of our knees before you take the next step. It sounds complicated when trying to describe it in words, but to see how it's actually done, watch any Blaxploitation film from the 1970's. You will see how a "pimping" strut is actually done.

Other than the fancy leather sandals and "robotic" walk, Kurt seemed like a normal, nice guy. He greeted me with a firm handshake and told me that he heard that I was a really smart kid and got really good grades in school. Of course, I smiled right away and thanked him. As much as I tried not to be nervous, I just couldn't help it. Thankfully, my mom knew that I would be nervous meeting Kurt for the first time. She didn't expect for me to want to stick around and talk for too long. A few minutes after Kurt and I got past "nice to meet you," my mom sent me on my way to go outside and play with my friends. Rather than push me too hard on the first introduction, I guess she decided it made more sense to take things slow.

Looking back on the first time Kurt and I met, I realize that my mom definitely did the right thing by taking the slow approach when it came to getting to know the new male figure in her life. Based on how critical I was of past new boyfriends, things probably would have backfired if she would have moved too quickly. Meeting the new guy dating your mom is probably awkward for any son or daughter at any age. It is only natural to be nervous, protective, and even judgmental towards a stranger who is attempting to become a part of your family. Just the simple fact that I paid attention to the type of shoes my mom's new boyfriend was wearing was a clear sign of how critical I could be as a son.

Even the way Kurt talked didn't get past my radar. He "talked white" is how we referred to it in my old neighborhood. It's sad that, even today, being a black man and speaking proper English clearly and in a manner in which people can understand what the hell you're saying is referred to as "talking white." I often wonder, "How did such ignorant seeds get planted in our communities?" If you are going to label speaking proper English as speaking "white," I challenge folks to at least try to define what that means. Anyone who has a TV or doesn't live under a rock, knows that not all white people talk the same or speak perfect English. It all depends on where you live, where you are from, and most importantly, your education. "Talking white" could mean sounding like Tom Brokaw or sounding like Larry "the Cable Guy." Skin color does not determine a solid grasp of the English language.

Even today, if I ran into my old friends from the neighborhood, there is a good chance that some of them would probably tell me that I talked differently or "talked white." Well, I got news for you old friends —I interact with lots of white people on a daily basis and sometimes I don't understand what the hell some of them are saying. It could be because of a strong southern accent or just plan, broken English. No one race or ethnic group has total ownership over proper or improper English.

As my mom's "proper English speaking" boyfriend, Kurt, started being around the family more and more, I quite naturally started to warm up to him. I even started liking his proper English! It became obvious to me that this was a quality man who wanted more than to just causally date my mom. I could see how Kurt enjoyed being around my big family and bonding with my uncles, who were around the same age as him. My mom had mentioned to me one day that Kurt's parents had passed away and the only person in his family that he was really close to was his sister. This explained a lot as to why he showed a great appreciation of our closeness as a family. This was something that he was obviously missing in his life.

The next several months into my mother's new relationship flew by really quickly. Kurt had become pretty much a part of the family. He and my mom eventually moved in together and things took off very quickly from there. They got engaged and I had to come to grips with the fact that I was going to have a father in my life. This meant a new world for me and I was full of mixed emotions. I told myself that I would get used to it and eventually it would become normal for me to have a dad. At the time, most of my cousins had fulltime dads and it usually seemed like a plus. They lived in nicer homes and had bigger TV sets. Life seemed pretty cool having both, a mom and dad around.

Just as I began to get excited at the idea of my mom getting married and me having a fulltime dad in my life, is when my mom hit me with the news. She told me that Kurt was going to have to leave the country for a several months. He had to go out to sea for ship duty. His desk duties at the Department of the Navy were coming to an end. Kurt was being deployed on the USS Nassau and headed for Saudi Arabia. All of this sounded crazy, especially to a ten year old who had barely ever left the projects. This would become my very first taste of military family life.

When the day finally came for Kurt to fly out for deployment, I rode with my mom to take him to the airport. On the ride there, neither one of them showed much emotion. Kurt acted like he was coming back tomorrow and my mom acted like he wasn't leaving at all. It seemed like they both were fighting to hold it all in. That all changed once we all got to the gate just before boarding. My mom and soon to be dad hugged and kissed like I had never seen before. In all honesty, it was probably a bit too much for public display. None of that mattered though. This was no normal trip and therefore no time for normal goodbyes. Kurt was not only going to be gone for months, but he was also going out to sea during very dangerous times. It was 1981 and tensions between the Soviet Union and the United States were escalating. The two countries were locked in a Cold War. The planet was living in constant fear that a nuclear war could break out at any time. To assume that this deployment was just like any other would have been a mistake.

After waiting for my mom to get out all of her last goodbyes, I finally decided that it was my turn to say goodbye to Kurt. Before I could figure out what to say and without thinking, I just ran over to him and hugged him as tightly as I could. This was the first time that I cried for a man because I was going to miss him like a father. When Kurt and my mom saw me crying, they both started crying. It was a sign to them both, that I had emotionally accepted Kurt as my new dad. Knowing that I was going to be calling this brave man in uniform "dad" made me feel so proud. To me, that uniform represented being a man —a selfless man. A man willing to stand for and defend something bigger than himself. This was a man I could look up to.

    Judging by how upset my mom was when we said our goodbyes to Kurt that day at the airport, I knew it was going to be a tough several months for her. It was completely understandable. Basically, her start at a new life was headed out to board a ship that was headed to the other side of the world. What fiancé wouldn't be upset? All she could do was count down the days and try to stay positive. Of course, some days had to be easier than others. I could always tell the good days. Out of nowhere, my mom would all of a sudden start talking about Kurt and their big plans together. Their plans are obviously what kept her going.

    To my surprise, they had even started planning for their wedding that was to take place once Kurt returned from sea. Somehow, my mom had found a way to keep this little secret all to herself for months. It was only by accident that I stumbled upon their plans. Looking for something in my mom's closet one day, I noticed several boxes and bags of wedding decorations stuffed in the corner. When I asked her about the mysterious baby blue plates, ribbons, and fancy tableware in the closet, she had no choice but to spill the beans. I knew that they were going to married, but I just didn't know that they had already picked out plates! She explained that the reason that they didn't tell anyone about the wedding is because Kurt wasn't sure exactly when he would be home. Being privy to exact return dates was just not something his duties in the Navy allowed. Unpredictability —This would become my second taste of military family life.

The days and months seemed to drag on without Kurt around, but my mom passed the time by staying busy. When she wasn't working, she spent her time thinking about the wedding and house hunting. Living in a small apartment in Southeast, D.C. was not in my future dad's plans. Before he left, Kurt and my mom talked about where they might want to live. Knowing my mom, she probably wanted to buy something as close to my grandparents as possible and knowing Kurt, he probably wanted to buy something as far away from the hustle and bustle of D.C. as possible. He was a quiet, to himself kind of guy. Space, land, and lots of trees seemed to be more of his speed. Most of my uncles and aunts already lived in the Maryland suburbs, but they were still no more than a fifteen minute drive from D.C. It seemed that none of them wanted to be too far away from grandma and granddad. Kurt had other plans for his family. He and my mom were considering the more rural parts of Prince George's County Maryland. It was because of their conversations before he left, that my mom chose to spend most of her house hunting time looking at houses in the most southern parts of Prince George's County. As if it wasn't already bad enough that I was going to be leaving all of my friends and the action in the projects, but now my mom was trying to move me out into the country.

It had been almost six months since my mom and I took Kurt to the airport to depart for his sea duties near Saudi

Arabia, but Kurt was finally coming home. It was a day of happiness, celebration, and relief the day we picked him up from the airport. For my mom, her new light could shine once more. But the celebrations didn't last long. Only a few days after he returned, Kurt found that he would have to go back out to sea again in a couple of months. The unpredictability of military family life had raised its ugly head again. The only good news was that after this next tour, he was going to be stationed in Norfolk, Virginia for at least a year. For now, this would have to be enough for my mom to hold on to.

 With clouds of uncertainty hanging over their new relationship, both Kurt and my mom needed something that could provide some sense of stability. So before Kurt took off for this second tour, they both decided that they no longer wanted to wait for a formal wedding to get married. Under their current circumstances, it just made more sense to just head to the courthouse to make it official and save the festivities for another time. It was more important to them to make sure that when Kurt left for duty this time, he was leaving as a husband and when he returned, he would be coming home to a wife. Now with the deal sealed, they could put all of their efforts into finding a house. With only two weeks left before heading out on a ship, Kurt and my mom managed to find a home and even go to closing. Under tremendous pressure, "The New Guy" was making things happen. Change was on the horizon —Suburbs here I come!

ESCAPING THE CRAB BUCKET

The year was 1983. My life was getting ready to go in a completely new direction. My mother no longer had a "New

Guy," but a husband. A husband who was a U.S. Navy sailor, fresh off the ship from a tour of duty. This was the man that GOD had chosen to give us a new perspective on life.

That new perspective would start out in the small city of Clinton, Maryland, which was located in southern Prince George's County. Clinton was only about a forty minute drive from my grandparents' house in Southeast D.C., but it seemed much further away. Back then, Clinton was a very rural and very "white" community. Other than us, there was only one other black family that lived on our street. Coming from the "all black" projects, I felt like I had moved to Mars. The gravel roads and dark woods at night didn't help much either. Before Clinton, my world was made up of asphalt streets and nocturnal neighborhoods that were lit just as bright at night as they were during the day. My new street was barely even paved. How was that even possible? It was 1983, the age of VCR's, cordless phones, and Atari —How tough could it be to pave a road? As a kid from the projects of D.C., I didn't see how I could ever get used to this life.

We moved to Clinton right after I graduated from sixth-grade. Fortunately, it was still summer break so that gave me some time before school started back up to try to get used to my new neighborhood. I spent most of my time riding my bike up and down the street, avoiding talking to any of my neighbors if I could help it. Getting comfortable with my new environment took a priority over making friends. It was obviously going to be a step by step process for me to fully embrace my new home. I felt that if I could just spend the summer coming to grips with the fact that this new life was going to be permanent, it would be easier for me to open up to new friends. Besides, "What choice did I have?" At the end of summer, I was going to be attending middle school with some of these kids in the neighborhood anyways. There was no way I could keep this antisocial charade going for too much longer.

Summer soon ended and my first day of middle school on Mars had finally arrived. I don't remember much about the school bus ride there, but I remember getting off the bus in front of the school and feeling sick from nervousness. The next thing I remember, is walking into a large school lunch room, packed with loud kids waiting for instructions of what to do on their first day of school. Eventually, a lady with a loud, shrieking voice told all of us to quiet down and sit at our assigned tables. Before I left for school that morning, my mom told me that I was on "Team B," but I didn't know what that meant until now. All of the students had to sit at designated lunch tables, which were divided by teams and grade levels. Looking around with a clueless look on my face, I finally spotted the table for Team B, Grade 7 and grabbed the first seat I could find. As soon as I sat down, I began to take it all in. The racial diversity of the students and teachers in that lunch room was nothing like the monolithic gatherings at my old elementary school. There, all of the teachers and all of the students were black. This was new territory for me. Not only was I starting a new school, but I was beginning a new reality. Up until this point in my life, the only other time I had a chance to interact with kids that weren't black was during a fifth-grade summer camp. This multicultural summer camp, I was fortunate enough to attend, was designed for gifted and talented kids from all over the D.C. metro area. The program was held at the prestigious National Cathedral School in Washington, D.C. Thankfully, because of this summer camp, I wasn't totally unprepared for my new reality of middle school life on Mars.

Anticipating my anxiety and fears, my mom shared with me a few choice words of wisdom a few days before my first day at middle school —"Treat everyone the same and you better stick up for yourself if somebody puts their hands on you." Somehow, she knew that if I followed and enforced those simple rules, everything else would fall into place. The way we were raised, allowing someone to put their hands on you was not to be tolerated. It was well understood that if I didn't stick up for myself in public, there would be a price to pay at home. Being the smart kid that I was, I knew that price and allowing myself to get handled by another kid was just not an option.

Fortunately, on the first day of school, most kids are interested in making friends rather than starting trouble. This was obvious as I looked around at all of the kids in the lunch room on that first day back from summer break. The room was filled with only loud laughter and smiles. This first day, for me, presented the perfect opportunity to break the ice and to make new friends who could help me ease into my new surroundings. That opportunity presented itself when I noticed a chubby white kid sitting across the room from me, wearing the same grey and blue Adidas jacket as me. He even had the matching Adidas pants, which gave him huge cool points in my book. Unfortunately, I only had the jacket because my mom couldn't find the matching pants in my size. Pants or no pants, this was a potential opportunity to make a friend. I would just have to wait for the right time to introduce myself.

Soon after everyone took a seat at their assigned tables, the homeroom bell finally rang and it was time to head to class. As I stood up from my lunchroom table and began walking towards the exit doors with the other kids, I noticed that my white "Adidas twin" brother was walking towards me. He was smiling as he approached me and said, "Nice jacket!" I smiled back and responded, "Nice pants!" He told me his name was Mike and we agreed to look for one another in the hallways or during lunch breaks. History was being made right before my eyes and I didn't even know it. Mike had officially become my first "white friend." Looking back on that day, the idea of labeling someone a "white friend" seems so strange considering the diversity of the friends in my life today. Who would have ever thought that something as simple as having matching Adidas jackets would end up being the pin to burst my "having-only-black-friends bubble?" Because of Mike, my preference of friends based on skin color had finally come to an end.

After running into one another on almost a daily basis, Mike and I soon became really close friends. We realized that we had a lot more in common than just matching Adidas jackets. Both of us were really into BMX bikes, break dancing, and surprisingly, getting good grades. I told him about growing up in the projects and the "creative" things that we did for fun. Even though we were raised in two extremely different worlds, you would never know it based on how we clicked from the start. We both embraced positive fun and had no interest in hanging out with the so called "cool" kids, otherwise known as the trouble making kids. I had more than enough of that crowd living in D.C. Mike told me that he grew up in Clinton and lived in a neighborhood right around the corner from the school. Having lived in the tightknit community his hold life, Mike knew lots of people and had lots of friends. Mike's friends would eventually become my friends. For a black kid starting out in what I perceived as a new "white world," it appeared that I couldn't have picked a more perfect "first white friend."

At the time I met Mike, I was only a twelve year old kid in the seventh grade, but I knew, through the grace of GOD, that surrounding myself with good, quality friends was my best shot at staying out of trouble. Unfortunately, it didn't take long before realizing that suburban life doesn't guarantee a trouble-free life. For me, I wasn't so much looking for a guarantee, but a chance. A chance to avoid the dark paths and places in which our surroundings and choices in friends can sometimes lead us.

Looking back, I can honestly admit that Mike's friends were far from angels, but they at least had basic respect for themselves and other people. Aside from the typical dumb things that kids get into, none of Mike's friends were into fighting, stealing, or being "too cool" to do homework. Truthfully, I never really understood how the so called "cool kids" got away with not doing their homework. My mom would have knocked the "cool" right out of me if I even thought about not doing my homework. My mom took education seriously, and obviously, so did the parents of a lot of Mike's friends.

New to middle school and new to the suburbs, I tried my best to hang out with the non-trouble making kids. Being friends with Mike, sure did make that a whole lot easier. Because of him, my positive circle of friends grew. These were kids who enjoyed life, but also did their homework. It didn't make a difference to me that most of them just so happened to be white. Skin color no longer mattered to me, I just wanted to be around fun, positive people. Sadly, sometimes some of the other black kids in school would give me a hard time for hanging out with white kids. I found this to be crazy considering the fact that I grew up in an all-black public housing project and found a way to overlook skin color, but these suburban black kids couldn't. This was especially confusing since most of them grew up right here in the mostly white suburb of Clinton. What was their excuse for being closed minded? Who were they to question my "blackness" based on who I chose to hang around? The lack of diversity that I experienced growing up used to be the excuse for my insecurities regarding race —What was theirs?

Even at the young age of twelve, life was teaching me that living with insecurity and fear is a choice. Someone can be fortunate enough to be raised in a diverse environment, but still succumb to ugly attitudes and choices driven by fear. Moving to the suburbs, the last thing I expected to experience was disdain by those in my own race, just because of who I hung around. My natural assumption was that black kids would look out for other black kids, especially in a majority white middle school environment. Unfortunately, this was not the case. It was obviously naïve of me to think that just because I shared the same skin color with someone in my school, we would automatically become friends. This didn't happen with white kids, so why would it happen with black kids? True friendships are irrespective of race, but are built upon a shared personal value system.

Mike and I shared, what we considered, an "all about the fun and staying out of trouble" value system. The so called "cool kids" and bullies in our school didn't share these same values. As a result, they felt the need to delegitimize our values by sometimes mocking and making fun of us. Because we didn't walk around the school looking "hard" or looking for trouble, we weren't considered "cool." Looking back, that "cool," "acting hard" shit was way overrated. Getting good grades opened more doors than being "cool" ever could.

One of the most harmful aspects of having a negative personal value system is that you tend to want to keep or bring others down to your level. For example, a punk kid who doesn't like school will often tease or make fun of a student who excels in school. The goal is to lessen the perceived value of getting an education in order to justify his or her own personal weakness or disdain for learning. They often attempt to hide their weaknesses in numbers. As long as the punk kid is alone in his twisted value system, his weakness remains exposed. For them, influencing others to question the value of an education is seen as a win. The goal being, "If I can get enough people to join me on the bottom of the barrel, then I won't have to think about my own weaknesses." Growing up, we used to refer to those too weak to rise above their own circumstances, but who thrived on dragging others down, as having a "crabs in a bucket" mentality. This old saying refers to how crabs in a bucket react when another crab attempts to climb out or escape. Crabs that remain in the bucket will use their claws to grab onto the crabs that are attempting to escape and hold onto them, ensuring that they all meet the same fate.

When I moved to the suburbs and started hanging out with Mike and other white friends, I had no idea how many "crabs" I would stir up. Getting bullied was nothing new to me, but I had never before been given a hard time for who I chose to hang out with. Coincidently, I had never experienced being black and having both black and white friends either. I guess you could say, "This 'crab' had definitely climbed outside of his bucket." The fact of the matter is, whenever you go against what's easy, you're going to encounter some form of resistance. The good news is, this is where your strength is built. The few "crabs" that did attempt to keep me in the bucket ultimately failed. I continued to climb, making friends of all colors. In fact, I may have even pulled a few "crabs" from the bottom to join me outside of the bucket.

RAKE THE LEAVES: THE GOOD FIGHT

"A hard head makes a soft behind."
- Mom

With each passing day, I was settling in more and more in my new hometown. The suburban life of Clinton, Maryland, surprisingly, was starting to grow on me. My relatives still joked about us moving to "the country," but I got used to it. In all honesty, compared to Southeast, D.C., Clinton was "the country." Instead of asphalt and pavement, we were surrounded by big yards and big trees.

It wasn't long after I moved to the suburbs that I soon realized that somebody had to take care of those big yards. At my house, that somebody ended up being me. Before moving to Clinton, the closest I ever got to yard work was watching my grandmother take care of her rose bushes in the front yard. Truthfully, it wasn't much of a front yard, but more like a square patch of grass with a one foot by five foot strip of dirt butting up against it. Regardless of its size, it was special to her and that's all that mattered.

My yard in Clinton was a lot more than a square patch of grass. The front and back yard combined made up almost an acre of lawn. To make matters worse, huge trees with lots of leaves surrounded both. Compared to the small yards in the projects, my front and back yard were like two football fields. I didn't have to be a lawn expert to realize that with a big yard comes big work. All of that grass in the summer was going to have to be mowed and all of those leaves in the fall were going to have to be raked. I was getting ready to find out what real yard work was like.

During the summer months, it was all about mowing. My stepdad bought a brand new, shiny red lawn mower for our new house, so I actually looked forward to cutting the grass every weekend. With each cut, I naturally developed a sense of pride in keeping our yard looking polished. My mom and I joked about making sure we kept a neat lawn. As one of the only black families on our street, we weren't looking to give our white neighbors any reason to complain. Aside from that, I think it made my mom proud to see her son taking care of the lawn when my stepdad wasn't around. The military family life had essentially made me the "full-time" man of the house.

As the first fall in our new home rolled around, I knew that I would have my work cut out for me with raking leaves. I never saw so many leaves in my entire life. Fall had just arrived and both, the front and backyard were completely covered. Even the driveway was hidden in leaves. At some point, I knew I was going to be asked to bust out the rake. The good news was that my dad was home for a few weeks, so I hoped that I wouldn't be raking alone.

The day finally arrived that I was asked to grab my rake. Fortunately, my stepdad told me that he would be grabbing his too. I was relieved beyond measure knowing that he would be helping me out. This would be the first major house chore that we would be doing together since moving into our new home. We both knew that it was going to be a lot of work, but we agreed to try to make it as fun as possible. My stepdad even broke out his boom box to play some music while we worked. He decided that Jeffrey Osbourne and Billy Ocean would be our soundtrack for raking leaves. A little "Caribbean Queen" and yard work —What could be so bad about that?

With the music pumping, I started with the front yard and my stepdad started with the back. Because the front yard was a lot smaller, I guess my stepdad figured I wouldn't panic if I started there. I could tell that he didn't really know what to expect from me when it came to doing hard work. In a sense, we were both still feeling each other out. At this point, the thought never crossed my mind to back out of my responsibilities. Raking leaves was going to be like any other chore given to me, at least that's what I thought.

Two hours in, things seemed to be running like clockwork. The music turned out to be perfect for keeping the mood upbeat. I even had a pretty good system going where I would rake four piles at a time and then bag them. This kept me from getting burned out by trying to rake too much for too long. Bagging gave my back and arm muscles time to recover. By all accounts, it felt like we were on a roll.

Heading into hour number three, I made the mistake of pausing to assess our progress. I quickly realized that we were barely halfway done. This immediately zapped my spirits. I was sure we were at least three quarters of the way done. Now with my momentum lost, I decided to ask my stepdad if we could finish the rest tomorrow. In my mind, I thought it was a good chance that he would say yes, considering that we were almost halfway done. It seemed like a perfect pause point for us to pick it up tomorrow. I was getting tired and I figured he was too. I thought, if we stopped now, we could have the rest of Saturday to enjoy. Call me crazy, but it sounded like a good plan to me.

Having convinced myself that I had come up with the perfect idea for finishing up the rest of the leaves, I decided to discuss my brilliant plan with my stepdad. Before I could even fully roll out my proposal, I was hit with a firm, unequivocal

"No!" "These leaves need to be raked up today," my stepdad said with a stern, fatherly voice. I was expecting him to at least give me a good reason we couldn't finish raking tomorrow, but all I got was a firm "No!" This cold, unexplained "no" response was something I wasn't used to. Typically, with my mom, if I innocently asked a reasonable question, she would at least explain her reasons for saying no. I took my stepdad's response really hard because I thought that I was doing a good job. I thought he would have been proud of me for not complaining one single time. For whatever reason, my new stepdad decided that this was the moment that he would lay his law down.

Coming from the projects, I couldn't have imagined in a hundred years that I would be getting into trouble for not wanting to rake leaves. I wasn't afraid of work, but the idea of raking leaves all day just pushed me to my breaking point. Plus, I wasn't used to my stepdad forcefully telling me what to do. His real "daddy hat" wasn't quite broken in yet as far as I was concerned. I was still a mama's boy, nobody scared me but her. In my mind, our father-son relationship was still in the testing phase. I still wasn't comfortable taking orders that direct from anyone except my mom. My stepdad and I had clearly entered unchartered territory.

My first reaction when I realized that my stepdad meant business was to run and tell my mom. I figuring she might take up for me knowing that I had been raking leaves for at least two hours already. But my gut was telling me that she might not have my back this time. My stepdad, Kurt, was new at this dad thing, so she might have felt obligated to take his side. Not wanting to take a chance with mom, I suddenly decided to stand my ground on my own. I threw down my rake and told my stepdad that I was tired and done! My anger had overruled my fear of my stepdad's response. This was out of character for who I was raised to be. For the first time, I was shrinking away from my responsibilities and doing it directly to the person who was supposed to have just as much authority as my mom. Not knowing what my stepdad's response would be, I kept a safe distance just in case. Being a military man and a big believer in discipline, I knew I was playing with fire.

Truthfully, I think my stepdad was more shocked at my bold reaction than I was. There was at least thirty seconds of silence as we stood there in the middle of that half-racked backyard. Not knowing what else to do, I started crying and proceeded to march towards the backdoor of the house. Suddenly, I heard a calm, but firm voice say, "Come back over here, we are finishing raking all these leaves today." I started crying even more, as I kept walking toward the house with my head down. I told my stepdad again, "I ain't raking no more leaves!" Again, in a scary calm tone, my stepdad finally says —"You know what they say, a hard head makes a soft behind." I knew this phrase very well. My mother and grandmother used it quite often. This was the last thing they said before a belt or hand would make its way to your behind!

Not having completely lost my mind, I was not interested in my stepdad's version of what happens on the other side of that warning. Humbly, I sucked in my pride, wiped away the tears and I walked back towards my stepdad, who was surrounded by piles of unraked leaves. We both grabbed our rakes off the ground and got back in the fight until every leaf in the yard was raked and bagged. It took the fear of my stepdad's voice to put me back in the fight. Instead of fighting him, I chose to fight my desire to quit. This was a fight I knew I could win.

It took us at least three hours to finish the rest of the leaves, but we finally did it. When we finished, my stepdad didn't say much, but I could sense that he was proud of me for respecting his rightful authority as a father. For me, I was proud that I could show him that his stepson was no quitter. This entire experience ended up being about a lot more than raking leaves. It was a battle that served a higher purpose. A purpose that would not have revealed itself without the battle. Who could ever imagine that something as insignificant as raking leaves could lead to a stepfather becoming a real father in the eyes of his son? Who would ever think that the desire to quit could forever be erased the moment a son picks up his rake from off the ground? I surely couldn't.

We never know where our battles are going to take us or what purpose they will reveal. For me, what seemed at first like nothing more than a stubborn son and his stepfather fighting over yard chores, ended up laying the foundation for mutual respect and love between a father and son. This GOD delivered prize, like so many other priceless prizes, often only reveal themselves on the other side of our battles. Be thankful for the good fight.

TOP GUN

"There is no limit to the ingeniousness that is born out of freedom and the need to defend it."

Clinton, Maryland is a city that barely sticks out on a map, but it just so happens to be located right outside of one of the most famous military bases in the world, Andrews Air Force Base.

Today it is known as Joint Base Andrews. The military facility serves as home base to Air Force One, the official aircraft of the President of the United States of America. Living so close to Andrews Air Force Base was one of the coolest things about living in Clinton. Being able to see and hear fighter jets roar over your house every day was like being at an airshow every day. Unlike some of my "noise sensitive" neighbors, I actually looked forward to the daily roof shaking sounds of the fighter jets burning by. For me, it was a distinctive source of comfort. In the midst of a cold war with the Soviet Union, those roaring jet engines represented U.S. might and security. I was proud to know that the sounds that shook my house every day, came from the very thing that was protecting my country every day.

Before moving to Clinton, I didn't know that a plane could actually make a house shake. The sounds from some of the fighter jet and cargo plane flyovers would be so strong that we sometimes thought our windows were going to break. It was a bit scary at first, but we got used to it. Quite often, when I would hear the sound of a fighter jet flying in the direction of our house, I would sprint out into the front yard to see if I could catch of glimpse of it streaking across the sky. Sometimes, the planes would fly so fast that I would hear what sounded like loud explosions in the air. Later, I would find out from my stepfather that those explosions are called "sonic booms." This is the loud noise that is produced due to the extreme air pressure that builds up around the jet as it reaches the speed of sound, referred to as Mach 1 for aircraft. For the non-aeronautical astute, that's 717 mph!

Needless to say, living close to Andrews Air Force Base was good stuff. Being able to see fighter jets, cargo planes, and bombers fly through the sky from your front yard was definitely a unique neighborhood perk. Not everyone gets to sit in a front row seat every day to witness the pure awesomeness of the U.S. military. Also, not everyone gets to live next door to an air base that just so happens to put on one of the best air shows in the country. People from all over came to see the Blue Angels and the other amazing aircraft perform at Andrews.

When we first moved to Clinton, we didn't realize how big of a deal the air show was. I guess, living so close to the base, we kind of took it all for granted. In fact, the first time we attended an air show, it was by accident. On the actual day of an air show, my mom and I just so happened to be driving onto the base to go grocery shopping at the commissary. Not knowing there was an air show taking place, we got stuck in all kinds of traffic before finally making it to the commissary. As we walked towards the door, we were shocked by all of the people and cars lined up outside of the commissary. I thought to myself, "This show must be a big deal if the crowds are this big." All of a sudden, I no longer wanted to go grocery shopping, but wanted to hang out in the parking lot to watch the show. Feeling somewhat anxious, my mom told me, "Boy, hurry up inside this store before we get stuck in all this mess." I knew she was probably right, so I quickly grabbed a shopping cart and made my way into the store. I told myself, "Oh well, I guess I'll have to catch the show next time."

As we walked up and down the grocery aisles, filling our cart with food, I could hear the planes flying overhead. It was hard for me to focus on anything else except what was going on outside. It even seemed like my mom was a little curious. It felt like she was going down the aisles a little faster than usual. She had to be at least a little curious with all of the excitement going on at the base. I couldn't wait to get back outside in that parking lot. One thing for sure, I knew this was going to be the slowest I ever unpacked a shopping cart in my life.

Finally, we made our way to the checkout line, which was surprisingly short for a weekend. I guess, unlike us, everyone else was spending their Saturday watching the air show. We checked out very quickly, but we still had to bag all of our groceries. Back then, unlike civilian grocery stores, the commissary required you to bag your items yourself, or get one of the non-commissary employed baggers to do it for you. These people worked strictly on tips. It was a decent gig for summertime or part-time work. Once all of the groceries were bagged, it was finally time to make our way towards the exit. From the moment the automatic sliding exit doors opened, my head was aimed straight towards the sky. I almost got hit by a car twice in the parking lot. My mom had to constantly tell me to look where I was going until we safely got to the car.

Halfway through unloading our cart, my mom and I were nearly knocked to the ground by the roar of an F-14 Tomcat that came tearing right over top of the commissary. I will never forget that sight as long as I live. Blasting by with the wings retracted, the fighter jet couldn't have been any more than 100 feet above the commissary roof! My emotions became so high, my eyes teared up. "That's my team, this is my country," are the unspoken words that played over and over again in my head. As a thirteen year old boy, the spark of patriotism was lit that morning in that commissary parking lot. It hasn't flickered since.

The sight, sound, and power of that F-14—an amazing symbol of American superiority and achievement, humbled me with appreciation for this country. Many years have passed since standing in that commissary parking lot on that fateful Saturday afternoon, but the impression that was left is as fresh as new. I have come to realize that as we make our crazy way through life, we experience countless events, but very few leave a lasting mark. For the most part, events typically turn into nothing more than happy or sad memories. But there are some experiences or moments that we stumble upon, which not only leave a lasting impression, but shape who are or who we become. For me, seeing that F-14 blast across the parking lot sky was one of those moments. As I stared in awe, all I could think about was the fact that "man" designed and built that awesome machine. I felt such a sense of pride and patriotism that I lived in a country where there is no limit as to what can be built or achieved. To be able to engineer and create something that can fly 1,544 mph —over two times the speed of sound, and turn on a dime, proved to me that anything is possible in this great country.

    Being on Andrews Air Force Base during that air show and being in that commissary parking lot at that moment was no coincidence. It was the right time and I was at the right place to receive GOD's calling for the type of person I was to become —someone who appreciates the men and women who sacrifice and serve to protect this nation and someone who believes in the potential and possibilities that are only possible living in a free country.

- CHAPTER 7 -

FAST TIMES AT SURRATTSVILLE HIGH

Every generation has its most cherished decade where memories of the good old days can be triggered by something as simple as an old-school song. For me, some of my most cherished memories are from my 1980's high school years —What a time to be alive! No matter where I am or what I'm doing, if I hear a Duran Duran, Journey, Heart, or Eurythmics song, my clock goes backwards. I get goose bumps right away reminiscing about Friday nights at the skating rink or riding bikes with my friends. We didn't have a care in the world. Back then, life was simple and music was everything.

High school life during the 1980's was an almost surreal experience. This was a time in American culture when there was no such thing as life imitating art, it was just life. At the heart of this life was the "high school" experience. The entertainment industry at that time understood this better than anybody. Out of the 80's, came some of the most successful comedy movies of our lifetime. Breakfast Club, Fast Times at

Ridgemont High, Ferris Bueller's Day Off, and Sixteen Candles, just to name a few, were all based on 80's high school life. These classic films were extremely popular back then and continue to be today.

During the days when music videos ruled the earth, everything seemed to move along to the beat of one big amazing soundtrack. There was something about the mix of music and culture during that time that was both "cheesy" and inspirational. Just listen to some of the rock ballads from the 80's or watch one of the music videos. The songs back then were more like 'ballads' rather than songs. It was musical cinema, which included dramatic lyrics like, "We're dancing on the ceiling," "Hungry like the wolf," or "I am a warrior." Listening to lyrics like that, who wouldn't want to put on a muscle shirt and a pair of parachute pants and attempt to dance on a ceiling.

As fun as the music videos and movies made it look, admittedly, I was a little terrified of starting high school. I knew that a lot of the fun was typically had at the expense of freshman. All I could picture on my first day was getting my lunch money taken by some big kid in a jean jacket with feathered hair. Fortunately, that never happened. On my first day as a high school freshman, I did, however, see something that would have been unimaginable in middle school. I saw a kid for the first time in my life smoking a cigarette inside of a school! There I was, making my way up the stairs to my homeroom on the 3rd floor, when all of a sudden, I see this kid sitting on top of a heater unit, puffing away. I couldn't believe the nuts on this kid. How could he just calmly sit there, wearing his Iron Maiden jean jacket and shades, puffing away, without being scared of getting caught? It was strikingly obvious that this kid had heavier things on his mind than a teacher smelling his Marlboro smoke. As Axl Rose would say —Welcome to the jungle!

As a freshman, it became very clear to me that I had a lot to learn about this jungle. Finding my way was tough at first because the rules of this jungle weren't always so obvious. As everyone knows, high school kids are often known for either making up their own rules or making sure they have fun breaking the ones that are in place. Those students who expect to stay out of trouble will quite often find themselves somewhere in the middle of that spectrum. That's exactly where I aimed for as a freshman. I didn't want to be a "goody-goody" and I didn't want to be a rebellious "hard-head" either. I wanted to stay under the radar until I understood the terrain of the jungle a little bit better.

Rule-breaking and high school have always gone hand-in-hand. Rebellion is almost a rite of passage during our tumultuous high school years. Back in the 80's, being rebellious usually wasn't anything more than smoking in school or skipping a boring class. Rarely would rebellious behavior equate to violence. Sadly, things are different today. Smoking and skipping class have been replaced by physical violence and a complete disregard for authority. Teachers back then, for the most part, were feared and respected. The threat of detention would usually be enough to get control over students when things got out of hand. After a long school day, there was nothing worse than having to stay after school in detention when all of your friends got to go home after the bell. Having served a few detentions, myself, back in the day, I can tell you that it was extremely embarrassing. Sitting in a classroom after the bell rang and seeing your friends peek through the classroom door window as they walk down the hall, making funny faces at you sucked.

MR. MECKLEY

One of the most feared, but respected teachers in my high school to hold afterschool detention was a teacher named "Mr. Meckley." Mr. Meckley was known throughout the school for not taking any crap from anybody, students or teachers. He ran his normal class, as well as his detention class, in one of the mint-green temporary classroom trailers, on the side of the school. This mint-green trailer was the perfect setting for Mr. Meckley's class. It had all of the hallmarks of a military barrack, which is how Mr. Meckley ran his classroom. These "temporary" classroom trailers or so called "temporaries" had been there for as long as anyone could remember. Covered in mint-green metal siding and resting on cinder blocks, these classroom units were only supposed to provide temporary classroom space until expansion of the main school building was complete. Well, based on the amount of rust draping down the metal siding and the deteriorating floor boards, these temporary structures looked as old as the school itself. As far as expansion of the main school building, there wasn't a peep of new construction taking place. Not a single hammer being swung anywhere.

    It wasn't until my sophomore year that I got my first chance to enjoy the comforts of one of the infamous, rusty mint-green trailers. Twenty-nine other students and I met in one of the trailers every morning for homeroom with Mr. Meckley! Initially, of course, everyone was terrified of being in his homeroom class because we had all heard about how strict he was with his normal class. Surprisingly, I didn't find him to be as mean as everyone painted him to be. I actually found him to be a nice guy who gave respect when it was given. He would only lay into you if you were being disruptive or out of line in his class. I figured, as long as I followed his rules, I had nothing to worry about.

Unfortunately, some of my classmates got off on breaking rules. One morning during homeroom, one of them brought out the Mr. Meckley that we all heard about and feared. Just like any other day, at 9:05am we started by standing for the Pledge of Allegiance. The Pledge was recited throughout the school over the intercom system every morning. In every classroom, the teachers always set the example for the students by standing in front of the class, facing the American flag with their right hand over their heart and reciting the Pledge. Compared to other teachers, it didn't go unnoticed that Mr. Meckley took the reciting of the Pledge of Allegiance very seriously. From the moment it was time to stand, the flag had his full attention. Being typical, silly high school kids, we would snicker at his seriousness. Under our breaths, we would quietly laugh, making sure not get caught. We all knew it was dumb and dangerous to laugh at Mr. Meckley, but we couldn't help it. No one could even imagine what he would do if he caught us. But like every other morning, this morning was no different. The silliness was too good to resist.

As we all struggled to hold back our laughs while reciting the Pledge that morning, our routine ritual suddenly came to an abrupt stop. Not even halfway through the Pledge, our hearts nearly stopped beating, as we saw Mr. Meckley suddenly turn away from the flag and began storming towards the back of the classroom. All I could come up with was that he saw somebody laughing at him. It turned out to be worse. A kid named Joey was sitting during the Pledge. Mr. Meckley must have seen him out the corner of his eye. None of us even noticed Joey sitting, but Mr. Meckley surely did.

Storming from the front of the classroom, Mr. Meckley's boots sounded like they were going to break through the flimsy floor boards. Suddenly, in his most ferocious voice he says to Joey, "If you don't get your skinny ass out of that chair and stand I will put my boot right in the crack of your ass!" The classroom went dead silent as we all looked at Joey to make his next move. Joey was known for being rebellious and a hard-ass, but I didn't think this was a fight Joey ought to pick. Based on his terrified reaction to Mr. Meckley's screams, it seemed that he agreed. Joey stood up immediately as Mr. Meckley got right up in his face and told him, "In my class, you will stand your ass up for the Pledge, you got that!" Joey's eyes immediately teared up out of fear and embarrassment. I guess every hard-ass eventually meets his match.

We were all a bit shaken up and not quite sure how to respond to what we saw that morning. The only thing we could do was just stand there at our desks in silence as the Pledge continued over the intercom. Once the Pledge ended, Mr. Meckley apologized for losing his temper, but did not apologize for his stance on standing for the Pledge of Allegiance. He explained to us that he was a Vietnam veteran who had lost many friends in the war. He considered sitting during the Pledge to be the ultimate disrespect to the flag, the country, and to those who have sacrificed for this country.

As a high school kid, this was the first time I had ever heard someone speak so passionately about loving and respecting your country. In that rusted mint-green trailer, we were in the presence of not just a teacher, but a real hero. A real hero who fought for this country and decided to dedicate the rest of his life to teaching kids. Mr. Meckley was someone who deserved respect and had every right to demand it. I will be forever grateful for the seed of patriotism that Mr. Meckley planted in my heart. It continues to grow.

MY FIRST "TRIP"

High school only lasts four years, but a lot of crazy things can happen in that short span of time. In 1988, I was on my third year of craziness. As a junior, I got to party a lot more than I did during my freshman and sophomore years. I was now even cool enough to hang out with the seniors, who were known for throwing the best parties. Even my girlfriend at the time was a senior. The days of trying to fit in were well behind me.

My junior credentials opened up all kinds of new doors. One of the biggest doors to ever open was the opportunity to join the seniors on their spring break senior class trip to Daytona Beach Florida! Typically, senior class trips were reserved only for seniors, but the school made an exception for this one. For a junior in high school during the 80's, this was the chance of a lifetime. At the time, Daytona Beach was one of the hottest destinations in the country for spring break. College and high school kids came from all over to experience the craziness. Movies like the classic 1983 comedy "Spring Break," made the Florida beaches that much more appealing. The drinking, sex, and partying in this movie was an advertising magnet for fun in the sun.

Other than the very obvious reasons to want to join the seniors on this trip, I was also very excited by the fact that they would be traveling by bus. As crazy as that sounds, this was a huge bonus for me because, at the time, I was afraid to fly.

Back in those days, if I couldn't get to a destination by car, bus, or bike, I wasn't going. This bus trip to Florida seemed like the perfect vacation, custom-made just for me. The only thing left to do now was get permission from my mom. My stepdad was away on military duty at the time, so the decision would be solely up to her.

    I knew that this trip was going to be a tough sell to my mom. Florida was a long way from home. In fact, further than any place I had ever gone before in my life. My mom wouldn't be able to just drive to pick me up like she would from a friend's house or the skating rink on a Friday night. Daytona Beach Florida is over 800 miles from Clinton, Maryland. I had to find a way to make this trip less of a big deal. The ingenious plan I came up with was to get one of my good friends to come along with me to Florida. My friend Andre was the perfect choice. We lived in the same neighborhood and just like me, he wasn't a senior. Also, his parents knew my parents, so our friendship was more than just about us. My thought process was that if he could get his parents to let him go, there was a good chance my mom would feel guilty not letting me go.

    When I first mentioned the plan for going on the senior spring break trip to Andre, he was crazy excited. Also, he was a lot more optimistic than I was as far as his parents letting him go. Andre's parents were both in the military, so traveling wasn't such a big deal to them. My mom, on the other hand, wasn't a big traveler. For her, Florida was a world away. Because of this, I decided that I would wait until Andre asked his parents before approaching her. With his parents' approval, I knew that my chances could only improve with my mom.

    It only took two days after I first shared my ingenious Florida spring break plan with Andre for him to seal the deal with his parents. Now it was my turn to make my case to my mom. Instead of mentioning the trip to her as if it was my idea, I made it sound like it was Andre's. Basically, I told her that he was already going on the bus trip to Daytona and I wanted to join him. As predicted, the first thing she asked about was Andre's parents and their thoughts on the trip. I told her that they were cool with it and probably would feel even better if I went too. Talk about laying it on extra thick, I had no shame in my game.

After a lot of begging and a little bending of the truth, I finally convinced my mom to say yes! I couldn't believe it. When I told the good news to Andre, he couldn't believe it. Everything seemed to be lining up for us to go to Daytona. Now, all we had to do was get our parents to put down the deposit and make sure they didn't watch the movie "Spring Break" before the day of the trip.

After weeks of bragging to our friends about going to Daytona Beach, the big day finally arrived. Andre, myself and about fifty or so other crazy excited high school students were all set to make our way to Daytona. We had to meet up with our buses bright and early on a Friday morning for the long ride. Most of the students, including myself, got dropped off by their parents at the bus pickup. I can clearly remember how everyone standing around the buses in the parking lot that morning had big smiles on their faces, except for the parents. It was as if they were dropping us off at an army recruiting station, afraid that their kids would never come back the same. Fast forward thirty years, now as a parent myself, I can only imagine the thoughts that must have swirled around in our parents' heads as their kids prepared to board those buses. There was no way to know who or what would be waiting for us when we stepped off of that bus in Florida. For a parent, it's moments like this where past, youthful experiences will often come back to haunt you.

Unlike our worried parents, we were looking forward to everything waiting for us in Florida. For us, this was game day. The call to board those buses couldn't come soon enough. While our parents worried about our safety on this trip, all we worried about was getting a window seat. Finally, when the call came to board, everyone rushed through their goodbyes and sprinted to the side of the buses. That's when we all got the bad news about there being assigned seats. Big smiles quickly turned into angry frowns. We were all disappointed of course, but this was probably a wise decision on the part of the trip organizers. A bunch of students fighting over seats wouldn't have been a good way to start an 800 mile bus ride.

Anyone who has ever driven from D.C. to Florida knows that there isn't much to look at along interstate 95. This lack of scenery was like fuel to a fire for a bus load of rowdy high school students on their way to Florida. For the fearless teacher chaperons, this journey was like riding inside a box of dynamite on wheels. With nothing exciting to see on the outside of the bus, we had no choice but to create our own fun on the inside of the bus. This translated into a bus full of loud, uncontrollably kids telling nonstop "your mamma" jokes. The chaperons did their best to maintain control, but the excitement over what awaited us in Florida made it nearly impossible to maintain any sense of calmness. Even though the chaperones tried to keep a straight face, there was a sense that they were just as excited as us at times.

There were all kinds of personalities on this trip. Each one of us brought our own little bit of craziness on board. On one end of the spectrum, you had your raging class-clowns and on the other end, you had your quiet, blowup-the-school types.

Throw in the racial makeup of the group, it all made for a wild bus ride. Even though the majority of the kids that went to my high school were white, oddly, most of the kids on this trip were black. I was shocked that we were in the majority on this trip. Black people aren't typically known for being big beach fanatics. Let's all admit, tanning and swimming aren't usually "our thing."

It turned out that this trip was about more than just jumping in the ocean or getting a good tan. This was a chance to let loose. Also, it was quality time away from our parents. But most importantly, it was the perfect opportunity to act like a fool. Sitting on that bus, I must have heard a thousand "mom-jokes" told in the span of an hour. It's just a simple fact, whenever you get a bunch of black teenagers together for a good time, you're going to be hit by a nonstop barrage of "mom jokes." This bus trip was no different. If I didn't know any better, I would have thought I was on a bus full of stand-up comedians en route to their next stand-up act. Because of the nonstop laughter, it was nearly impossible to get any sleep during the long drive. Every five to ten minutes, someone would burst out laughing uncontrollably because someone's mom was getting pounded. For hours and hours, the nonstop party continued. I wouldn't be surprised if our cool, calm and collective bus driver had contemplated driving us off a cliff a few times during the trip.

After almost ten hours of laughing and barely any sleep, we finally arrived in Daytona Beach Florida. My mom's famous "field trip" fried chicken managed to sustain me the whole way. She was happy that I took her chicken with me on the trip, but she wouldn't have been happy about all of the crumbs I let fall on the seat and floor beneath me. I just hoped that with all of the excitement on the bus, no one would notice.

Complete pandemonium erupted on the bus as soon as we pulled onto Daytona's main strip. At this point, I was confident that my chicken crumbs were no longer visible to the naked eye. I remember our bus driving down the main strip and seeing all of the muscle cars, mullets, and girls in neon colored bikinis strolling the strip. This was 1988, 80's fashion was at the top of its game.

The Daytona strip was everything that I imagined it to be and more. It was a haven of exotic cars and exotic girls. As soon as your eyes became fixed on one beautiful thing, something else would immediately grab your attention. Even with the hot girl I was dating sitting a few seat rows in front of me, I couldn't help but stand up and look in awe at the sights as we drove down the strip. Judging from my girlfriend's non-reaction, she must have understood my pain. As rude, selfish, and inconsiderate as my actions were, I guess she felt that under the circumstances, she had to give me a one-time pass on this one.

Our jaw-dropping bus cruise down the strip came to an end once we arrived at our hotel. The long journey that started out in a parking lot in Clinton, Maryland was finally over. As soon as we pulled in front of the hotel, the chaperones on the bus could barely keep us in our seats. They informed us that we had to remain on the bus until the entire group was checked-in. For a bunch of restless rowdy kids that had been sitting on a bus for over ten hours, this was not welcomed news.

After almost thirty minutes of doing everything in our power to keep from bum rushing the front of the bus, we finally got the good news that we were all checked-in to the hotel. Unfortunately, before we could get off the bus, we had to listen to a long list of rules and instructions for this trip. At this point, we were so riled up and ready to hit the strip, we could care less about rules or safety. All we wanted to do was change into our beach clothes and get the party started! For most of us, those rules went in one ear and out the other. Sensing that nobody was really paying any attention, the chaperones threw in the towel and gave us the green light to head to our rooms.

The crowd waiting for the elevators was packed, so Andre and I took to the stairs —luggage and all. Before he and I even got to our room, we were already plotting a plan to ditch my girlfriend. A unanimous decision was made between the both of us that the Daytona strip was worthy of our undivided attention. Now I was beginning to understand that old saying, "Don't bring sand to the beach." Ironically, I should have been the "sand" because, technically, my girlfriend invited me! After all, she was a senior and it was her class trip. I was a junior, who should have been counting his lucky stars that I was even in Daytona. The last thing I should have been doing was plotting how to be a pretend "player." What was I thinking? The answer is very clear —I wasn't.

For the first couple of days at the beach, I remained on my best behavior. Most of the time, my girlfriend wasn't far from my side. Andre, my girlfriend and I spent most of our time during the day walking the strip and checking out the amazing late 60's, early 70's muscle cars. We weren't old enough to hit the bars, so sightseeing was our thing to do. Even if we could go into the bars, I wasn't a drinker yet. The only thing close to drinking I had ever done at this point in my life was taking a few sips of my uncle Tootsie's Miller High Life when I was nine or ten years old. He would always offer me sip when we were sitting around eating crabs. My family would always get a kick out of watching my face wrinkle up as I took a few swigs. Fast forward to my junior year in high school, my reaction to the taste of alcohol pretty much stayed the same. Unlike a lot of my high school friends, I was in no rush to experiment with getting drunk or high. I had this strange belief that drinking would interfere with my good time, not enhance it. Talk about being a parent's dream child.

    At the naïve age of sixteen, I had a hard time accepting the fact that drinking and drugs can affect your reality. Even with all of the evidence life had presented me thus far, I developed this idealistic belief in high school, that human beings are always capable of controlling their minds. Drinking and drugs were just excuses we could use for explaining erratic behavior. Remarkably, I wasn't alone in this naïve way of thinking. My friend Andre also held similar skeptical beliefs about the effects of alcohol and drugs. We were both very analytical for our age, but at the same time, clearly foolish. Our ridiculous ideals, like most youthful ideals, were based on inexperience. This trip to Daytona was about to provide all of the experience we would ever need.

    Speaking of experience, Andre and I had a hotel roommate on this Daytona trip that had plenty of it. Danny was a super nice, quiet white kid who was heavy into "Heavy Metal." Because he dressed the part, Danny looked a bit scary if you just met him. The truth is, he was one of the nicest guys I knew in high school. A lot of kids gave him shit because of the way he dressed, but I always thought his look was kind of cool. Danny would wear ripped up jeans, skull chains, and Iron Maiden shirts every single day. He was all "Heavy Metal," but behind the clothes was a gentle, shy guy who was very approachable. Also behind the clothes was a very "experimental" guy, who was quite fond of experimenting with reality. On this trip to Daytona, "acid" (LSD) was Danny's substance of choice to test reality.

Even though the three of us were roommates, Andre and I barely saw Danny on this trip. In passing, it was always a quick what's up and then off to our separate ways. This was pretty much the norm until one day, the three of us ran into one another in our hotel kitchen. It was the first time that the three of us actually paused to engage in a conversation. Andre and I mentioned to Danny that we were getting bored with hitting the beach and strip every day. We were looking for something new to do. Without saying a word, Danny, all of a sudden, goes into the freezer and pulls out a zip-lock bag with little pieces of paper in it. He told us that he was planning on "tripping" that night in the hotel room and asked us if we wanted to join him. The first thing I thought was, "Dude, this guy is crazy." Based on the look on Andre's face, I think he agreed. That being said, Danny, at a minimum, had us extremely curious.

Acting like two kids who stumbled upon dad's gun, Andre and I nervously asked Danny if we could see the zip-lock bag. As soon as he handed to us, the first thing I noticed was the colored clown face that was stamped on each of the tiny pieces of paper. Each piece was about the quarter of the size of a postage stamp. I clearly remember the edges of each piece being perforated as if it was torn from a sheet. Next, I opened the bag to see if it had any type of smell. Surprisingly, there was no smell. I naturally assumed that if it was a drug, it should have some type of odor. There I was, acting like a drug expert with no personal experience with drugs whatsoever. When we asked Danny about the creepy clowns on the stamps, he laughed at our cluelessness. He told us that people who make sheets of acid will often stamp the pieces with their own unique "trippy" designs to distinguish their stamps from other suppliers. But more importantly, he explained that the mystical markings on the stamps add a nice touch to the "tripping on acid experience."

As skeptical as Andre and I were of what was actually in that zip-lock bag, Danny still had our undivided attention. We tried to hide our increasing curiosity behind laughter. The idea that a little piece of paper with a clown on it, kept in a zip-lock bag in the freezer, would allow us to experience an alternate reality with our "Heavy Metal" roommate sounded beyond laughable. We even began to mock Danny, calling him a sucker for buying "make believe drugs." At the time, the only thing I knew about acid or "tripping" was from stories I heard about Pink Floyd and Grateful Dead concerts. The idea of smelling colors and out-of-body experiences always sounded a bit too crazy to be true. Standing in that kitchen in Daytona Beach, I still felt that way, but I have to admit, Danny definitely had me curious.

Andre and I ended up turning down Danny's offer to "trip" with him, at least for now. We walked out of the kitchen that day, convincing ourselves that our "Heavy Metal" friend was nuts. The truth is, it didn't really matter at this point if he was nuts or not. Our curiosity was already planning our destiny. It was no longer a question of if we would tryout what was in Danny's zip-lock bag, but when. Instead of leaving our hotel room that day thinking about girls in bikinis, all we could think about was "Heavy Metal" Danny.

For the rest of the afternoon, Andre and I hit the beach and Daytona strip as usual. By most measures, it was a typical day —lots of cool cars and lots of hot girls. Late that evening, we returned to our hotel room to find Danny stretched out on the bed with the balcony door slid wide open and his music blasting. For a second, I thought the worst. Suddenly, he slowly turned his head towards us to tell us that he had just taken "a hit" of acid about fifteen minutes ago. Just like earlier in the day, he asked if we wanted to join him. Both, Andre and I looked at one another and said "Let's do this shit!" Danny immediately jumped up from the bed and headed towards the kitchen. He took two stamps from the small plastic zip-lock bag in the freezer. Next, he told us all we had to do was to put the tiny stamp on our tongue and wait for about fifteen to twenty minutes for the fun to begin. It all sounded way too easy for it to possibly work. In our minds, there was no way that this tiny, silly little stamp was going to change anybody's reality. Without further delay, Andre and I popped the stamps on our tongue and waited for the magic show to start.

From the moment we put the tiny stamps in our mouths, we couldn't stop laughing. It wasn't because of the effect of any drug, but at the idea that we would all of a sudden start "tripping." We were still in denial, regardless of what freak show Danny promised us. After waiting for fifteen minutes for something "psychedelic" to happen, we got nothing. Danny was hoping that the acid would kick in right away so that he could finally shut us up. Nothing would have been funnier to him than watching two non-believers all of a sudden lose it.

The longer it took for the acid to kick in, the cockier Andre and I became. Because it was taking so long, longer than Danny expected, he actually started wondering if in fact we were somehow immune to the drug. This wasn't the first time Danny had taken acid, so he was familiar with how it works slowly in stages in the beginning. According to him, it usually took at least thirty minutes for the drug to fully kick in. He told us that his "hit" was already starting to come on. Of course, we didn't believe him because we weren't feeling anything ourselves at this point. After anxiously waiting for twenty minutes for something to happen, I gave up. I told

Andre and Danny I was leaving and walking over to 7-11 to get something to eat. There just so happened to be a 7-11 directly across the street from our hotel. It was always the go-to place for late night snacks. As I left the room, I headed straight for the stairs, like always, to avoid the wait for the elevator. On the six flight walk down, I remember laughing to myself and feeling even more confident that the whole "acid thing" was a joke. Thirty minutes had gone by since I popped that clown stamp in my mouth and "acid" still couldn't lay a hand on me. I was convinced, Andre and I were right. The human mind is stronger than any drug. Boy, was I in for a scary surprise.

Walking into 7-11, I remember cruising the aisles for the perfect late night, junk food. I grabbed a bag of bar-b-que chips, a Slim Jim, a Sprite, and a pack of orange gum. There were about four people standing in line in front of me to pay. As I stood patiently behind the last guy, all of a sudden, out of nowhere, I burst out laughing for no apparent reason. Not only did I scare the people waiting in line and the dude behind the register, but I also scared myself. "What's wrong with me?" I thought. For a split second, I actually considered that maybe, just maybe, the acid was starting to work. "No way," I said, "this can't be happening." Even with this strange and sudden outburst of laughter, I remained stubbornly skeptical. Just like a kid who takes one sip of beer and pretends to be drunk, I convinced myself that I was subconsciously pretending to be "tripping." However, what I would experience shortly after leaving the 7-11, would be beyond anything that I could ever imagine pretending to be.

After pulling myself together, I finally made it to the front of the line to pay for my stuff. By the time I got to the cashier, he looked like he didn't even remember me as the guy who was laughing for no reason five minutes ago. I'm sure with the in and out drunk fools who would hit that 7-11 regularly, he didn't think too much of me. Besides, based on my snack choices, he probably assumed that I smoked something that would make me laugh. Even though this was Daytona, I couldn't help but to feel a little embarrassed as I walked out of the store.

It was getting late, so the only thing really left to do was head back to the hotel to eat my snacks and hang out with Andre and Danny. Standing in front of the 7-11, I had to wait on the curb for the traffic light to change in order to cross the street. It was a busy night on the strip, so traffic was nonstop. To cross without a walk traffic signal was nearly impossible. After waiting patiently for several minutes, the light finally changed. As I began to cross the street, suddenly I saw something that would completely blow my mind. Within my first few steps, looking around, I noticed that the cars that were stopped at the red light were at least twice as tall as me! These were normal cars, not trucks. I thought to myself, "What is wrong with me? First, I laugh for no apparent reason and now this!" Only a crazy person at this point would think that none of this could possibly have anything to do with the hit of acid they took thirty minutes ago. Folks, I was that crazy person.

In a determined attempt to regain my sense of scale, I glanced down at my own body and legs for reference. Unfortunately, this only added to the panic. My perception of my own height had gone from 5-feet 2-inches to about 3 feet! To make matters worse, this new height wasn't just perceived mentally, but physically as well. Touching my torso and legs, I immediately realized that my senses of sight and touch were in complete agreement. In other words, this new height was my new reality. Scared to death by what I was experiencing, I began to run towards the other side of the street as fast as I could. Even running at what I perceived as a fast pace, it was, strangely, taking me longer to cover a distance. Confused and terrified, I suddenly realized that because of my shrunken legs, the length of my strides had become a lot shorter. As a result, I had to move my legs twice as fast as before in order to cover the same distance. Everything I was experiencing in that moment was my new scary reality. LSD had taken control of both, my mental and physical interpretation of the world. All senses, even my sense of distance and time had been taken over. No matter how much I told myself that what I was seeing wasn't real, my new, inescapable reality said otherwise. Acid had turned me into a 3-foot person. As a result, my senses were adjusted to fit that new reality.

As out of my mind as I was that night, thankfully, I did make it across the Daytona strip in one piece. Once I reached the sidewalk, for some strange reason, everything went back to normal. I regained my height and the cars appeared to be their normal size. It was as if I had scared myself back to real reality. I tried my best to regroup as I made my way back to the hotel. All I kept thinking was, "Please don't let anyone see me like this." To avoid running into any of my classmates, I snuck into the side stairwell entrance of the hotel. Fortunately, I somehow made it up six flights of stairs without running into anyone. It was a miracle because there was usually always someone smoking or hanging out on the stairs. Once I reached my floor, I told myself that I wasn't going to tell anyone about what I had just experienced, not even Danny and Andre.

As I nervously walked into the hotel room, the first thing I noticed was Danny lying in bed, completely straight on his back. His long hair was parted perfectly in the middle, eerily resembling Jesus. I couldn't help but stare at him lying there in almost complete stillness. The only things that appeared to move were his feet. As I began to focus on them, something very frightening happened. His toe nails appeared to rapidly grow right in front of my eyes! I knew it had to be the acid coming on again, but I was still determined to keep quiet. Andre was out on the balcony, but came inside right away when he heard me come in. As soon as we saw each other, we both started complaining about feeling sick. Suddenly, Andre ran into the bathroom and started to throw-up. I felt like I wanted to throw-up too, but somehow, I fought back the urge. My heart immediately started racing because at this moment I knew that the acid was having an effect on both of us. There was no place to hide anymore —no more lies I could tell myself. Those little stamps in the freezer that I made fun of less than an hour ago were the real deal.

    Andre came out of the bathroom and immediately went into denial mode. He blamed being sick on something he ate. I could tell in his eyes that he didn't believe the lie he was telling himself. We both knew that it wasn't anything he ate, it was the acid. Not knowing what else to do, we both decided to go out on the balcony to get some fresh air. Neither one of us was yet willing to admit to the other that the drug was having an effect. Even though both of us were experiencing the same symptoms.

    After hanging out on the balcony for a few minutes, in near total silence, Andre and I walked back into the room. We both oddly came to a dead stop in front of Danny's bed, where he was still lying lifeless on his back. In a random instance, Andre and I turned towards one another, looking each other straight in the eyes, and began laughing uncontrollable for no reason. Within a few seconds of this laughter, our faces, all of a sudden, quickly turned from expressions of laughter into frowns of fear. Holding onto any little bit of control that we had left, we promised each other that we would get through this. We both took a deep breath and for the first time ever, admitted to each other that we were "fucked up."

Over an hour in, Danny was already well into his "trip" and obviously enjoying the ride. Andre and I were still having a hard time accepting the reality of the situation. I recall early on looking at myself in the mirror and crying out —"What did I do to myself! I want "me" back!" My greatest fear was that "me" would never come back. The ugly reality of drugs that I chose to dismiss, had come back to haunt me. Now I had done something to make that ugly reality my reality. Staring in the mirror, I saw a life of hard work and potential now at risk. Danny may have been enjoying this "trip," but I surely wasn't.

It didn't come as a surprise, once the acid kicked-in, that each of us would have a different experience with the drug. Like most experiences, the experience of "tripping on acid" depends a lot on what you take along with you on the journey. For Andre and me, we were saddled with "fear of the unknown." Having never taken acid before, we had no idea of what to expect. We weren't even sure if acid could do what we heard it could do. This explains a lot about our initial "scared-out-of-our-minds" reaction to the drug. For Danny, everything was smooth sailing. He had no fear. His attitude was —"acid, bring it on!" Danny's carefree spirit served him well on his acid journey.

As the acid really started to kick-in, it was looking more and more like Andre had more of a carefree spirit than we thought. At one point, I looked over at him and he had a big smile on his face, as he appeared to be enjoying the ride. He told me things would be a lot less scary if I just stopped fighting it. It turned out, he was completely right. Once I relaxed a bit, letting the acid take control, I became a lot less fearful. Meanwhile, amazed with his newly found "acid powers," Andre began doing Karate moves in the hotel room mirror. He told me that the acid was causing him to see every move in slow motion. Immediately, I jumped in front of the mirror and started doing my moves. We were both blown away by our newly found powers. Just like slow motion special effects on TV, every arm movement was followed by a succession of "ghosted trails." This was the most amazing thing I had ever seen! But, our night was just beginning. The hotel Karate show would be followed up by the dancing wallpaper hieroglyphics show, the melting gum show, the mirror body building show and many more.

 Two hours into our acid trip, we were suddenly startled back to reality by a knock on the hotel room door. Being the young dumb dumbs that we were, it never occurred to us, "What if someone comes to our hotel room while we are on acid?" Feeling scared to death as I slowly walked towards the door, suddenly, I heard my girlfriend's voice on the other side. Boy, were we lucky. I slowly opened the door, just enough for her to squeeze through, and told her to quickly come inside. Looking at my face, she started laughing at me right away because she thought I had finally gotten drunk for the first time. When I told her that I did acid, her eyes teared up right away and she started crying. All she kept saying was, "Why did you do that? Why did you do that?" Already, regretting what I had done to myself, this made the situation even worse. Just like me, my girlfriend's biggest fear was that I had done something that would permanently change who I used to be.

 Even under the influence of acid, my sober conscience could feel my girlfriend's pain. "Why did you do that?" echoed over and over again in my head. I couldn't stop feeling like I had taken GOD's gift of intelligence for granted. Throughout my childhood, I had been blessed with countless opportunities because of the ability to think and learn —"Did I just throw all of that a way?" Unlike me, for someone who had done acid before, they would have found peace in knowing that eventually the effects of the drug wear off. I had never even had so much as a buzz before, so tripping on acid seemed like the end of my world as I knew it.

Not too long after my girlfriend showed up, the acid finally took full control of my mind. Unlike an hour earlier, surrendering was no longer an option. In order to escape the frightening hallucinations I was having, I attempted to hide from everything and everybody in the room. For at least two hours, I hid under the bed sheets. I wouldn't come out for anything. My girlfriend had to lift the sheets in order to see to me. The situation was so crazy that she went from being scared for me to laughing at me. At first, I felt angry because she was laughing, but soon after, I started laughing myself. It was then that I started to feel less afraid. After over two hours of hiding under the sheets like a scared child, I finally emerged from my cave. Saying nothing to anyone, I got out of bed and immediately walked over to the bedroom mirror. Just like in the beginning of this whole acid experience, I made Karate moves with my arms. This time, I prayed that I wouldn't see any "ghosted trails." As my girlfriend stared at me standing in front of the mirror like a crazy person, I realized that my prayers had been answered —no "ghosted trails!" After almost five hours of terror, the acid was finally starting to subside. I could tell that I wasn't out of the woods yet, but it was a start. My girlfriend told me to lay back down and try to sleep the rest off, so I did.

The next morning, my girlfriend, Danny, Andre and I woke up to an eerie silence in our hotel room. Everyone, except Danny, seemed spooked by the shit that transpired the night before. For me, I was thankful that the nightmare seemed to be finally over. Of course, my girlfriend jumped out of bed with a zillion questions. I begged her not to talk about it, but that was asking the impossible. It seemed that when she started asking me questions about what it was like, I immediately began to have flashbacks. My mind snapped back and forth between tripping and normal. It was obvious that I wasn't out of the woods yet.

Thinking that maybe food and some fresh air would help get the drug out of my system, I suggested that we all take a walk across the strip to McDonald's to get some breakfast. My hope was that a change of environment might help me feel like me again. It all seemed like a good idea until I walked inside the restaurant. Right away, as soon as I stood in line, the flashbacks began. Looking up at the menu boards, the letters appeared to continuously shift left and right. I tried my hardest to mentally push back against what I was seeing, but it just wouldn't stop. Immediately, I became paranoid that someone would notice me acting strangely and would think that I had lost my mind. Unlike being locked in a hotel room, there was nowhere for me to hide in McDonald's. I was now at the mercy of the public, vulnerable to judgment.

Refusing to let things get to a point where I could be hauled off in a crazy van, I bolted out of McDonald's, leaving Andre and my girlfriend standing in line. Once outside, I began to panic and cry because I started to lose hope that the hallucinations, paranoia, and flashbacks from the acid would stop. I told my girlfriend when she came outside after me that, "The 'old me' is gone." Looking confused, she asked, "What do you mean?" I told her that the acid had killed who I used to be. It may have sounded crazy, but in that moment, this was something I truly believed. Thankfully, two hours later, after a bit more rest, hope once again returned. The "old me" made a comeback.

It should come as no surprise that I spent the rest of my trip in Daytona strictly focused on cars and hot girls. No more acid tripping for me, ever. Those foolish ideals that Andre and I once boastfully held onto, may as well have been flushed down the toilet. We now knew without a doubt that getting high on drugs is real. No amount of mind control can save you if you put the wrong things in your body.

Looking back on my first and only experience with LSD, I will be the first to admit that I am probably making the whole thing a bigger deal than it should be. Say what you like, but I had damn good reasons for being scared out of my mind. Number one, it was the first time I had ever done drugs. I had no experience in adjusting my reality. Number two, as a child, I grew up in an environment where drugs snatched away the lives of so many. Living in the projects, I knew people who ended up walking the streets, losing their family, or going into a mental institution —all because of experimenting with and using drugs. So, there I was in Daytona, putting myself in a situation that could allow the same thing to happen to me.

My onetime tango with LSD was one of the scariest experiences of my life. For almost twelve hours, my senses of sight, hearing, touch, taste, and smell were detached from reality. In other words, I got a glimpse inside a mindset that was longer compatible with this world. As scary as that sounds, it was even scarier going through it. So much so, that when I returned home from Daytona, I actually went to the library to read up on LSD. I wanted to know, "How could a single, tiny stamp with no noticeable traces of a drug be so potent?" The answers that I found were beyond interesting and worth reading up on.

    I wish I could say that LSD spooked me so much that I never ever played around with drugs again, but that would be very far from the truth. I had a lot of life and trouble waiting for me down the road.

- Chapter 8 -

The Divorce

Stability is something we naturally long for as human beings. From the moment a baby is born, it seeks stability in its new world. That stability usually comes in the form of a mother's nurturing and love. That nurturing and love is eventually associated with a certain face and touch. It is the consistency of this love that establishes the stability for that child to grow and develop in essential areas of their lives. If a father is present, the child will naturally attempt to expand its circle of stability beyond the mother. This life process continues, eventually adding siblings, family members, and friends to this circle.

For a brief period in my own life, I got to experience one of the most sacred sources of stability that a child could ever have. From middle school, up until my junior year in high school, I got to experience what a lot of black kids, unfortunately, think is only possible on the Cosby Show —Having both, a mother and a father in the home. Sure, my stepfather wasn't a doctor like Bill Cosby's character, Cliff Huxstable, but he took care of his family just the same. As for my mom, lawyer or no lawyer, Clair Huxstable couldn't lay a glove on her. Unfortunately, by the time my senior year in high school rolled around, our "sitcom" family life came to a crashing end —My parents were breaking up.

Just like in the case of any painful divorce, things between my parents got real ugly, real fast. Sadly, my younger sisters and I would be caught in the middle of the drama. Both of my sisters were really young at the time, so the real pain wouldn't come to haunt them until a few years later. For me, the divorce was immediate devastation. The pain coupled with an already rebellious teenage attitude tempted me to lose all hope. With one year left in high school, it would take everything in me to keep it together.

How does this happen? How can a mother and father abandon the very thing that sustains their children? The answers to these questions don't really matter when you're a child going through it. For me, the "why" was irrelevant. All I knew was that I was losing the very source of my happiness and wholeness. That dream of having a mom and dad that somehow came true, was no more. At the impressionable age of sixteen, I would have to find a way to pick up the pieces, to somehow move on with life.

As much as it hurt at the time to admit it, the days of relying on my parents for happiness were over. I had to start leaning more and more on my friends for happiness. The friends that I had at the time essentially became my new family. Of course, my mom, grandparents, and relatives were still there for me, but I preferred to spend more time with my friends. They were very good at helping me take the focus off of myself. More importantly, they also showed me that life can go on without a happy home. For me, that life would eventually include partying and afterschool drinking with friends. As much as I believed that partying with my friends was helping me get through the pain, the truth is, it was only masking over it.

Not all of my friends were just friends to party with. A lot of them actually showed a genuine concern for my well-being. My neighbor and close friend Paul was one of those concerned friends. We were very tight. Paul lived directly across the street from me and knew all about what I was going through with my parents getting a divorce. Not having a perfect family himself, he sympathized with my situation. Paul had known my family ever since we first moved into the neighborhood from D.C. When we met, my parents were technically still newlyweds. So, sadly, Paul actually witnessed firsthand the beginning and end of my family. Being the type of friend that he was, not once did he ever judge my family for what we were going through. Instead, he made a mature decision just to be there for me.

Throughout the painful divorce ordeal, there were many times that I found myself leaning on my friend Paul, either for advice or just a good time. I could depend on him for both. The times in which he revealed himself to be a true friend are too numerous count. But, there was one time in particular in which Paul proved to me the caliber of friend he truly was. This unforgettable moment with my friend occurred on a random night when he and I were driving around Clinton in his car looking for something to eat. Somehow, we got on the subject of my parents splitting up and all of a sudden, I just lost it. I became overwhelmed with anger and sadness at the same time. With tears rolling down my face, I told Paul that I didn't care about anything anymore. I even told him that I was dropping out of high school. Out of all of the dumb things that were pouring out of my mouth, this may have been the dumbest. I had only one year left to graduate. Surprisingly, Paul remained silent throughout my entire pity party. In fact, he didn't say anything until several minutes after I was done. Once he was sure that I had gotten it all out, all of a sudden, in an angry, but mature voice, Paul told me that I sounded like a damn fool. Looking me straight in the eyes, he asked me, "Why would you let stupid decisions made by your parents ruin your life?" When I didn't respond, he went on to say, "You have your whole life in front of you. I wish I had the grades that you have. Finish high school, go to college and don't look back!"

After hearing those words come out of Paul's mouth, the weak position of feeling sorry for myself was no longer a positon I wanted to take. His blunt words empowered me. In the spirit of a true friend, Paul balanced his tough love with praise. He reminded me of all that I had accomplished up to this point. This taught me the importance of remembering past blessings when we are going through tough times. They can be a powerful source of strength to get to our future blessings.

I'm confident in saying that Paul's words that night forever changed the course of my life. They were a wakeup call to take charge of my own life and to use my talents to create the life that I wanted and deserved. Instead of supporting my pity party, my friend showed me tough love at a moment in which I needed it the most. Paul made me realize that it is a sign of weakness to allow failures of others to be used to justify your own. Even if those failures are those of the ones we love.

"Thank you Paul, you are missed my friend."R.I.P.

THE KNOCK ON THE DOOR

I once read a quote that said, "There are two types of pain in this world: Pain that hurts you, and pain that changes you." For me, the breakup of my parents fulfilled both. Throughout every dreadful stage of my parents' divorce, it took every ounce of optimism in me to cope with the pain. Even with the help of empowering friends like Paul, there were days when I just couldn't overcome the hurt, no matter how hard I tried. I was poignantly reminded of my family's predicament by things like getting a knock on the door from a county sheriff attempting to serve divorce papers or having a WIC delivery truck show up at our house for a government food drop off. With no father around, money had gotten so tight that we had to rely on the WIC supplemental food program for a portion of our groceries. These were sad times.

    Struggling to keep my head up through it all, it seemed nearly impossible that the pain I learned to live with could get any worse. But one day, unfortunately, it would. Life as I knew it was about to make a dark turn. A turn where there is typically no coming back. It all started in our home one night when I was woken up by loud banging on the front door at around two o'clock in the morning. The noise also woke up my two sisters, who started crying hysterically. I didn't get out of bed right away because I assumed that all of the noise had to have woken up my mom too. I just knew that it wouldn't be long before I would hear, "Who the hell is knocking on the door this late?" Instead, I heard nothing, except for my sisters crying. When both of my little sisters suddenly came into my room looking for mommy, that's when I knew something was wrong. That's when I knew we were all alone.

As frightened and confused as I was, I did everything in my power to comfort my sisters as the loud banging on the front door continued. With my mom nowhere to be found and my sisters scared to death, I nervously walked into the living room to look out the window to see who was banging on our front door. Immediately, I saw two police cars sitting in our driveway. Feeling afraid, but somewhat relieved at the same time, I slowly opened the door. I was relieved because it was the police that was banging, but afraid because of why they might be here. One of the officers immediately asked me if anyone else was in the house. I told him that it was just my sisters and me and that I wasn't sure where my mom was. Strangely, he asked me again if I was sure nobody else was in the house. I told him that I was sure, as I fought back my tears. Next, they asked me if they could come inside to take a look around. I told them yes, as I moved out of the doorway to let them in. The police officers came into my house cautiously with their flashlights shining in every direction. One of the officers asked if my sisters and I were okay and if anyone was hurt. I told him no, but he obviously wanted to make sure since my sisters were still crying uncontrollably. By the way the officers were checking everything out, I could tell that they were looking for possible signs of violence or a struggle that could have taken place.

After almost thirty minutes of the police searching the house, I still had no idea of what was going on or the whereabouts of my mother. But I was smart enough to know that the police knew something that they weren't telling me. Their reluctance to mention or even ask about my mom was a frightening sign. Up to this point, all they seemed to care about was making sure no one else was in the house. There was no concern whatsoever for the whereabouts of my mom. For reasons unknown, I was being purposely kept in the dark. All I could do for now was try to stay strong for my sisters, as I waited for answers.

Finally, after searching the house from top to bottom, all of the police officers gathered around in my living room and asked me to bring my sisters with me to join them. As soon as we walked into the living room, one of the officers took my sisters off to another room. I assumed to either comfort them or shield them from what they were about to tell me. Sadly, it turned out that it was because of what they were about to tell me. The officers standing in the middle of my living room at 3 o'clock in the morning were there to tell me that my mother was in the hospital. She was there because she just tried to commit suicide.

"At any second now, I will be waking up from this bad dream," I thought to myself. Unfortunately, that wake up never came. Instead, pain set in, confirming that I was indeed awake. My emotional collapse into a state of complete helplessness was real. There was nowhere to run from the devastating news delivered by those police officers. Unintentionally, they had just snatched away the very breath of life from my lungs. This was my mother they were talking about —the person who gave me life. Even though she was still alive, it didn't hurt any less. To know that she was in so much pain that she was willing to leave me and my sisters, broke my heart. Not only because of the thought of losing her, but also because of how much she must have been hurting in order to even think about attempting to end her own life.

As I tried to come to grips with what the police officers were telling me about my mom, I soon noticed an out of place white envelope, mysteriously sitting next to the phone in the living room. Somehow, no one in the house noticed it that night except for me at that very moment. As soon as I picked it up, I immediately recognized my mom's handwriting on the front. The envelope was addressed to me. When I opened it, inside was my mother's wedding ring and other pieces of her most precious jewelry. Also inside was a note from her apologizing for having to leave me and my sisters. The contents of that envelop crushed me to my core. This was essentially my mom's last cry —Her final surrender.

After reading that letter, there was nothing left to the imagination. In her own words, my mom was letting me know that she had given up. Contrary to what I had thought my entire life, my mom was not invincible. In fact, no one is when put under the right amount of pressure. Most of us grow up thinking that our parents are invincible and often forget that they are human beings just like their kids. For my sisters and me, we had to learn this the hard way. By a loud knock on the door at 3 o'clock in the morning, we learned just how fragile a parent can be.

I truly believe it was GOD's saving grace that kept me from seeing that envelope until after the police officers had a chance to tell me my mom was okay. I can't imagine how hard it would have hit me if I would have seen it one second sooner. Just the thought of reading that letter and assuming that my mom had already committed suicide is something I just can't imagine. The hopelessness would have been unbearable. Thankfully, life had other plans. Instead of being left hopeless, GOD granted me comfort in knowing that now my mother was safe and getting the help that she desperately needed.

With absolutely no chance of my mom coming home that night or anytime soon, my sisters and I were going to need a place to stay. I wasn't eighteen, so my sisters couldn't stay in my care. The police officers asked me which one of my relatives they could call to come pick us up. My Aunt Carrie Lee lived the closest, so I had them call her. I don't remember if the officer who made the call told my aunt the details of the situation over the phone or not. I'm assuming he probably didn't. Having her drive in a complete state of panic wouldn't have been a good idea.

Not even thirty minutes after the police officer made the call to my aunt, she was at our front door. It was obvious that she wasted no time getting there —she was still wearing her pink hair rollers. Regardless of what details the officers may have left out over the phone, my aunt had to have known that something was seriously wrong. No one gets a call from the police at 4 o'clock in the morning unless there's something wrong. As soon as my aunt walked in, before she could even say hello to me, the officers immediately pulled her off to the side to talk to her. Judging by the sudden blank look on her face, it was obvious that she was getting hit with the details of the sad news about my mom. I'm sure it broke my aunt's heart to hear that her younger sister was in so much pain that she wanted to take her own life. The only reason, I'm guessing, that she didn't collapse on the floor is probably because she felt the pressure to stay strong for us. At one of the most desperate moments in our lives, my aunt knew that my sisters and I needed her strength now more than ever.

Once the police were done updating my aunt on the condition of my mom, she finally made her way over to my sisters and me to ask if we were okay. I hesitantly shook my head up and down and immediately started to cry. "Everything is going to be okay baby," my Aunt Carrie Lee told me in her naturally comforting voice. She told me to grab some things for me and my sisters so that we could go stay the night at her house. Right away, I began wiping away my tears, as I made my way to the bedrooms to pack our bags. While packing, all of a sudden I was pleasantly shocked by the smell of coffee coming from our kitchen. This instantly put a smile on my face and refilled my heart with hope. Coffee was special to my Aunt Carrie Lee. As it was to my grandmother and as it is to me. There was only one person in my house that night that would have thought to put on a pot of coffee under such sad circumstances. That person was my aunt. She knew the power of a warm and loving cup of coffee. It was amazing that something as simple as the smell of coffee could lift me up from such a dark, low place. For any of the officers that may have still been concerned for our wellbeing, thanks to my aunt and her coffee, they could now leave rest assured that we were in good hands.

When I woke up that morning at my Aunt Carrie Lee's house, as soon as I opened my eyes, I knew that it wasn't just a bad dream. I was waking up to a real-life family nightmare. From the upstairs bedroom, I could hear my aunt downstairs in the kitchen talking to one of my relatives on the phone. By now, I was pretty sure that most of my family had heard the bad news about my mother. When I walked into the kitchen, my aunt told me that she had been up all morning on the phone with the family. So far, all we knew was that my mother was being kept at Malcolm Grow Medical Center on Andrews Air Force Base. The well-known hospital facility, established in 1958, was named after Malcolm C. Grow, the first Surgeon General of the United States Air force[1]. The medical staff there had spoken to my aunt several times that morning, assuring her that my mom was getting the best care possible. Unfortunately, they also told her that my mom wouldn't be allowed to have visitors until the next day. Even worse for me, no one under

---

[1] Outpatient Information Guide: Malcolm Grow Medical Clinic. 2012.

eighteen years old would yet be allowed to see her. As a son who wanted more than anything to see his mom, this was heartbreaking news to wake up to. But I had to quickly remind myself to be thankful that at least I still had a mother alive to see.

That next day, my grandparents, uncles, aunts, and most of my cousins all met over my Aunt Carrie Lee's house before making the sad trip to visit my mother in the hospital. All of us were anxious to see her, but more anxious to find out how she tried to kill herself. At this point, no one knew any specifics of what took place that night. The hospital was only about a twenty minute drive from my aunt's house in Suitland, Maryland. For the short trip, we all piled in three cars and made our way towards Andrews Air Force Base. As soon as we arrived at the hospital, right away, the staff told us that everyone under eighteen would have to hang out in the waiting room areas, while the adults took turns going back to see my mom. As anyone could imagine, it was hard for me to sit still in that waiting room. Knowing that I couldn't see my hurting mom, who was in a room only a few feet from me, was very upsetting. Adding to my frustration was the fact that my older family members, who were able to go back to see my mom, were very tightlipped when it came to giving me any ugly details. All I was being told by everyone at the hospital, including my own family, was that my mom was in a very fragile state and that she would be staying in the hospital until she gets the care that she needs. Obviously, there was a universal decision that it was best to keep me in the dark with regards to any ugly details. For now, I would just have to settle for the promise that everything was in GOD's hands.

After a long, painful week of being kept in the dark, I was finally allowed to visit my mom in the hospital. I was joyful that this moment had finally arrived, but afraid of what it might reveal. Walking into the visitor's area of the psychiatric ward, I couldn't help but notice the arts and crafts scattered all around the room. Later on, I found out that arts and crafts are often used as part of medical psychiatric treatment. When I first saw my mother, she was sitting at a table surrounded by some of this art. She smiled right away when she saw me, but her smile couldn't hide her sadness and confusion. I could tell that she was far from her normal self. Her eyes were blank and she spoke very slowly. It broke my heart to see my mother like this.

Quite naturally, the first thing I expected my mother to talk about when I saw her was what happened on that dark, sad night. I was beyond shocked when the first words that came out of her mouth were "Look at these paintings I did." This left me speechless. "Had my mom lost her mind?" I thought. She may have felt like showing me her paintings was a positive thing, but in reality, her detachment from her situation only made me more frightened. The paintings offered me no comfort whatsoever, but only played into my fear that my mom had lost her mind.

BRIGHT LIGHT IN THE PARK

"GOD cracked open the sky."

It took almost five years before my mother opened up about what happened on the darkest night of her life. That haunting moment in time when she attempted to take her own life somehow came up during a random conversation we were having one fateful evening. Out of nowhere, my mother brought up the night she snuck out of the house around one-thirty in the morning, while my sisters and I were sleeping, drove about two miles to an empty, dark neighborhood park parking lot, put a gun to her head and pulled the trigger. This was the night that the devil sought to rain down defeat over my mother. But GOD had other plans.

My mother opened up by first talking about her drive down to Tanglewood Park. This was a neighborhood park less than two miles from our house with a parking lot far enough back from the main road for a car to park out of sight. A little after one-thirty in the morning, under the cover of darkness, my mother drove to the back of this empty parking lot, where she knew that no one would be able to see what she was about to do. In her defeated mind, she had found the perfect spot. With tears in her eyes, my mom went on to describe the pain she felt, sitting there all alone in her car, crying out with a gun to the side of her head. At this point, she was only a trigger pull away from taking her last breath. With no one and nothing around to stop her, she pulled the trigger.

What my mother described as happening next was impossible for me to comprehend at the time and probably difficult for most people to believe. Looking me straight in the eyes, my mother told me that when she pulled the trigger as hard as she could to fire the gun into the side of her head, the entire sky lit up outside of the car. In that empty, dark parking lot, a light emerged so bright that it blinded her. As the gun remained pressed against the side of her head, she suddenly couldn't move any part of her body. In my mother's own words, "GOD cracked opened the sky" the instant she pulled back on that trigger. This was the moment that GOD took my mother's battle and made it HIS. After that, my mom would wake up in a hospital bed on Andrews Air Force Base, with no recollection of how she got there. Having witnessed GOD's awesome power myself, I don't doubt for a minute what my mom experienced in that dark parking lot on that dark night.

LIFE AFTER THE BRIGHT LIGHT

My mother ended up spending over two months in the hospital after that bright light in the park. For a brief period during that time, my sisters and I had to bounce around between relatives. With my mom not being around, we had few choices. Eventually, my stepdad ended up having to come back home to take care of us. As much as I wanted him being there to provide some level of comfort, a home was just not a home without my mom around. Sadly, it didn't take long before I started feeling resentful with my stepdad being back in the house. Most of my anger stemmed from thoughts of my mom being laid up in the hospital, while my stepdad got to play dad. Fairly or unfairly, I couldn't help but to blame him for a lot of the pain that my sisters and I were being put through. Life at home going on as usual without my mom around was just not going to happen. It would be just a matter of time before I found an excuse for not being able to live at home with my stepdad anymore. Without even realizing it, I started pushing the rules, hoping for an overreaction on his part. In my mind, the divorce had made my mom the sole rule maker. Any attempt by my stepdad to change her rules was seen by me as an affront to her.

All of my life, I worked hard to follow my mom's rules because she rewarded me in kind. For my stepfather, rules were meant to be followed —no reward necessary. When I turned sixteen and got my drivers license, one of the rules was to be at home by 10:00pm. If, for some reason, I couldn't, then I had to call home. This was an inflexible rule put in place by my mom. She made a pact with me that if I followed this rule for a year without messing up, then she would let me stay out past 10:00pm, as long as I called home. At this age, this was the reward of all rewards! It was my dream to be able to hang out late with my friends. Proudly, I passed my mom's test with flying colors. It was tough, but my hard work had earned me a new privilege. This privilege continued under the care of my stepdad, at least until the night I decided to make this privilege a right.

Things changed forever between my stepdad and me the night I decided to party all night with friends in Georgetown. This long night would inevitably provide me with the excuse I had been looking for to part ways with my stepdad. Anger or something I drank that night convinced me that it was okay to stay out without calling home. For some miscalculated reason, I decided that night it was time to make my own rules. I no longer had to come home or call if I didn't want to. My friends and I made the decision that this was going to be an all-nighter. We were going to shutdown Georgetown and then head to Chris' house to do more drinking. Chris was a close friend, whose mom was always out of town, so it was the perfect spot to crash. It was a given that by the time we all got back to Chris' house, it would be too late and too risky for anyone to drive me home. Also, I was too scared to go home this late, fearing that I would wake up my stepdad. Finding myself in an inescapable predicament, I decided to take a chance and crash at Chris' house. I knew that regardless of what I did at this point, my stepdad was going to be upset. My only hope was that he would consider me staying the night at Chris' the safest choice. If I got in trouble for anything, maybe it would be just for not calling home. Regardless of what was going to happen, I was determined to remain optimistic about the outcome.

When I got home the next morning, I was terrified of walking into the house. As soon as I opened the front door, I saw my stepdad standing in the kitchen. I quietly said hello and walked straight towards my bedroom. His disappointment and annoyance was obvious in his hello. All I could do now was go fiddle around in my room and wait for the scolding speech that was sure to come. Ten minutes quickly passed, then twenty, and finally thirty minutes passed and nothing! No yelling, no lecture —nothing! "How could this be?" I thought. My stepdad was a strict guy who believed in rules and respect. I kept asking myself, "Why isn't he storming into my room and letting me have it? Why isn't he standing in my room doorway telling me how wrong and inconsiderate I was last night?" Sitting there on the side of my bed, I couldn't come up with any answers. As crazy as it seemed, it was starting to look more and more like I got away with my crime.

After hanging out in my room all day and hearing nothing from my stepdad, I was confident that I had escaped punishment. So confident, I decided to ask him for permission to go out with my friends for a second night. Well, like any presumptuous criminal, it was just when I assumed that I got off clean, that my luck came to a screeching halt. My stepdad immediately started laying into me about not coming home or calling the night before. His words reflected more disappointment than anger. It was obvious to me that my disrespect towards him hurt. I sincerely apologized for not calling home and admitted that it was inconsiderate. I promised him that I would never do it again. Regardless of my sincere apology, it became obvious that my stepdad had already made up his mind that I had to be punished. It was the only way he could be sure that I got the message loud and clear.

Deservedly so, there had to be consequences for my actions. I actually agreed with my stepdad and was prepared to accept my punishment. That was until he read me my sentence. Not only did he tell me that I couldn't go out that night, which I kind of expected, but I also wouldn't be allowed to go out at night again until he said so. In other words, my nighttime privileges were over. For my stepdad, one screw up was one time too many. All I could do was stand there with my mouth hanging open. This punishment was over the top compared to how my mom dealt out punishment. Her discipline could be tough too, but the consequences were always clearly defined. There was no unending or random timeline of punishment. Also, unlike my stepdad's, my mother's discipline always took into account my ever increasing ability to know right from wrong. She always trusted me to make better decisions the next time. I felt like my stepdad's discipline was missing this element of trust.

After hearing my stepdad lay down his sentence, with no clear date for parole, I walked away from him steaming with anger. In my mind, I worked too hard for the freedom to be able to hang out with friends at night to have it all taken away for messing up one time. As I stormed down the hallway towards my bedroom, I made up my mind that I could not and would not accept this punishment. It was way beyond reasonable in my opinion. This may have been an arrogant position to take, especially coming from the kid who decided to go out, get drunk, and not call home, but I was sticking to my guns.

With nowhere to go, I felt trapped sitting in my bedroom. All I could do was sit there on the side of my bed, waiting for my anger to boil over. After sitting there for about twenty minutes, seething with anger, my mind suddenly snapped. There was no way that I could stay in that house anymore with my stepdad not trusting me. The decision was made —I have to go. Immediately, I grabbed my book bag from the closet and started filling it with as many clothes as I could. Next, I quietly called my friend Chris (Yes, the same Chris who I was hanging out with when I got into all of this trouble.) from my bedroom phone to ask him to pick me up. No questions asked, my friend told me that he would be there in fifteen minutes. Fifteen minutes later, I brushed off my fear and headed for the front door. As soon as I got outside, I saw Chris sitting in his car, parked a bit up the street, waiting for me. When we pulled off, an inside voice told me that I would never see my Atari, fish tank, and bedroom again. Sadly, that inside voice would turn out to be right.

As a teenager, feeling like I had to leave the place I called home hurt me badly. It still hurts today. Walking out that front door and leaving my sisters behind, crushed any remaining sense of family stability I had left in me. But at the same time, I knew that I had no choice. It was either leave now or allow my anger towards my stepdad to escalate the situation into something worse. In some strange way, I even felt like I was doing my stepdad a favor by leaving. He could now go on with his life without me being around to selfishly remind him that he could never fill my mother's shoes. It's often said that "hurting people hurt people." My stepdad and I were definitely hurting.

With my mother still in the hospital and me no longer living at home with my stepfather, I was officially in charge of my life now. If freedom is what I wanted, now I really had it. But freedom always comes at a cost. For me, that cost was having to leave the only place I could call home. At first, sure it was fun crashing at different friends' houses, partying, and staying out late. But the fun eventually started losing some of its appeal when I realized I was living out of a book bag.

Once again, the lack of stability in my life had brought me to my knees. Burned out from sleeping on friends' couches, I decided it was time to raise the white flag and call grandma. Of course, as soon as she heard my voice over the phone, she knew something was wrong. I told her that I wanted to go home, but I couldn't stay with Kurt, my stepdad, anymore. Right away, my grandmother told me to come stay with them until my mother got out of the hospital. Staying with my grandparents was going to be a big change for someone that was getting used to stumbling in the house at two o'clock in the morning. But at this point, I felt like I had no choice.

Living with grandma and granddad, like the good old days, was smooth sailing for the first few weeks. I was reminded of how nice it was as a little boy to have so much love in the house. Unfortunately, I was no longer that little boy. As the days passed, the behavior of a rebellious teenager eventually collided with the rules of old school grandparents. Staying out late and trying to tip-toe drunk into the spare bedroom every other night didn't go unnoticed. It wasn't long before I got the "There's nothing but trouble in the streets after midnight" speech. That's when I knew that my days of staying at grandma and granddad's might be numbered.

Just like a typical naïve teenager, I took for granted my grandparents' concern for my wellbeing. They were looking out for me, but all I was looking for was fun. I felt like partying was the only way to keep my mind off of my mom and rolling out on my stepdad. "If there was just someone in my family who I could stay with for a while, someone who could provide stability, but at the same time, understand what I was going through, my life could go on," I thought.

Soon enough, that prayer was answered. The same aunt who came to my rescue the night my mom attempted to take her own life, came to my rescue again. My Aunt Carrie Lee, who was the epitome of laid back, invited me to stay with her until things got better. She welcomed me and my baggage with open arms. Right or wrong, she also sympathized with me and my frustration trying to live under my grandparents' rules. Aunt Carrie Lee was full of youth and life. I didn't have to explain to her what I needed to feel better —She just got it. It wasn't long after my aunt first offered me a place to stay that I was moving the few things I owned into my new bedroom.

What was supposed to be a temporary, stable place for me to stay until my mother recovered, ended up being my home for almost two years. As it turned out, my mother and I would end up never returning to our home in Clinton, Maryland. The fallout from my mom's suicide attempt and the divorce, left my stepdad with the house and custody of my younger sisters. My mother was left with nothing. She ended up having to live with friends and eventually my grandparents. This was a painful time, but my mom did what she had to do to get back on her feet. Unfortunately, as she was fighting for her comeback, her teenage son was running faster and faster towards trouble.

- CHAPTER 9 -

A FOOL'S GOLD

Youth, ignorance, and anger can be a frightening combination. The mixture of all three at the same time usually leads to trouble. Add in a little bit of false teenage sense of invincibility, you are talking serious trouble. Unfortunately, trouble is just part of the teenage journey. We all walk the journey, but unfortunately, some of us take the scenic path.

One of the most costly parts of being a teenager tends to be the lack of consideration for the consequences of our actions. It's not unusual for a teenager to be big on risk taking and small on accountability. Combine this with idealism and impulsiveness, you have an unpredictable creature on your hands. At one time, I was one of those creatures and so were most of my friends. As teenagers, we pushed the limits. Any advice or warning given by an adult was usually considered outdated at best and hypocritical at worst.

Even with the natural pushback I gave as a teenager, I still tried my best to maintain a basic level of respect for my friends and family. One of the most important things my mom ever taught me was the importance of respect: giving it and demanding it. Starting as a kid in elementary school, I was taught to always respect others, but also to stick up for myself and fight for respect if I had to. Growing up in the projects, I had no choice. Weakness only invited more disrespect. I learned at a young age that the perceived tough kid rarely gets tested. Demonstrating a posture worthy of respect can be a powerful deterrent.

"Peace through strength" —that's how the official policy of the United States during the 1980's Cold War with the Soviet Union is best described. Looking back on those scary times, I can't help but notice a striking similarity between the position that the U.S. military took to insure respect from the Soviet Union and the position that a tough kid on the playground in the projects takes to insure his respect. In both cases, the projection of strength creates an environment less inviting to disrespect or confrontation. It's worth mentioning, however, that strength can never guarantee the absence of confrontation, but whenever one party has more to lose, the chances of confrontation are greatly reduced.

During the Cold War, under the leadership of Ronald Reagan, the United States understood this principle. By the U.S. projecting maximum strength, it was demanding maximum respect. As the Soviet Union attempted match or surpass U.S. strength, it came at a cost they were unable to pay. Economically and militarily, the Soviet Union could not sustain its challenge to the economic and military might of the United States of America. As a result, they ended up in a positon with more to lose, thus reducing their desire for conflict and war. Without a single punch being thrown or shot being fired, mutual respect had ultimately insured the peace.

Unfortunately, during my high school years, unlike during the Cold War, sometimes a punch or two had to be thrown in order to get respect and a sense of peace. Mutual respect was often undervalued to say the least. For the teenage mindset, the potential costs associated with the lack of mutual respect is rarely, if ever considered. A youthful sense of invincibility tends to hide any potential price associated with the lack of respect. It is only when assumptions regarding "price" become actual "costs" that respect can be demanded.

During my senior year in high school, I crossed paths with someone who I can definitely say made a lot of assumptions about "price" when they made the decision to steal from me. Little did that someone know, they were stealing from a person who was in a very unstable and volatile state of mind. A person who was going through a very tough time, who was just itching for someone to take their anger out on. I doubt if the young, high school punk who chose to steal from me put any thought whatsoever into how I would respond or the potential consequences of his actions. With brazenness, he was confident in his decision to disrespect me. I was determined to let him know that he made a serious misjudgment in his confidence.

THE THIEF: COMES TO STEAL

In John 10:10 of the Bible it says that "The thief comes only to steal and kill and destroy." The thief the Bible is referring to is the devil. You can never predict when or where you're going to cross paths with the devil. Of all places, the last place I thought would be at an all-girl Catholic school. I could never have imagined that one day, I would be sitting in my car in a Catholic school parking lot and all of a sudden, my car is surrounded by an angry group of thugs who decide to attack and rob me. Well, on one perfect sunny afternoon, about an hour after school let out, this is exactly what happened to me.

It was 2:30pm, the final bell had just rang. The sun was out and my car was clean, which meant it was time to cruise. My good friend Chris and I decided to take a drive up to La Reine Catholic High School to see a girl I had just started dating. Her school let out an hour after ours, so this gave us plenty of time to make the twenty-minute drive and get a prime parking spot right at the entrance before the bell rang. Because La Reine was an all-girl Catholic school, I didn't have to do too much arm twisting to get Chris to join me. The school, located in Suitland, Maryland, was a very popular afterschool destination for a lot of the local high school boys. It didn't come as a surprise to me that a bunch of young, Catholic high school girls dressed in short plaid skirts could draw a crowd. Although, it did come as a surprise to see the level of competition and jealousy that came along with that crowd. For a lot of the boys who hung out at La Reine afterschool, it wasn't just about seeing girls, it was also an opportunity to show off. For me, I admit, it was a little bit of both. Sure I was there to see a girl I was dating, but you best believe, I had every intention to do my own tiny bit of showing off. Before I drove one foot into that school parking lot, I made sure my little Nissan Sentra was spotless and my tires were soaked in "Armor All." Back in the day, where I'm from, no car, no matter how clean, was complete without that "Armor All" tire shine. The bottom line, boys and girls alike, I was there to impress.

While sitting in our car, styling and profiling, Chris and I soon realized that the girls coming out of school weren't the only ones honing in on the "Armor All" tire shine. We both began to notice a crowd of jealous looking guys walking towards our car from the direction of Suitland High School. This was the public high school located right next door to La Reine and known for having its fair share of rough dudes. As the boys from Suitland got closer and closer to my car, their contempt for all of the attention we were getting became obvious. It was pissing them off that my girlfriend and all of her friends were only focusing on us. I could tell in my gut and by the stare in their eyes that trouble was headed our way. Growing up around violence and rough dudes, I knew this type of stare very well. Instinctively, I knew that it was just a matter of minutes before things got ugly.

Trying to remain calm and prevent the crowd from noticing my nervousness, I calmly told my girlfriend that I had to get going. Unfortunately, because of the group of people standing in front of my car, I couldn't pull off right away. By that time, three thugs from the crowd had already made their way up to the side of my car. Randomly, one of them asked me, "Is this your car?" I knew better than to show fear, so I answered confidently, "Yes it is." Meanwhile, my friend Chris in the passenger seat, had "scared" written all over his face and justifiably so. He immediately looked at me and says, "Jermaine, we have to go!" I slowly tried to pull off, but the crowd didn't budge. I had hoped that the crowd would move and disperse once they knew I was serious about leaving. Unfortunately, that didn't happen.

Leaving was never going to be enough for the thugs in this crowd. These were not your typical high school boys jockeying for girls. This was a mob of jealous punks willing to do anything to impress girls. Obviously, they were feeling like I had one-upped them for whatever reason. It could have been my car or maybe the gold chain I was sporting outside of my t-shirt. I did notice the same thug who asked me if this was my car, staring at it. Because I was so caught up in trying to impress the girls, it never occurred to me that wearing a shiny gold herringbone chain in front of a bunch of punk-ass high school boys was probably not a good idea. Between the Armor All tires and the gold chain, I had really dug myself in a hole.

Feeling like I had exhausted all other options, I decided to stomp down on the accelerator, causing the engine to rev loudly, which cleared the crowd standing in front of the car immediately. Now, they knew I meant business. It was then that one of the thugs surrounding the car yelled out, "Get his gold chain!" At this point, anyone still standing in front of the car was getting run over. The time had come for me to do what I had to do to get out of there. As I began speeding through and past the crowd, I suddenly felt a sharp pull on my neck. Immediately, I slammed on the brakes because I knew exactly where that pull came from. Someone had snatched the gold necklace my mom had given me from around my neck. Right away, I felt around on my shirt and realized it was gone. When I looked back in my rearview mirror, I could see the thugs in the crowd daring me to back up. Standing in front, was one of the three thugs who initially came up to the side of my car. He was holding and dangling the gold necklace that he had just snatched from around my neck. "Come get it, come get it," the crowd chanted as I looked back. Without thinking, I opened my car door to do just that.

When I boldly stepped out of my car, everything seemed to go silent. The crowd seemed more shocked than I was scared. I could tell that a lot of them were in disbelief that I actually stopped and got out of the car. As I stood there, torn between Chris begging me to get back in the car and the crowd taunting me, all I kept thinking was "How could I get this guy alone —without his friends there to help him?" Since getting him alone wasn't in the current deck of cards, I had to bring myself back down to earth. Either that or put myself in a situation where I could get seriously hurt or even worst, killed. My anger wanted me to confront this thug at all cost, but my brain told me otherwise. I knew that if I would have walked even halfway towards the guy holding my gold chain, his friends in the crowd would have jumped me and probably beat me unconscious. Regardless of how angry I was, I knew that I was no match for a crowd. The only logical choice I had was to get back in the car, swallow my pride and leave to fight another day. So that's exactly what I did.

    As Chris and I sped out of the parking lot, thinking that the confrontation was at its end, the punk-ass delinquents in the crowd threw rocks at my car. It wasn't enough for them that they stole from me and made me leave. They wanted to inflict as much embarrassment and damage to me as possible. These weren't high school students, these were animals with no respect for anything.

    The entire ride back to Chris' house in Clinton, I couldn't stop shaking with anger. All I kept thinking about was that some punk-ass dude had taken something very special from me to make it his own. The only comfort I could find was in telling myself that one day I would have my revenge. Someday, someway, and somehow, I would find a way to hurt the guy who stole my chain. The guy who grinned, taunted, and dared me to take back what was mine —his day was coming.

    Not long after we made it back to Chris' house, a few of our knuckle-headed friends showed up. Right away, we began telling them about what happened up at La Reine. Of course, some of my hardcore friends wanted to jump in the car and drive back up there, but the rest were just like "Jermaine, let it go." I must admit, it's nice to have hardcore friends who have your back when shit gets real, but heading back up there was not a very bright idea. No matter how hardcore, a couple of buddies is no match for a crowd of thugs. For now, it was looking like revenge would have to wait.

As the days passed, instead of moving on from what happened up at La Reine, I began to imagine ways to hurt the person who hurt me. Bad thoughts swirled around in my head for weeks. Eventually, months passed and my anger still festered. I refused to listen to the advice of some of my good friends, who suggested I put it all behind me. I'm not sure how much of it was anger or pride, but my need for revenge was consuming me. I had fallen into the trap that so many other teenagers fall into at that age: The refusal and inability to consider the consequences of my actions. In my case, it was my "future" actions. At seventeen, up to this point, it didn't occur to me that if I hurt this dude who had stolen from me, that I would do more harm to myself and my future than any gold chain is worth —mom given or not. My anger and need for payback was leading me towards a cliff.

THE THIEF: COMES TO KILL

The devil has a fondness for attacking the angry and weak. I showed up on his radar the moment I allowed my anger to devalue life and my weakness to crave revenge. It was just a matter of time before he would attempt to zero in for the attack.

His first move came when I was out driving around with friends late one evening and we all noticed a group of newly opened stores near the Shopper's Food Warehouse. With nothing else to do, we decided to pull in and check them out. Most of us were broke, so the most we could do was window or cabinet shop. The first store we checked out was the Asian specialty shop. They sold everything from Kimonos to Ninja throwing stars. Of course, the weapons caught our attention right away. The only time we had seen weapons like these were in Karate movies. I couldn't believe that they were even allowed to sell some of this stuff. They had throwing stars, daggers, nun chucks, and every type of knife you could imagine. For me, the knife cabinet stood out more than any of the others. While my friends were gazing and gawking at the unique Martial Arts weapons, I was consumed with the knife display. As much as I would have liked to have thought that the reasoning for my high-interest in the knives was based on innocent fascination, unfortunately that wasn't the case. Anger and hatred had drawn me to the knife display.

Sure, time had passed since that awful day in the Catholic school parking lot, but not my need for revenge. To me, each of the knives in that display cabinet offered its own unique touch for exacting my revenge. It became obvious that I had turned a dark and dangerous corner on this dead end mission. No longer was it a question in my mind of whether or not I should hurt the person who stole from me, but rather, which knife in that cabinet should I buy to do it? Because I wasn't eighteen yet, I would have to get one of my older friends to buy it for me, which wasn't a problem. All I had to do was come up with a little bit of cash.

A week later, with cash in hand, I was ready to do a little knife shopping. I was ready to buy something that had the power to destroy my future, but more frightening, the power to kill. All that was left to do now was to get one of my older friends to take a ride with me up to the Asian specialty shop.

The first person I asked was my friend Eddie, who was over eighteen and knew how badly I wanted to hurt the guy who stole my chain. I didn't have to ask anyone else because, without hesitation, Eddie agreed to take the ride with me. Right away, we jumped in the car, along with one of my other friends, and we all headed up to the store. As soon as we got there, I had to make sure that it appeared Eddie was buying the knife for himself. Not being eighteen, I couldn't give the store clerks any clues that he was buying a knife for me. It was tough hinting to Eddie which knives I liked, but he knew my price limit was twenty dollars, so that narrowed things down quite a bit. After several minutes of amateur hand and eye signals, I finally made my pick. I signaled to Eddie that the bronze-colored folding knife with the word "SURVIVAL" etched on the blade was my choice. It was the coolest looking one in the display case that was priced under twenty dollars. Within five minutes of making my pick, the cashier was ringing us up and we were on our merry way.

When we got in the car, it was tough to come to grips with what I just bought. This wasn't just a new knife, this was something I picked out for the sole purpose of hurting or possibly killing someone. Just holding it in my hand gave me pause. For some reason, I developed an uncomfortableness with my new sense of power. Sure, I held and shot guns before with my stepdad, but never with the specific intention of using it to do harm to someone. Instead of emboldening my desire for revenge, holding that knife calmed that desire. I suddenly realized that wanting to do harm to someone takes on a whole new meaning when you actually equip yourself with the means to inflict that harm.

As it turned out, what was supposed to be a high-fiving ride home from the Asian specialty shop, celebrating the purchase of my new knife, ended up being a serious moment of self-reflection for me. At least, that's how I would have described it at the time. The truth is, my sudden awakening had nothing to do with self-reflection, but everything to do with GOD'S Grace. Even though Eddie was able to put that knife in my hand, GOD was able to put peace in my heart. Peace that would provide a glimpse of clarity and a conscience as I weighed the cost of my revenge.

THE THIEF: COMES TO DESTROY

Equipping me with the means to kill, was obviously not enough for the devil's plan to move forward. He would have to come after my Faith next. The devil knows that the surest way to destroy is by undermining Faith. If he can shake our Faith in GOD, then he can destroy us. My Faith would now become the focus of the devil's attack.

The one thing that grounds us under any type of attack is our Faith. The devil knows this and that's why it's often the focus of his strongest attack. During the turbulent times of my parents' divorce, my Faith was often the only thing that kept me going. These were hard times, filled with a lot of uncertainty. It was tough to keep the Faith and stay positive. This was no secret to the devil. He knew that under the right pressure and circumstances, he could get me to question my Faith. At the age of seventeen, I had no idea of the devil's wicked plans that had already been set in motion.

Not too long after buying that knife, I found myself glued to the TV one day, watching a talk show that featured a guy named Anton LaVey. He was the author of a book called "The

Satanic Bible." With a bald head and super pale white skin, this guy looked every bit of satanic. As evil looking as he was, he was a very charismatic and convincing speaker. I was young, curious, and naturally rebellious, so I couldn't help but to want to learn more about the strange looking author and his shadowy book. Instead of sounding evil like I expected, I found the things that he was saying to be appealing, especially to my frustrated and rebellious side. It appeared that his message and his book were specifically targeting young, inquisitive, and vulnerable minds —go figure.

A few days after watching Oprah interview Satan (joking), my curiosity grew so strong that I had to have a copy of Anton LaVey's book, "The Satanic Bible." One day after school, I decided to take a trip to the Barnes and Noble at Forestville Mall with my partner in crime Chris to see if I could find a copy. I was too embarrassed to tell Chris what book I was buying, so I kept him in suspense the whole ride up there. Even when we walked into the store, I wouldn't tell him. It was only after I searched every aisle, fiction and nonfiction, with no luck, that I decided to tell him. Like I expected, Chris thought I was out of my mind. His reaction to me wanting to buy this book was worse than his reaction to me wanting to buy a knife. Regardless of his reaction, I could sense that he was very curious about the book.

"The Satanic Bible" seemed like it was nowhere to be found in the Barnes and Noble. Having come too far to give up now, I courageously walked over to the information desk to see if they could help out with my hunt. It was more than embarrassing telling the innocent looking black girl behind the counter the name of the book I was looking for, but I didn't care at this point. Predictably, when I told her the name, she looked at me like I was crazy, but went on typing the creepy title into her computer anyways. She told me, in what seemed like her best professional voice, that they didn't have any copies in the store, but that she could order it and have it in two days. It sounded like a plan to me, so I gave her the okay to make the order and two days later, I was back there to pick up my book. Step by step, I was falling right into the devil's plan.

    I couldn't wait to get home to crack open that book. As soon as I walked in the door, I went straight to my room to start reading. Sadly, I had never had such a sense of urgency to read a book in my life until now. Not the Bible or any other book had sparked my interest like this one. The devil was clearly having his way, at least for now. But his way would soon come to an end once the FATHER steps in with his GRACE.

    From what I remember about this dark, deceitful book, there was a lot of material devoted to convincing the reader that there is no GOD. It begins by encouraging the reader to revel in a point of view of inescapable cynicism with the goal of getting the audience to question everything. Even the most basic foundations of life and decency are put to question. One of the quotes from the book that I remember was: "Question all things, for the belief in one falsehood is the beginning of all stupidity." I liked the quote so much at the time that I even put it on the cover of my class notebook. This statement was a brilliant trap for young minds that often question matters of Faith and GOD.

    Besides encouraging disdain for GOD, "The Satanic Bible" also contained chapters encouraging disdain and hatred for your enemies. Forgiveness for those who have wronged you was described as the ultimate form of weakness. In short, this book was like a cookbook with specific instructions on how to destroy your life. And for an angry, young fool such as myself, this book had every recipe. Between this book and the knife, it was looking more and more like everything was moving along perfectly according to the devil's plan.

Unfortunately for the devil, I threw a wrench in his plan the day I decided to bring a crucial piece of his plan out in public. My fascination with "The Satanic Bible" naturally made me want to show it off to my friends. As far as I knew, none of them had ever seen or read it. One school morning, I decided to take the seductive book to school for a few of my friends to see. I had to make sure that none of my teachers or "big-mouth" friends saw it, so I wrapped it in a book cover made out of newspaper. My friends in homeroom were the main people I wanted to show the book to. Every morning, we would get into these deep, philosophical conversations about things we knew absolutely nothing about. I thought to myself, "My new book would fit right in with one of these conversations."

Our homeroom was in an art studio, so the class was divided into four large tables that sat eight students each. It was an awesome homeroom because everyone could share and talk at each of the big tables. The only downside was, whatever you shared and talked about was instantly heard by eight people. If you thought that high school gossip passed around fast by telling just one person, imagine telling eight at the same time. I was taking a huge risk pulling this book out in homeroom. My thought was, wrapping it in newspaper would prevent any loud reactions at the table. Unfortunately, it caused the opposite. Before I could even pull the book out of my book bag, a loud kid at my table asks, "What's that!" Instead of panicking, I calmly passed him the book, hoping that he would keep quiet once he realized what it was. He did, but he couldn't stop his mouth from hanging wide open.

Instantly, "Let me see! Let me see! What is it! What is it!" echoed around the table. I knew that it would be just a matter of seconds before the teacher walked over. Just as I predicted, she started making her way. "Here comes Mrs. Turner! Put it away! Put it away!" I told everyone. Somehow, I managed to get my friends to instantly snap into "here comes the teacher" mode. Before Mrs. Turner even got two feet from her desk, thanks to my quick acting friends, that "Satanic Bible" had magically vanished to another galaxy. She would have no idea what all of the commotion was about by the time she reached our table. Once she got there, she immediately asked, "What's going on over here?" Like typical lying teenagers, we all responded in typical guilty harmony, "Nothing Mrs. Turner." "Wow!" I thought, "My friends just saved me from getting into a whole lot of trouble." If Mrs. Turner would have found out what I brought into her classroom, I'm not sure what she would have done, but I'm sure, for me, it wouldn't have been good. After that close call, I decided to wait until after homeroom to get my book back from whoever was quick enough to hide it. I was too nervous to ask for it back right away because I didn't want to cause another scene.

There were only ten minutes left of homeroom, but the fact that I didn't know who had my book made it extremely difficult to sit through those last few minutes. Finally, when the 1st period bell rang, I was expecting whoever had my book to just hand it to me. Naturally, I assumed it would be the kid who I originally passed it to, but he said he didn't have it anymore. He told me that when Mrs. Turner started walking over, someone grabbed it from his hand underneath the desk. It sounded a bit suspicious, but I had no way of knowing if he was telling me the truth. All I knew for certain was that now I had to face the prospect that my book could be in the hands of anyone sitting at the table that morning. With no one coming forward, it was starting to look like whoever had it, had no intention of returning it.

The situation with my missing "Satanic Bible" caused me to become really scared at first. "What if someone has decided to keep the book so that they can show the teachers or principle?" I thought. This would be a tough and embarrassing situation to explain away. I was definitely afraid of this happening. Despite the obvious reasons for being afraid, I also had deep reasons for being angry. Embarrassing book or not, someone had stolen something that belonged to me. This was unacceptable as far as I was concerned. Eventually, my anger overtook my fear and I made sure that everyone that was a potential suspect knew that. Suddenly, I no longer cared about causing a scene in class, I was going to get my book back.

"Who has my book!" I angrily asked my so-called homeroom friends sitting at my table. I thought for sure that someone was going to give it up now, sensing my level anger. Still, no one came forward. Not knowing who else to blame, I began to focus all of my anger on the only person I gave the book to. This, otherwise, good friend swore to me for the second time that he didn't have it. Maybe he didn't, but I was pretty sure he had at least a clue about who did. I even threatened to fight him right there in class if he didn't tell me something. To my surprise, he didn't even flinch at my threats. I thought, this was an unusual response for someone who was guilty. If he had it, I would have expected him to have an arrogant smirk. If he knew who had it, I would have expected him to give me a clue so that I would stop accusing him. He did neither. His calm, confident demeanor was that of someone who was willing to fight to protect his name, not defend his theft. At least, that's what my gut was telling me. For all I knew, he still could have been lying, but at the very least, he succeeded at getting the focus off of him.

"What could I do now?" I thought. If no one was willing to come forward with my book, anger could only get me but so far. By me not being able to tell and get help from the teacher, my options were limited. There I was, desperately wanting to get something back that belonged to me, but I was too ashamed to say what it was. This was when it all started to click. This was the moment that GOD's GRACE revealed its presence and power. The anger that I was feeling about something being taken from me was replaced by calmness and release. I began to ask myself, "How could something that supposedly espouses the seeking of truth be something to be ashamed of?" Also, I wondered, "If the things described in 'The Satanic Bible' were somehow a beacon or light of truth, then why did my classmates <u>instinctively</u> know that they had to hide it?" These were just some of the questions that led to my release from a thing that was meant for my harm.

Later on in life, I would come across a scripture in the Bible that would help me understand why the devil was unsuccessful in his evil plans during my rebellious youth:

"You are of GOD, little children, and have overcome them, because He who is in you is greater than he who is in the world." —John 4:4

During my high school years, it was obvious that the devil knew me, but he must have forgotten about "He who is in me." The "He" who would place a knife in my hand to erase the sweet taste of revenge. The "He" who would use a book meant for my harm to draw me closer to Him. Today, I look back and I am so thankful that GOD removed that book from my life and any desire in my heart to replace it. Astonishingly, I never found out what happened to that book. No one ever came forward and I never even heard a rumor about who may have taken it. It was as if the book just vanished under the table that morning in homeroom. Whatever happened to it, GOD made sure that I would never lay eyes on it again.

As painful and violating as it was to have something stolen from me, I was fortunate enough, through the Grace of GOD, to realize that my emotions were leading me astray. An insatiable need for revenge had placed me on a dark path. This is to not say that the person who stole from me shouldn't have been punished, but at what cost? Should I have thrown my life away for the sake of getting revenge or a gold chain? Should I have destroyed another person's life? The answers to these questions seem pretty obvious to me today. During my rebellious youth, not so much.

Eventually, that "SURVIVAL" knife ended up in a shoebox and gold chains went out of style. Looking back, I wouldn't change a thing about my experience and reaction to what happened in that Catholic school parking lot. Because of it, I was given a testimony. Because of it, I got to witness GOD's Grace. Ironically, that quote from "The Satanic Bible" that demands the reader to "Question all things" ended up bringing me closer to GOD, not further away as it had intended. GOD decisively defeated me in my rebellion.

- CHAPTER 10 -

BEAUTY FOR ASHES

It was called "crack." If you didn't know someone using it, you knew someone selling it. Anybody who grew up in or around Washington, D.C. during the crack cocaine epidemic would probably agree with this statement. During the late 80's and early 90's, crack cocaine took Washington, D.C. and other major cities in America by storm. The violence, murders, and carnage that accompanied the crack epidemic were unlike any other drug plagues to ever hit this country. It was during this period that Washington, D.C. became known as the "murder capital of the world." The city that historically took on the name "Chocolate City" for its majority of black residents had now earned a new title. You couldn't turn on the 6 o'clock or 11 o'clock local news without hearing about a drug or gang related homicide. The streets of our Nation's Capital had essentially become a war zone.

The casualties of the conflict were crack dealers and customers alike. For the dealers who were willing to risk it all for the quick dollar, it was often jail time or even death. For their customers, it was typically the same outcome, but just a different ride to get there. Being hooked on "crack," it didn't take long before you were living a life that was spiraling out of control. The seduction of the drug and its quick high were so addictive, a person would often be willing to do anything for their next fix. I personally had friends and acquaintances, who were so hooked on crack, that they stole and even sold their body to get a fix. On the other side of the equation, I knew people who sold crack and even killed for the profits they made from it. For many of us around during the reign of crack cocaine, the violence and destruction became painfully personal.

HUSTLING

It was hard to find any community that was untouched by the crack epidemic. For me, living in the suburbs at the time, proved to be no great escape. Even though there weren't drive-by shootings, the impact that crack had on the stability and culture of the suburban community was undeniable. All of a sudden, you had suburban high school kids acting like gangsters. It became cool to dress and look like a drug dealer, even though you were living with your parents in a single family home. Some of my high school friends went all the way and actually began selling crack or "hustling," as it was called. They would take the risk, not so much for the money, but for the image they could portray. Wearing a pager, jewelry, and the hottest clothes was a way to show their admiration for the drug life. Sadly, I would venture to guess that some of their parents probably moved to the suburbs to escape that life. Never could they imagine that something called crack cocaine would come along to cause their kids to look up to that life.

Thankfully, I never sold drugs in high school, but that's not to say I wasn't tempted. The "drug dealer image" was quite seductive to young eyes. It was sometimes tough to say no to the nice clothes, expensive Timberland boots, and steady flow of pocket cash. Just like a lot of my friends who didn't hustle drugs, I would occasionally put on a front as if I did. Back then, a pager and a fake car phone antenna were all you needed to play the role. I couldn't afford a pager, but I did have enough to buy a five dollar fake car phone antenna from Trak Auto to stick on the rear windshield of my car. All of my friends knew that it was fake, but that didn't matter. It was all about portraying an image. This was during a time when car phones and portable cell phones were over-the-top expensive. The only people who could typically afford them were wealthy folks and drug dealers. For the rest of us, the fake car phone antenna was our symbol of success and power.

It's hard not to make fun at some of the silly things we used to do in high school to appear to be something that we weren't. The truth of the matter is, there's really nothing funny at all about wanting to look like a drug dealer. It became obvious that crack was not only impacting the culture of my generation, but our value system as well. No longer was it cool to flip burgers or wash dishes for extra cash. Working at McDonald's just couldn't compete with making five hundred dollars a day checking a pager and making a few calls.

THERE GOES THE NEIGHBOROOD

Selling crack, especially in the inner cities, produced conditions that were ripe for violence. As more and more people got hooked on the highly addictive drug, the deadlier the drug market became. Increasing demand produced increasingly aggressive competition. Violence linked to competition hit the streets of Washington, D.C. much harder than in the suburbs where I lived. I had grandparents still living in D.C. at the time, so I routinely got to see up close the urban destruction brought on by crack. My old neighborhood in the projects had essentially become a war zone. In fact, it was home to one of the biggest drug strips in the D.C. area —The 58th Street strip. Crossing over busy East Capitol Street and connecting the Northeast to Southeast quadrants of the city, 58th Street was known for its almost daily drive-by shootings, murders, and open-air drug markets. The infamous drug strip made regular headlines on the 6 o'clock and 11 o'clock news. For me, I didn't have to watch the news to find out about the latest shooting on the 58th Street strip, my grandparents lived just three housing units down from it.

 As dangerous as my old neighborhood had become, I still considered it home. A lot of the friends who I grew up with still lived there. I was still close to most of them, even the ones caught up in the drug game. Because of that, I never felt afraid being back in the projects. It was no big deal to me to hang out on 58th Street with my old friends. That being sad, I was smart enough to realize that the old neighborhood wasn't what it used to be. It was always a rough place, but there's a big difference between rough and dangerous. Unfortunately, it had become more of the later. During catch-up conversations with my old friends, I would hear about who got shot or who just got locked up. Sadly, it never seemed to be a big deal, but just another day around the way. I guess my old neighborhood friends had become numb or just used to their sad reality.

My old friends weren't the only ones who had grown numb to their reality. The frightening sights and sounds that my grandparents had somehow gotten used to were unreal. Finding bullet holes and bullets lodged in their backdoor frame or hearing screams from someone in the alley who had just gotten shot —just to name a few. I can't help but to think, "What if one of my grandparents had been standing in the doorway when those bullet holes were made?" "What if those bullets hit a few inches to the left and came through the doorway?"

I could never have imagined how violent my old neighborhood would eventually become. Crack came in and wreaked havoc on every inch and every corner of the projects. Sadly, a lot of the young men who brought about this havoc were people I grew up with, they were friends. They were kids who I played on the playground with, who I chased after ice cream trucks with, and who I rode big wheels up and down the streets with. "How could this happen?" I wondered. Crack was a beast and it was swallowing the public housing projects of D.C. whole.

The temptation to hustle was overwhelming for young men living in the projects. Who wouldn't want nice clothes and a nice ride when everything else around you is poor and broken? I had friends living with their grandmother, but were driving around in brand new SUVs that they paid for in cash. For a young man living in the projects with no hope, how do you say "No" to that game? Even for someone like me, who was about to graduate high school and head to college, I couldn't help but to envy someone my age who could afford a brand new, customized SUV.

I never hid my awe over the success and money my friends in the projects made selling crack. Being a broke high school kid getting ready to be broke for at least four more years while attending college, I just couldn't help it. To my surprise, my friends in the projects had a certain amount of awe for me as well. Being someone from the projects just like them, but who somehow made it out and was headed to college, was something my old neighborhood friends admired. They gave me a lot of respect for playing the long game.

This understanding and mutual respect between old friends taught me a very valuable lesson about life. We always have to be mindful of our current circumstances and the effect they have on our overall perspective and outlook on life. For a person selling drugs, life is played as a short-sighted game —high risks, immediate gratification, and fast money. For a college bound kid, life is seen as a long-sighted game consisting of hard work and sacrifice, which hopefully will lead to low risk, sustainable prosperity and wealth. I recommend choosing your perspective wisely. Don't let temporary circumstances cause you to make decisions, which can lead to permanent problems.

MY "ALMOST" RODNEY KING MOMENT

Unfortunately, in my old neighborhood, the short-sighted crack game wasn't going anywhere anytime soon. Selling crack paid and it paid well. You couldn't drive a block through the projects and not see a Benz or BMW with Hammer or BBS rims on it. For a cop patrolling the projects, you didn't have to be Sherlock Holmes to figure out who the likely sellers were.

The buyers were just as easy to spot. Out-of-state tags or being "white" driving through the projects was a huge red flag to the police. It was normal for cops to pull people over without probable cause if they didn't look like they belonged in the neighborhood.

One day leaving my grandparents' house for the drive back to the suburbs, I somehow managed to fit the description of "someone who didn't belong in the neighborhood." I always knew that I probably would get pulled over one day because I looked young and had Maryland tags on my car. It was just a matter of time. On this particular day though, I was completely caught off guard. It all started the moment I made a left turn out of the projects onto East Capitol Street, heading towards Maryland. That's when I saw the flashing lights in my rearview mirror. "No big deal," I thought. I knew I hadn't done anything wrong. Driving a little silver Nissan Sentra, I knew it couldn't have been because of my car, it wasn't expensive. It couldn't have been my nice rims or "chromed-out" rocker panels because I had neither. I thought, "The Maryland tags had to be it."

Taught to always be respectful of police officers, I pulled over right away. It's always scary getting pulled over by the cops, but my confidence that day rested in the fact that I knew I didn't do anything wrong. Also, I had been randomly pulled over a few times before, just not in the projects. Before the officers even got out of their car, I had already gotten my license out of my wallet and registration and proof of insurance from the glove box. My intention was to have everything ready to hand them as soon as they got up to my car. Unfortunately, my preparedness ended up pissing the officers off. When they approached the side of my car and saw that I already had my credentials ready to hand to them, they took it as a sign of arrogance. Immediately, they became irritated that I was a step ahead of him. This was when I knew that this wasn't going to be a typical stop.

After handing the officer on the driver's side my license and registration, he suddenly asked me to get out of the car. This was the point at which my nervousness turned into fear. "Why do you need me to get out of the car?" I calmly asked the officer. Suddenly, in an angry, loud voice I heard, "Get the fuck out of the car and keep your hands up to the side of your head!" Terrified and confused, I slowly opened my door and stepped out of the car. Next, I was told to walk to the back of the car and put my hands on the trunk and not to move. While one of the officers patted me down and searched my pockets, presumably for drugs, the other officer on the passenger side began searching every inch of the inside of my car. I knew that they weren't going to find anything, but the smartest thing I could do was keep my mouth shut. They were looking for any reason at all to escalate the situation. Once the officer who was checking me found nothing and the officer searching my car found nothing, the last place left for them to search was the trunk. I was told to stand on the side of my car with my hands on the roof while they did their last search. Much to their disappointment, nothing was found in the trunk either.

Appearing surprised and obviously disappointed that their hunch didn't pay off, the police officers finally gave up on their search and told me to get back in my car and wait. Both of the officers then returned to their car, I'm assuming to run my license and plates. As I sat there, my eyes welled up with tears of anger. I wasn't a lawyer, but I knew that what I had just went through violated every single civil right in the book. I wanted to hate those officers, but inside, I knew that they were in a fight themselves. Having to patrol one of the most dangerous crack infested spots in D.C., they were up against a tough enemy. An enemy that took advantage of the laws the cops were expected to follow. I wasn't making excuses for the behavior of the officers, but I understood the tough dilemma they found themselves in. Unfortunately for me, doing something as simple as making a left turn put me in the middle of that dilemma.

Ten minutes after sitting in my car, trying to regain control of my emotions, both police officers finally got back out of their car and began walking towards the driver's side of my car. I wasn't sure what to expect, but I was praying that they were just going to hand me back my license and registration and tell me to go on my merry way. Well, in a roundabout way, those prayers were answered. In a courteous, calm voice, completely different from the earlier voice, the officer who originally told me to "get the fuck out of the car" explained that the reason they pulled me over was because I didn't use my left blinker. "Yeah right," I thought to myself. "They didn't pull me over for a stupid blinker, they pulled me over on the suspicion that I was buying drugs, period." The big red-flag was raised the moment I made a left turn out of the projects to head towards Maryland. Those cops spotted my out-of-state tags, got a hunch and went straight in for the kill.

Regardless of the fact that the officers wouldn't admit to the real reason for pulling me over, in that situation, I was willing to take what I could get. Arguing would have been the dumbest thing in the world to do. Because I held my tongue, both officers even apologized for any misunderstandings. It seemed as if they felt somewhat badly for the way they initially treated me when first pulling me over —as they should have.

Looking back on that day, sure, I can understand that those officers had a job to do, but that job should never, ever have come at the expense of the rights of a presumed innocent individual. The utter powerlessness that I felt when my rights were wrongly taken away was indescribable. I was completely at the mercy of another individual, who just so happened to have a gun. There were no superior officers or judges present at the scene to hold the officers accountable for their actions or behavior. It was just them and me, my word against their word. What if these officers were having a bad day or what if they were under pressure to make an arrest? Where would that leave me?

Even though I was wrongly pulled over and searched, choosing to remain calm and respectful to the guys with the guns served me well. Cooperation is typically the quickest way to diffuse any interaction with the police. This doesn't mean that you have to unconditionally agree with everything a police officer does, it simple means that you should use the only power that you have when dealing with an officer —your brain. I wholeheartedly believe that the majority of law enforcement officers are decent, honest individuals who proudly look forward to serving and protecting our communities every day. These selfless and brave officers put their lives on the line for our safety without hesitation. Unfortunately, there are rare situations, like the one I experienced, where power can be abused. These infrequent cases can sometimes tarnish the relationship between citizens and law enforcement. For me, I refuse to let these rare occurrences overshadow my respect for police officers and the critical role they play in providing safety to our communities.

INNOCENT NO MORE

Throughout the beginning of my senior year in high school, I managed to steer clear of crack cocaine, both selling it and using it. This was true for other drugs as well. After my crazy junior year spring break experience with LSD, drinking beer was more than enough to fill my plate. It was also easy to get. At my high school, everybody had connections or knew places that didn't "card." Liquor stores in D.C. were a lot more lenient than those in Maryland at checking I.D.'s. A good rule of thumb back then was, the worse the neighborhood, the less likely they would check your I.D. I would always get a kick out of taking my suburban white friends with me to a liquor store in a rough part of D.C. Seeing them scared to death, while trying to buy beer, was the perfect way to have some laughs before heading back to the suburbs to party.

    Up to this point in my senior year, everything seemed to revolve around beer. It was only natural that I would become curious about other things to party with. Beer, which had been enough to fill my plate, would no longer suffice. My tolerance had grown and so did my plate size. Thus, making room for other things that were a lot stronger and more ominous than beer.

    The first dish I added onto my plate was malt liquor, which wasn't a big step up, but a step nonetheless. It was a lot more efficient than beer. Instead of having to pound ten beers to get drunk, now all I needed was a six-pack of Schlitz Red Bull Malt Liquor. Just drinking one, nearly gave me the same buzz as drinking a six-pack of regular beer. Because of the high alcohol content, Red Bull Malt Liquor ended up being a cheaper drunk than regular beer. For this reason, it was not only popular with broke suburban high school kids, but with broke grown-ups as well.

It was only a matter of time before I would get bored with beer buzzes and malt liquor. Eventually, the nonstop high school partying would lead me to try other things. Things that would give me a new type of thrill. To get the ball rolling, I started with pot. When that became normal, I then moved on to pot laced with PCP. Once I got used to that, I decided to try out the unthinkable —crack. Sadly, I had come a long way since my good old days of just drinking beer.

Pot was an easy, quick high. Unlike drinking beer, you didn't have to deal with a bloated stomach and having to pee every five minutes. Instead, it was just a matter of taking a few puffs and the next thing you knew, you were either laughing at or doing the stupidest stuff. One time, I remember being so high that I laughed uncontrollably for almost thirty minutes just watching a friend eat Oreo cookies. Not doing anything crazy with the cookies, but just simply eating them. Another time, a friend and I got so high while driving around, that we got out of my car at a busy traffic light intersection to have a Star Wars lightsaber fight. Two of my youngest cousins made the mistake of leaving their toy lightsabers in the backseat of my car that day. This is just some of the crazy shit pot had me doing, but there was a whole lot more. None of it would compare to the things PCP would have me doing.

My experimentation with pot jumped to another level one night when my friends and I somehow ended up at a party made up of an older crowd. The party was in College Park, Maryland, not too far from the University of Maryland campus. About twenty minutes after we got there, I noticed someone passing around a joint that smelled completely different than any other joint I had ever smelled before. Right away, it got my full attention. "What is that they're smoking?" I asked the guy standing next to me. Suddenly, the guy holding the joint yelled out "boat!" "Boat" or "love boat" is the street name for pot dipped in PCP. This wasn't my first time hearing about it, but it was my first time smelling it.

As someone who was feeling a bit cocky with having a handle on alcohol and now pot, I decided that the time had come to once again step up my game. "This was a different kind of party, so why not try something different?" I thought. In my already high state of mind, it only made sense for me to ask for a hit of "boat." Besides, I thought, "How much stronger can this so called "dipped pot" be?"

The second I put that joint up to my lips, I could taste the chemicals. Unlike regular pot, both, the smoke and smell were unnatural. It reminded me of formaldehyde, the chemical used in my middle school science class to preserve dead frogs used for dissection. But that didn't stop me. I inhaled the PCP laced joint anyway. It wasn't long after taking my first few hits that I began to notice a dark change in my mood. Suddenly, my party vibe was replaced by feelings of aggressiveness and invincibility. Way before this first experience smoking "boat," I heard stories about people doing some crazy stuff while being high PCP —everything from running down the street naked, to appearing unfazed after being shot multiple times. I had a hard time believing most of those stories. That was until I found myself outside of the party, later on that night, punching a brick wall for no apparent reason.

I don't remember who or what stopped me from hitting that wall that night, but I couldn't have been more than a few punches away from breaking both of my hands. Anyone at that party who saw me, had to know right away that I was out of my mind on drugs. For anyone there who actually gave a shit about me, it had to be a sad sight to see.

There was no doubt at this point, especially in my inner circle of friends, that my partying had reached a whole new level. I was no longer known as just a beer and pot guy, but as a serious partier who would try almost anything to get high.

BIRDS OF A FEATHER

Trying anything new, will inevitably bring about opportunities and friends that are new. In my experience, trying new drugs is no different. Unfortunately, those opportunities and friends aren't usually good ones.

One of the first things I noticed when I started getting high on a regular basis was the sudden change in my circle of friends. A lot of my longtime friends, who I used to hang with, all of a sudden grew distant from me. I'm guessing that the whole "smoking drugs thing" was just a bridge too far for them. Even those friends who I considered the biggest partiers, made it crystal clear to me that they pumped their brakes at beer. Unfortunately for me, I had my foot on the gas.

With some of my old friends gradually growing distant from me, I couldn't help but to think of an old saying my grandmother used to say to me growing up. "Birds of a feather flock together," is what she would say to me whenever I hung out with kids who basked in trouble. It was her way of warning me that you become who you hang around. I never could have imagined that years later, some of my friends would be afraid of becoming like me.

My interest in getting high, inevitably, led to me hanging out with those who were unconcerned with my best interest. To these friends, I was just someone to party with and vice versa. Even though these so-called friendships were destructive in nature, close bonds formed nonetheless. One such bond formed between my friend "Bones" and me. We were like two peas in a pod when it came to getting drunk and high. With Bones as my partner in crime, the fun never seemed to stop. Some of my old friends, who I used to hang out with, couldn't believe it when I started hanging out with Bones. He had a reputation in high school of being crazy and a drug dealer. At the time, both of which fit perfectly with my invincible state of mind.

As Bones and I kept on getting closer and closer through partying, he started opening up to me about his involvement with drugs. Like many other young black teenagers during that time, Bones dabbled in selling crack. To him, it wasn't a big deal, but just an easy way to make money. No different than any other side hustle. His nonchalant attitude was always contagious, even when it came to something as serious as selling crack. Bones had a talent for making everything not a big deal. This seemed to always work for him. His attitude was, nothing was a big deal until it becomes one or someone else makes it one.

In those first few months of hanging out with Bones, I never knew or bothered to ask him where he got his supply of crack to sell. It was of no concern to me, but it should have been. I was the one with the car, driving him, me, and his crack supply around. As long as he passed a couple of dollars to me here and there for beer and gas, I really didn't care. That all changed the day Bones decided to ask me if I would take him over to "his boy's spot" to pick up something. That "something" would turn out to be a plastic bag full of crack.

We had been drinking all afternoon that day when Bones asked me to take him to his pickup spot. It was a Friday, so as usual, we were pre-drinking down in my aunt's basement. I had a habit of referring to it as "my aunt's basement," but actually, it was my basement too. I had been living at my aunt's house ever since my parents split up. For Bones and me, my aunt's basement was the perfect spot to hang out before hitting the Friday night party seen. My aunt had cable and a nice stereo system hooked up down there. Bones and I would blast music videos playing on BET, while throwing back beers. On this particular Friday afternoon, I threw back quite a few and Bones knew it. That's probably why he thought this was a good time as any to ask me to take him to "his boy's spot."

Three beers later and feeling more relaxed than ever, Bones and I were in my car, blasting NWA's "Straight Outta Compton" tape —on the way to "his boy's spot." We played that NWA tape so much that it became clear and see through. All of the song titles were completely worn off. We couldn't even tell side A from side B. The only way to know the side was to pop in the tape to hear what song played. It was 1989, NWA's "Straight Outta Compton" was the hottest tape out. Even with the NWA cranking and the beers flowing, I was still somewhat nervous about where we were going. Bones could tell, so in his typical nonchalant fashion, he told me there was nothing to worry about.

"Just wait right here, I'm going to run in here real quick and I'll be back down in fifteen minutes." That's what Bones said when we parked on the side of an apartment building in Marlow Heights, Maryland. As soon as Bones got out of the car, I told myself, "There's nothing to worry about. All I have to do is wait in the car and everything will be fine." For the next fifteen minutes, I stared at the clock on my radio like a hawk. As soon as that clock went one minute past the fifteen minute mark, I went into panic mode. We were in Marlow Heights. At the time, one of the roughest parts of Prince Georges County, Maryland. Located not too far from the Maryland-D.C. state line, it was the perfect hub for crack dealers.

Sitting in my car, scared out of my mind waiting for Bones, I began to nervously look around for the police. That's when I saw Bones coming out of the apartment building and walking towards the car. Feeling like I just saw Jesus, I quickly unlocked the passenger side door, Bones jumped in and we took off. "We did it!" I said in a loud voice of relief. Once we got out of that apartment complex parking lot and onto the main road, Bones suddenly pulled out a bag from his inside jacket pocket. It was a large plastic ziplock freezer bag full of tiny bags of crack rocks. Bones looked at me grinning and said, "I can sell each one of these tiny bags of crack for $25 dollars." There were at least two hundred tiny bags in that Ziploc bag. Young and dumb, we forgot to even think about what would happen if we had gotten pulled over. We were so caught up in how much money could be made from selling what was in that bag, the police were a distant thought.

Getting caught driving around with that amount of drugs in the car would have meant mandatory jail time. Being young, drunk and ignorant, would not have shielded us from the potential life changing consequences. Some say that when we get older, we spend too little time living "in the moment" and too much time thinking about tomorrow. The opposite can be said about when we are young. We dangerously spend too much time living "in the moment" and far too little time thinking about the future. For me, this was especially true under the influence of drugs and alcohol.

Halfway driving back to my aunt's house, out of the blue, Bones admitted to me that he was always nervous going to his "pickup spot." He told me that there was always a chance of being setup by your own supplier or that they could be under police surveillance. Also, he mentioned the possibility of getting robbed leaving the pickup spot. Other drug crews would often know the location of competing suppliers and would sometimes target pickups. In his list of reasons for being nervous, Bones somehow left out the obvious —police and going to jail. This didn't shock me one bit, it was typical Bones.

Apparently, all of these were risks that Bones and other smalltime drug dealers like him were willing to take. Having the latest pair of Timberland boots, the hottest Sergio Tacchini sweat suits, and extra cash in your pocket to blow on greasy carry-out food and beer was somehow worth it. The truth is, none of those ridiculous things are worth jeopardizing your future. For the young, naïve, and invincible like Bones and I were, the future was something that rested in the hands of angels.

EXPERIMENTING WITH THE DEVIL

The time it took us to get back to my aunt's house from the drug pickup spot, was just enough time to get in five more NWA songs. "Straight Outta Compton" had become the official soundtrack to my first drug run. Bones and I celebrated our successful return by heading right back down to my aunt's basement to drink more beer and watch more BET videos. We only had a couple more hours to kill before it was time to head down to the Roy Rogers in Clinton. This was the meetup spot for all the weekend parties. Everyone from our high school would meet there every Friday and Saturday night to find out who was having a party.

During those last couple of hours of drinking before heading down to Clinton, Bones and I engaged in one of our typical drunk, philosophical, and nonsensical conversations. This time, the subject was "Why do people get hooked on crack?" Of course, it didn't take long before the conversation turned into a passionate debate. Neither one of us had any hard facts as to why crack was so addictive, but that didn't stop us from spouting our opinions. I was a stubborn debater and so was Bones. With no one willing to cede the debate, Bones decided to make his argument using real evidence. All of a sudden he reached into his jacket and pulled out the Ziploc bag of crack and popped it on the coffee table. He then looked at me and said, "Let's answer the question for once and for all."

Bones had really put us in a pickle this time. This was no longer just about winning an argument, but a dare to see how far we were willing to go to be proven right. Other than smoking crack ourselves, "How else could we really understand why people would sell the clothes off of their backs, steal, or turn to prostitution to get a hit of this stuff?" Pandora's Box had been opened, but we were too drunk and stupid to realize it.

There was no turning back now. Our youthful inquisitiveness had gotten the best of us. Feeling like he had no choice, Bones finally reached into the Ziploc bag and pulled out a single tiny bag of crack. Immediately, he looked at me and said, "I can't believe this little white rock is causing people to lose their minds!" I replied, "It looks like a piece of soap. Can I see it?" For the next few minutes, we passed the tiny bag of crack back and forth, until finally, our curiosity reached the next level. Suddenly, Bones said out of nowhere, "We should smoke one and see what happens." He asked me if I was scared to do it. Without flinching, I said, "Hell yeah I'm scared! You go first!" All of a sudden, Bones grabbed one of the empty beer cans on the coffee table and asked me to go find one of my aunt's cigarettes laying around the house. I quickly ran upstairs into the kitchen and found a halfway smoked cigarette in the ashtray on the kitchen table. By the time I got back downstairs to the basement, Bones had already folded the beer can in half and punched small holes in the crease of the fold. When I handed him the cigarette, he twisted a small amount of the tobacco over the holes in the crease of the can. "What are you making dude?" I curiously asked. Bones told me that he was making a "ghetto bong" to smoke the crack with. It was becoming more obvious by the minute, that Bones was no amateur with any of this stuff. Either from personal or secondhand experience, Bones knew enough to let me know that this wasn't his first rodeo.

As soon as we were finished making our "ghetto bong," Bones broke the single piece of crack into three smaller pieces. He then placed one of the small pieces on top of the mound of tobacco that covered the small punched holes in the crease of the can. "You ready?" Bones said to me. Suddenly, he put his mouth up to the opening of the can, held a lighter overtop of the piece of crack, and then began to inhale through his mouth. I couldn't help but notice the fire from the lighter being drawn towards the burning crack rock, as Bones sucked air into his mouth. He continued pulling in smoke until all of the crack had melted and burned away with the tobacco.

After Bones finished taking his hit, I stared at him, waiting for something crazy to happen. To my surprise, nothing happened. Other than a goofy smile on his face, he seemed to have the same drunk buzz as he had before smoking the crack. "Bones! What did it feel like?" I asked. He said that he didn't feel anything and asked me if I wanted to try it. Since nothing crazy happened to him, I said, "Sure, why not?" Bones picked up one of the other small pieces of crack and teed up the "ghetto bong" for my hit. Without pause, I lit up that piece of crack and inhaled smoke until there was no more rock left. Confused, just like Bones, I felt nothing. I thought to myself, "Was this a weak stash or were we smoking it wrong?" After taking those first hits and feeling nothing, we decided to load up the bong again.

After taking the second hits, we couldn't help but notice the uncontrollable craving to do another. It was as if a voice inside was telling us, "This next one will do it. Just one more, then you'll feel it." That's when all of a sudden it clicked. Bones and I finally realized that this was the trap that crack sets for you. It never gives you that satisfied high that you are seeking. Unlike pot and alcohol, where you eventually get a sense of fulfillment, smoking crack is like chasing a rabbit. Its high is quick and elusive. Every hit is a tease as to how good the next one will be.

Bones and I were playing with some serious fire down in that basement. Truthfully, the only thing that kept us from smoking that entire bag of rocks was the fact that he had to sell it. As crazy as Bones was, there was no way he was going to piss around with his supplier. With no other option but to close that Ziploc bag, we packed our shit up and headed down to the Roy Rogers in Clinton. We both made the decision to not tell anyone about what we had done. It was best for both of us to just laugh it off and pretend that it never happened. Smoking crack was looked down upon, even by our drunk, pot smoking friends. No one wanted to be associated with a crackhead.

BEAUTY FOR ASHES

A few days had passed since Bones and I added "smoking crack" to our party resume. Even though we made the decision to never do it again, this didn't mean that we would never be tempted. Our first test was only a couple of days away. Another Friday night of partying was quickly rolling around. This time, Bones and I had plans to meet up with some girls we had partied with a few times before. One of the girls told us that her parents were going out that night, so the plan was to bring beer and hang out at her house. When Friday finally rolled around and we showed up at their house, we suddenly realized that the parents hadn't gone out. In fact, they were staying in the entire night. With the parents being home, our only choices were to either find another place to party or drink in the car. Bones and I didn't know of any parties going on that night, so we all decided to drink and party in my car.

    Instead of driving around drinking, for some strange reason we decided to just park a few houses down the street and get tore up there. Just far enough down so that the girl's parents didn't see us. For the next three hours, we drank, partied to music, and talked about everything under the sun. When the subject of getting high came up, that's when the conversations all of a sudden went philosophical and off the deep end. It started out with everyone taking turns talking about the craziest drug they ever tried. With my crazy experience with acid down in Daytona Beach, Florida, I knew for sure, I was going to be the top dog with this one. Bones had never done acid, and I was pretty sure neither one of these girls had either. Well, I ended up being dead wrong. Not just one of them, but both of them had done acid before. Bones ended up being the odd man out this go round.

As someone who never liked to be outdone, Bones felt compelled to uphold his street credit. In this case, it was more like his "drug" credit. He had to somehow make himself look like the most experienced person in the car that night when it came to using drugs. Knowing Bones, I had a pretty good idea of what drug he was going to bring up to do just that. No one in the car had yet mentioned it, even though it was the most talked about drug of our generation. Crack was the 300 pound gorilla in the room, and Bones was just about to release it.

It was barely a week ago when he promised to never tell anyone about us experimenting with crack. But like most guys and their promises, things quickly change in the presence of girls. Impressing them typically becomes a priority over all else. Bones figured that these girls, like most other people, were probably too afraid to try crack. By telling them that he tried it before, was his way of outshining everyone else's drug story.

I knew as soon as Bones opened his mouth about trying crack, he was going to mention me doing it with him. Barely five seconds into his story, that's exactly what he did. I didn't care about any of the other drugs I had tried, but admitting in front of those girls that I smoked crack was embarrassing. The only excuse I could come up with was that we were really drunk that night we smoked it. It was a lame excuse, but as it turned out, it didn't really matter. One of the girls came out and admitted that she smoked a little bit of crack before too. With everyone's cards now on the table, things quickly spiraled out of control from there. The next thing we knew, Bones was pulling out the Ziploc bag.

"Let's smoke some! Let's smoke some!" said the girl sitting in the back seat next to Bones. Suddenly, everybody sitting in the car had a big smile on their face, including me. That's when I knew that my experience with crack was going to be more than a "one-time-fling." The temptation to do it again was overpowering.

Between the four of us that night, we smoked at least ten to twelve rocks. None of us, including Bones, cared one bit that we were smoking crack that we didn't pay for. We were seduced way past the point of responsibility. I can still remember the almost "trance-like" look on everyone's face as we passed the bong around. Every time someone finished a hit, the next person waiting for their turn had a look on their face of pure desperation. The pull of this drug was beyond enticing. I even found the smell of crack burning to be seductive. Its smoke had a sweet smell that can best be described as a mix between burning wax and soapy perfume. It's been over thirty years since I experienced that smell, but I can still remember it as clearly as the smell of a cup of coffee in the morning.

A lot of the memories I have from that night are crystal clear and some are nonexistent, like, for example —How I got home? It wasn't until I woke up that following morning that I even realized that I had made it home. With no memory of driving, coming in the front door, walking upstairs to my bedroom, or getting into bed that night, it almost seemed like a dream. If it wasn't for waking up smelling like beer and an ashtray, I could have been easily convinced that is was.

I remember opening my eyes that morning and struggling just to lift my head up from the pillow. Even with all of the alcohol and drugs I put in my body the night before, something woke me up really early. The sun had barely risen, but my room was bright enough for me to see that I was still wearing the same clothes from the night before. I was unable to stand up right away, so all I could do was sit there, on the side of my bed, in my smelly, smoke-filled clothes until I could pull myself together.

As I began to get some strength and focus, I immediately started wondering, "How did I get home?" "There's no way I drove my car back last night," I kept saying to myself. I knew there was only one way to find out, but I was really afraid to do it. I was going to have to go outside to look for my car. The thought of seeing it was more frightening than not. If it was somehow parked out front, I was almost certain that it would be damaged or crashed. My biggest fear was that I hit something or somebody driving drunk and high back to my house. That was something I would not have been able to handle.

Finally, after getting enough courage to face my fears, I quietly made my way downstairs to see if my car was parked out front. The reason I had to be quiet is because my aunt was still asleep. I definitely didn't want her to wake up and see me like this. So, slowly, I walked towards the front door, opening it ever so carefully as to not make any noise. At first, I didn't see my car, but then looking a little further up the street, I saw a car that resembled mine, parked several cars up. The only way to be sure it wasn't mine, was to walk outside and get a closer look. As I walked up the street towards the car, I quickly realized that it was definitely my car. Immediately, I stopped in my tracks to see if I could see any obvious signs of damage. Nothing stood out, so I nervously walked closer. Once I got right up on the driver side and seeing no damage, I began making my way around to the passenger side. There was nothing! Not a single dent or scratch on my car! It was a miracle.

Shocked, but relieved that there were no signs of me hitting anything or running over anybody, I decided to open the passenger side door to take a look inside. When I opened it, I expected to see empty beer cans and trash on the floor. That was the norm pretty much after every Friday night. But what I saw that Saturday morning, was something so disgraceful that I froze in shame. Every inch and crevice inside of the car that my mom sacrificed so much to give me was covered in cigarette ashes and empty crack bags.

At that very moment in my life, I was standing at a fork in the road. I truly believe everyone experiences "fork in the road" moments. Those critical moments in your life where a crucial decision is presented to you and the choice you make in that given moment will have a profound and ever lasting effect on your life. We should all hope and pray that when those "fork in the road" moments come, God guides us to make the right decision.

> *"But He said to me, My grace is sufficient for you, for My power is made perfect in weakness."*
> —2 Corinthians 12:9

That morning, as I stared at the ashes covering the seats and floor of my car, it became obvious that I wasn't strong enough to resist something that was destroying the things I cared deeply about, including my own life. Even with the warning signs that were glaring brightly before me and the almost certain destruction that lay ahead, I knew that I wasn't strong enough to force a different direction in my life. Any decision that I would have made at this "fork in the road" moment, would have eventually been overruled by my weakness.

It is because of this weakness, that I wasn't given a chance to make a decision that morning. I wasn't allowed to decide which direction to take at the fork in the road. GOD chose the direction for me. He froze me there, holding the passenger door open, not allowing me to look away from what I had done. He wouldn't even let me blink. It was only after making sure that the painful image that I saw when I opened my car door was permanently burned into my conscience, that He would let me look away. Once GOD made sure that I would never ever forget this moment and the power of His Grace, He then snatched away every temptation and desire from me to ever do drugs again. GOD had something beautiful in store for my life that He wasn't going to allow to be destroyed. He gave me Beauty for Ashes.

- Chapter 11 -

In the Closet

By the time I turned sixteen is when I really started noticing that race was mattering less and less when it came to dating. At my high school, black guys where dating white girls, black girls were dating white guys and the two Asian kids dated whatever was left over. It seemed like the dating scene in Clinton, Maryland was steadily moving beyond racial barriers, at least for high school kids. Of course, there were the "non-mix-it-up" folks, who were always concerned about what other people might think. For them, dating outside of their race wasn't considered an option. I tried to date a few "non-mix-it-up" girls during high school, but usually I got nowhere. Most of them were more afraid of what their parents would do, more so than what their friends would say.

A lot of the parents in Clinton were "old school." That's just the way it was. This was a very rural community, where lots of folks were just set in their ways. Right or wrong, change was often seen as negative. When it came to interracial dating, it was often seen as wrong. I'm not ashamed to admit that even members of my own family were "old school" back then. Sure, they may not have been from a rural area like Clinton, but they were stuck in their "old school" ways nonetheless. I learned early on that open-mindedness is more than a function of where you're from.

By the time I graduated high school and made my way to college, race seemed like a zero issue in my world. Not because society had become perfect, but because of my mindset. By developing self-confidence, I had become strong enough to withstand racial insecurities, both, my own and those of others. Ever since my middle school days, I learned that looking at the world in terms of race or skin color is not a fun way to live. There is just too much excitement and craziness out there to look for it all in one color.

This became more obvious than ever when I got to college. As a freshman at the University of Maryland, I was exposed to all kinds of young people, not just of different races, but of different kinds of craziness. I had dorm-mates of every religion, ethnicity and cultural background. Each with their own unique way of contributing to the fun that was college life. Exposure to diversity was one of the big benefits of living on campus during college. But even for an open-minded, confident kid such as myself, the broad range of diversity took some getting used to.

It wasn't until my second semester that I really started to loosen up to weekend social life on campus. Before that, I typically spent the weekends with my old friends down in Clinton. Even as someone who prided himself on making new friends, I often chose "the familiar" over the new. It was just easier. Being with my old friends on the weekends, I never had to worry about saying, "Hi my name is Jermaine…Where are you from?" Instead, hanging out with my Clinton crew, it was always, "What up! The keg is over there." Going down to southern Maryland every other weekend wasn't just about seeing my boys, it was also a chance to catch up with a few girls too. I remained close friends with lots of girls from my hometown. A lot of them were really good friends of mine and a few of them, I often wished were more. My friend Gina was one of those girl "friends," who I couldn't help but to wish was something more.

During one of my weekend trips back to Clinton, I ran into Gina at a party. I had recently found out that she was no longer dating anyone. This was music to my ears since I had always had a crush on her. In fact, pretty much every guy from around the way did. She was very attractive, and therefore, somewhat intimidating. A lot of guys stayed away from her though because she always had a crazy boyfriend. This was why I never ever considered asking her out. The last thing I wanted was some crazy boyfriend coming after me. Now with her being single, running into her at that party was my first chance to safely escape the "friend-zone."

As soon as I saw Gina, immediately I started flirting and trying to lock her into a random deep conversation. My goal was to keep her attention all on me. I couldn't let any of the other guys at the party slip in. Somehow, the conversation got on the topic of interracial dating. I'm thinking, this could have had something to do with the fact that Gina was white and I was black —go figure. Gina was a very blunt, open person just like me when it came to relationships and issues of race. Her outgoing personality made her appear a little crazy, but I found it refreshing and attractive.

During our deep conversation, we talked mostly about race issues, but we also talked about family stuff. For the first time, I learned that Gina was a kid of divorced parents just like me. She lived with her mom and sister in Clinton, while her dad lived in Alabama. The fact that her dad lived in a southern state like Alabama triggered all kinds of alarm bells in my head. At first I thought, "Alabama! Let me get away from this white girl right now." But then, I calmly brushed it off. The last thing I was going to let happen was to let some dad eight hundred plus miles away scare me into not talking to his hot daughter. Besides, I wasn't even sure at this point if he was racist.

Unfortunately, those alarm bells that went off in my head earlier turned out not to be false alarms. Sadly, my stereotyping of a white dad living in Alabama was spot-on. Gina ended up telling me that night, in a straight up, non-roundabout way that her dad was indeed a racist. She told me how whenever she would go visit him, he would regularly tell "black jokes" in front of his friends and use the word "nigger" like it was going out of style. Hearing this, I didn't need to be Albert Einstein to figure out that her dad would lose it if his daughter ever dated a black guy.

After hanging out with Gina for almost two hours and learning more about her dad, probably much more than I needed to know, it was time for me to head back up to campus. I felt like neither one of us wanted our interesting conversation to end. My senses were telling me that this girl, who I had a huge crush on, enjoyed my company as much as I enjoyed hers. So much so, before leaving the party, I asked Gina to come visit me on campus one weekend. To my surprise, she instantly agreed. A week later, Gina was on my college campus looking for a parking space.

That first visit up to the University of Maryland, turned out to be the first date of many for Gina and me. If our connection wasn't obvious before that first date, it was obvious now. It seemed that I had finally found someone who was just as open-minded and silly as me. Every time we got the chance to hangout or go out, it was always about the fun. During those good times though, we never forgot about the deep racial conversation we had before dating. The fact that we were now officially a mixed couple, kept the topic of interracial dating fresh in our minds. Our biggest concern was Gina's dad somehow finding out about us. All of the other junk that came along with interracial dating was just par for the course. We figured we didn't have too much to worry about since her dad lived all the way down in Alabama. How would he find out?

    Sitting around eating one day, I randomly asked Gina what she thought her dad would do if he found out she was dating a black guy. In a fearful voice that I had never heard before, she told me that he would probably stop paying for her to go to Catholic school, not pay for her to go to college, and probably disown her. I thought to myself, "Wow! How can a dad do that to his own daughter?" This was the first time I could really empathize with Gina's fear of her dad. It wasn't so much about her fearing him personally, but more about fearing the power that he had over her future. From the point of view of a dependent daughter, she had a lot at stake.

    With so much focus on Gina's dad in the early stages of us dating, her mom barely came up in our conversations. I still had no clue whether or not Gina's mom would be cool with her dating me. To be frankly honest, I don't think Gina knew either. We both weren't really sure how to tell her mom or even if we should. The fact that her mom was extremely nice and pretty open-minded, Gina was somewhat confident that she would be open to her dating a black guy. But we weren't ready to take any chances, so for weeks, we pretended to be new best friends. Friends who just so happened to want to spend every single moment together. I find it so fascinating that teenagers can be so naïve in thinking that their parents were never young at one time themselves.

In the beginning of us dating, Gina and I would try to only go out or hang out in group settings with our friends. That way we wouldn't raise any suspicions with her mom. I was just a new face in her daughter's circle of friends. Too much one on one time and Gina's mom would have seen right through us. Up until this point, the only time we hung out without our friends was if Gina would drive up to see me on campus. Her car was a "1970-somethin" piece of shit that burned tons of gas, so driving up to campus and back home was not convenient for her at all. Somehow, we had to find a way for me to be able to drive down and hang out at her house sometimes. Our fear was that if I showed up there without friends, her mom would know for sure that we were dating.

Well, one Friday night Gina and I decided to take a chance and push past our fears. The plan was for me to show up at her house around seven o'clock to watch a movie and order delivery. Around seven-thirty, I was pulling up in Gina's driveway. I wasn't really nervous because she had already told her mom that I was coming over to hang out for a little bit. To put her mom at ease, Gina told her that I was spending the night at a friend's house later on that night. Nothing about our plan sounded too suspicious, we hoped. Besides, we were just two "friends" hanging out on a Friday night. Gina told me that as long as I was gone by eleven-thirty, her mom was cool with me being there. I thought to myself, "Wow! Her mom really is cool." My mom would have never allowed me to have some girl over my house watching movies at eleven o'clock at night. In fact, I would have gotten in trouble just for asking.

Unfortunately, instead of appreciating the fact that Gina's mom was okay with just the two of us hanging out, Gina and I decided that night to be typical teenagers and take advantage of the situation. We hung out until exactly eleven-thirty, hoping that her mom would fall asleep. Much to our surprise, the gamble paid off. When Gina peeked into her mom's bedroom, she was sound asleep. Suddenly, all of the ground rules went flying out the window. Our date would now include an all-night 80's music listening party in Gina's bedroom. The hit list included everything from New Edition to Aerosmith. As long as we kept the volume low enough not to wake her mom, we had nothing to worry about. At least, that's what we thought.

Our troubles began the second we got so caught up in the music that we forgot to pay attention to the time. Gina and I were shocked when we finally looked at the clock and realized it was three-thirty in the morning. "There is no way you're driving back to campus this late," Gina said to me. "It's just not safe." I thought to myself, "Cool, you don't have to twist my arm." So, Gina and I decided to roll the dice and sleep for a couple of hours before I would sneak out. Gina told me that her mom usually wakes up around seven-thirty, so I set my watch alarm for 6:00am. As long as I got out before her mom woke up, we were all good.

It seemed like the perfect plan, until it wasn't. Instead of waking up that morning to the beeps of a watch alarm, I was woken up by Gina in full-blown panic mode. Somehow, we slept through my watch alarm and Gina's mom was now awake! To make matters worse, we were trapped in Gina's bedroom of all places. My panic mode ended up leaving Gina's in the dust. Right away, we both started scrambling for some kind of excuse for me still being in that house. Unfortunately, everything we could think of sounded like a typical guilty boyfriend lie. "My car broke down," "I got sick," all of it sounded suspect. We were stuck with no easy way out. The jig was up.

Just when we thought things couldn't get any scarier, all of sudden we heard Gina's sister's voice outside the bedroom door, "Gina! Open the door! Why is your bedroom door locked?" Her older sister had come home that morning from spending the night at her boyfriend's house. Not knowing what else to do, Gina opened the door. Her thought was, if she didn't open the door right away, her mom would have heard the commotion and walked over. Gina quickly let her sister into the bedroom and shut the door. Right away, she begged her sister not to say anything to their mom about me being there. Gina's sister couldn't stop laughing at the situation we were in. It was the funniest thing in the world to her that her sister was hiding a black boy in her bedroom. Surprisingly, she actually made Gina and I laugh at our predicament. It was all we could do to keep from panicking.

Finally, after making fun of us, Gina's sister made the promise not to tell their mom. She even said that she was going to try to distract her while I snuck out. Boy, was that a lie. As soon as her sister walked outside of that bedroom, all we heard was, "Mom! Gina has a black boy in her bedroom! We have a visitor this morning." My heart dropped. I immediately looked at Gina, expecting her to lose it, but instead, she started laughing. It was the only thing left to do. Eventually, the whole house started laughing. "What kind of crazy family is this?" I thought.

At first, Gina's mom acted like she was too nervous to come into the bedroom to see us. She decided, instead, to stay in the kitchen, pretending to be shocked that I was still there. For some reason, we had a strange feeling that she wasn't shocked at all. Regardless, Gina and I were still nervous. It became obvious that her mom wasn't going to come into the bedroom to greet us, so we had to make the frightening walk to the kitchen to greet her. Walking down that hallway from the bedroom to the kitchen was one of the longest walks in my life. It almost felt like I was walking into that kitchen naked. My teenage games were now exposed. The "just a friend" bullshit was over. And I was relieved.

    Gina's mom admitted as soon as we stepped into the kitchen, that she suspected for a while that we were dating. As it turned out, it was us who had been naïve this whole time. Her suspicions actually served us well that morning. It took some of the heat off of us breaking her rules. Instead of being grilled about staying the night, we both were hit with a million questions about our relationship: "How long have you been dating? Does anyone else know? Have you ever dated a white girl before? Have you met his parents?" These were just some of the questions that came our way that morning. We felt like celebrities and aliens at the same time. It was obvious though, that all of the questions were coming from a place of curiosity, not a place of judgement. I must admit, I kind of enjoyed the direct questions. It was not only an opportunity for me to be truthful with regards to the issue of race, but also a chance to help someone else overcome their uncomfortableness with discussing it.

    Gina's mom ended up surprising both of us that morning by being so calm and cool with us finally admitting that we were dating. This was the last thing we expected, especially after getting caught in our failed "sneaky sleepover sneak out." That morning, I thought for sure that I ruined any chance that I may have had at dating her daughter. Instead, I was pretty much welcomed with open arms. Now, not only did I have Gina's mom's approval, but essentially her sister's too. I was "in like Flynn!"

Just when I thought things couldn't get any better that morning, Gina's mom invited me to go with them to the mall and out to eat that Saturday afternoon. "Am I in the Twilight Zone?" I thought. "Are they going to kidnap me or something?" It just wasn't making any sense that Gina's mom was being so nice to me so fast. Actually, it made all the sense in the world. Gina's mom was just that nice. She loved her daughter and loved even more to make her happy. Inviting me to spend the day with them was her way of making Gina happy. It was also her way of welcoming me to the family. And part of their family is what I eventually would become.

Never in a million years would I have ever predicted that one day I would grow so close to a "white family." Things like that weren't supposed to happen to a black kid from the projects like me. At least that's what I thought until I met Gina's family. Immediately after finding out about us dating, they went out of their way to make me feel like one of them. Her mom treated me like a son and her sister treated me like a brother. Eventually, I ended up not only looking forward to spending time with Gina, but her family as well. It seemed like every chance I got to leave campus, I ended up hanging out with Gina and her family. On the weekends, we were either going out to eat or going shopping. It was never a dull moment with my new "white family."

So far, it had been smooth sailing with our fun and family friendly interracial relationship. But Gina and I knew that it was only a matter of time before our commitment to that relationship would be tested. Unfortunately, that test came sooner than we expected. It all began the day we found out from Gina's mom that her dad was coming into town. Just out of nowhere, she told us that he was flying up from Alabama on Friday to visit family in the area and wanted to stop by on

Saturday to see Gina and her sister. Gina and I had already made plans for me to stay over on Friday night that we didn't want to break. We figured, as long as I was gone before her dad showed up on Saturday, we would be fine. Oh boy, this plan sure did sound familiar.

By eight o'clock on Saturday morning, everyone was up and about. My morning plan was to eat breakfast with Gina, hang out for a bit and then hit the road. As we all sat around the kitchen table, Gina's mom and sister couldn't help but to joke about Gina's dad possibly showing up early and catching me in the house. If, for some reason, that did happen, the backup plan was to just introduce myself as a neighborhood stopping by to pick up something. Sure, it sounded suspicious, but there was no way we were going to tell her dad the truth.

Her father wasn't expected to arrive until around twelve-thirty that afternoon, so as long as I was out of there by eleven-thirty, we assumed I would be fine. Of course, Gina and I pressed our luck and ignored her mom's warning to leave earlier than that. At around eleven-fifteen, all of a sudden the doorbell rang. It was Gina's dad! Instantly, all of us screamed, "Oh shit!" at the same time. I didn't know what to do, so I just ran into Gina's sister's bedroom. Gina ran behind me and told me to hide in the bedroom closet. This ended up being a perfect hiding place because her dad wouldn't have any reason to go into any of the bedrooms. Gina's parents were divorced, therefore, the family living room would be the extent of his visit.

After making sure I was hidden nicely in the closet, Gina left me there to walk back out into the living room to greet her dad. I was nervous and scared out of my mind, but I still made every effort to hear her dad's voice through the closet door. I wanted to know if his voice matched up with the racist images

I had of him in my head. To my surprise, the opposite became true. If I hadn't known about his racist tendencies or jokes from his daughter, I would have thought the voice I heard coming from the living room was that of a typical father. It was a voice that sounded like any other loving dad, who missed the sight and presence of his daughters. As someone who had grown to love his daughters nearly just as much as he did, it was sad that I couldn't meet him to let him know that.

The fact that a human being would have to hide in the closet from another human being because of no other reason, but racism will always be sad. Finding myself in that exact situation was one of the most difficult personal tests I had ever faced. I had a serious choice to make that Saturday morning. I could either sit in that closet, feeling sad, allowing myself to be a victim or I could say "fuck him," this is his loss for not meeting me. I chose the latter. Immediately, once I looked at my situation from a position of strength and worthiness, my whole perspective changed. In fact, I even started to laugh at my predicament. Just the thought of how ridiculous I must have looked hiding in the corner of a girl's closet and trying to look cool while sitting on top of a pile of girl's dress shoes, was enough to make me laugh.

As it turned out, I would have to keep those laughs up for almost three hours. That's how long Gina's dad ended up sticking around. Thankfully, Gina and her sister took care of me throughout the entire ordeal. They both took turns coming back into the bedroom to check on me. Somehow, they even managed to slip past their dad to sneak me food. In the end, the three of us made the best of what could have been a much tougher situation.

Sometimes, I look back on that day and I'm still shocked that I was able to remain so positive. In all honesty, I never felt like I had a choice. If I would have resorted to sadness or anger, I would have been handing another person power over me. Essentially, becoming a victim. Anytime you let another person turn you into a victim, you are headed down a dead end road.

GOD's grace gave me the strength to laugh that Saturday morning. He allowed me to see the situation for what it was —Gina's dad's loss. As a child of GOD, I found the confidence in myself to know the value of the love and friendship I could offer to anyone who was willing and fortunate enough to get to know me. No ignorant, closed minded person would or could ever rob me of that.

I never allowed my Saturday morning, three hour stint in the closet to rob me of how truly special Gina's family was to me. A family with experiences and a background that were completely different from my own. Differences that would forever broaden my perspective on life.

- Chapter 12 -

Taking New Territory

Just like cultures and traditions that get passed down from generation to generation, family expectations are also passed down. Our parents inherit a certain set of values and norms from their parents and those are then passed down to their children. Unfortunately, sometimes the things that get passed down to us can be limiting in terms of us fulfilling our true potential.

For example, in the case of education or career goals, parents with a limited sense of achievement may feel content with the fact that their children achieve just as much or only slightly more than them. This can be especially true in the case of older generations. Parents, such as my grandparents, often faced many insurmountable obstacles to personal achievement. They grew up in a time in America where poverty and discrimination put certain caps on achievement. For them, just seeing their children be able to get a decent public school education and stable job was a groundbreaking achievement.

For those of us who come from families or environments where expectations are minimized, even unintentionally, it is critical that we acknowledge these potential traps. Breaking the cycle of low expectations is not only important for our own success, but for our future generations as well.

COLLEGE

Growing up, the idea of going to college wasn't something I put much thought into. It wasn't so much that I didn't care, it had more to do with the fact that college was unfamiliar territory to me. The only thing I knew about college was what I saw on TV —white kids partying non-stop and black kids taking up political causes. It was always tough for me to understand how anybody found the time to do school work. Back then, I could do without the political stuff, but I did find the college party scene very appealing. I truly believe some kids go to college just for that reason alone. Even with the perks of partying, I was somewhat afraid of the idea of stepping into a whole new world. A world surrounded by unfamiliar people and unknown challenges.

    The world of college wasn't just unfamiliar territory to me, but to my mom as well. She, like her parents, didn't go to college. Because of that, both my mom and I had to rely on my high school guidance counselors to sell us on the idea of going to college. These counselors were very helpful, but also quick to point out that college wasn't necessarily for everybody. During the 1980's, trade school was still a respected option. I didn't feel like it was one for me though. Before my parents got divorced, my stepfather told me that I had two choices after high school: go to college or join the military. Trade school wasn't on that list. Even though my stepfather was no longer around to enforce those choices, I still felt compelled to respect his words. As tough as they were sometimes, I knew in my heart that they were for my own good. Therefore, I made a promise to myself to heed them when given the chance. The day that I found out that I was accepted into college was my chance.

Receiving my acceptance letter from the University of Maryland was more than just exciting news. It was an official invitation to face my fears. The question in my head still remained: Would I be up for the challenge? I knew that being able to go to college wasn't something that everyone gets to do. For the sake of my family and their sacrifices, I felt like I had no choice. The last thing I wanted to do was take this opportunity for granted. If I would have listened to my fears, I essentially would have been doing just that.

Fortunately, fear is not something that is outside of our control, but it can be if you let it. One of the most debilitating forms of fear is "fear of the unknown." Basically, this is just being afraid to try out or experience something new or different than what we're used to. We essentially become stuck in the familiar. For my mother and me, this type of fear hovered over our heads from the day I received my college acceptance letter, all the way up to freshman orientation day. It was like a dark cloud. No matter how much we pushed back against it, there it was lurking, trying to keep us from being exposed to something bright and new. Somehow, thankfully, we saw the bright light through that cloud. The bright light of opportunity.

No matter how nervous my mom may have been with the idea of her son going off to college, she always found a way to let her confidence in me shine through. Sometimes she had a funny way of expressing that confidence, but no matter what, it always meant the world to me. I can tell you from experience, there are very few things more powerful than a mother's expression of confidence in her own son. As a teenager, who was afraid of just the idea of going to college, my mother's confidence in me was everything. It gave me the push I needed to overcome my fears. If it wasn't for my mother's faith in me, my education would have probably ended at high school, instead of graduate school.

"All you have to do is take your behind in there and do what you're supposed to do and everything will be fine." Those were my mom's words to me right before she left me on campus for the first time. Her words were curt, but they hit me where it counted. "Do what you're supposed to do" was her way of saying "Do what you're mom expects you to do." Years later, I would come to realize that the power of my mom's words that day didn't come from the pressure, but from the expectation. When my mother expected me to do something, I did it. She expected her son to go to college. So that's what I did.

THE LIFE

Looking back, I realize that I would have missed out on a world of fun if I had let my "fear of the unknown" keep me from going to college. It was an experience that I will never forget. Sure, adjusting took me a little while, but once I got used to the life, my mom couldn't drag me off campus.

The freedom and non-stop partying was nothing like I had ever experienced before. Even as a freshman, I could see why college life was the subject of so many crazy Hollywood movies. Only on a college campus could nerds, pot smokers, athletes, drunks, and scholars all live in tranquil harmony. It was as if everyone there knew that this was the last stop before life got serious. College was not only a perfect environment for the young to let loose, it was also a place to express yourself and your values. For most of the guys on campus, including myself, those values typically circled around girls, beer, and music. This was often obvious by the way we decorated our dorm rooms. For me, it was wall-to-wall beer, Grateful Dead, Metallica, Led Zeppelin and Cindy Crawford posters. For others, it was colorful lava lamps, dark lights, and neon beer signs. A few even went all out and set up home stereo systems in their dorm rooms. I loved it all. To me, nothing was better than walking into your dorm after a boring day in class and hearing Led Zeppelin blasting from your friend's room down the hallway. This was the life.

THE FRIENDS

Living on a college campus, you can't help but to meet all kinds of cool people. I was lucky enough to become good friends with some of them. During my sophomore year, I became really tight with a group of guys that lived in my dorm. The four of us all lived on the same floor, next door to one another. From the moment we all met, we just clicked. It was non-stop laughs whenever we got together. None of us were old enough yet to get into the bars, so we made the most out of dorm life. Whether it was hanging out in someone's room blasting music, prank calling people, throwing water balloons at unsuspecting students walking in the quad, or just drinking beer, it was always a good time. The funny thing is, even though none of us were twenty-one, we somehow always found a way to get beer. No I.D., no money, rain, sleet, or snow —it didn't matter. We always found a way. A piece of advice: never underestimate the lengths that an underage college kid will go to get beer. It's a level of determination that exceeds all human understanding.

Looking back over my sophomore year, I can recall so many crazy fun times hanging out with the guys who lived on my floor. Even though most of our fun together took place inside the dorm, one of the most memorable times we had together actually took place outside of the dorm. It all started when a group of us decided that we were going to take a road trip off campus to hit a warehouse party. The party was on a Friday night and it was down in my old neighborhood of Clinton, Maryland. I heard about the party from some of my high school friends and figured it was the perfect opportunity to let my dorm buddies see how we partied down in Clinton. Also, it was a rare chance to let loose outside of our dorm.

This road trip was going to be our first time leaving campus to party as a group. Therefore, it was a pretty big deal. To make the trip happen, one of the guys in our group, asked his parents if he could borrow the family station wagon for the weekend of the party. There were only four of us going, but we wanted to do it up right. What better way to take a road trip than in a station wagon? Putting icing on the cake, my friend's parents' station wagon looked exactly like the Griswold family's station wagon in the movie "National Lampoon's Vacation." It even had the wood side paneling on the doors! I couldn't wait until my Clinton friends saw us pulling up to the party, rockin' those wood panel doors.

When that Friday finally rolled around, we loaded up that station wagon and hit the road. On the way to the party, we needed to make two stops. The first stop was my grandparents' house. I needed to pick up beer and wing money for the weekend. The second stop was any liquor store that didn't I.D. We were in luck because I knew of several liquor stores that fit that description, not too far from where my grandparents lived.

The quick stop at my grandparents' house would turn out to be the first time any of my college friends had ever stepped foot in a public housing project or the "hood," as they called it. While driving there, I joked with them in the car about there not being any white people where we were going and to duck if they heard any gunshots. They all laughed of course, but I could tell that some of them were a little nervous. My hope was to ease their nervousness by making fun of a situation that I knew was uncomfortable and unfamiliar to them. One of the strengths we all shared as friends, was our ability to not take ourselves or our circumstances too seriously. In this situation, that's exactly what I was attempting to do.

By the time I reassured my friends that I was only halfway joking about the gunshots, we were pulling up and parking in front of my grandparents' house. As soon as we walked in the front door, we were greeted with big smiles from my grandparents sitting on the couch. Once I introduced them to my goofy friends from college, those big smiles grew even bigger. It must have made them feel so proud to see me with friends from college —not from high school or the neighborhood, but from college. There I was, their grandson, now a college student, introducing them to my friends who were also college students. Friends of different races and different backgrounds, but not one thinking that he was better than the other. Just a group of friends loving life.

As much fun as we all were having hanging out with my grandparents, eventually it was time to hit the road again. We all graciously said our goodbyes, as my grandfather smoothly slipped me twenty dollars on the way out the door. Before shutting the front door behind us, my grandmother told me that she loved me. It wasn't unusual for her to tell me that, but this time it seemed special. I felt like she was letting me know that she was proud of me. Not only for hanging out with decent friends, but also for letting those friends know that I was not ashamed of where I came from.

I learned at a young age, a very simple truth: no one has a perfect upbringing —no one. Where you come from should never be something to be ashamed of or overly touted. Every family has issues and struggles. As you move through life and if you are lucky enough to get the chance to hang out with different types of people, this fact will become more and more obvious. Whether financial or personal, if you dig deep enough, you will find that life deals no one a perfect hand. Sometimes the people who appear to have it all are the ones who are screwed up the most. Everyone has a story. That's what gives life its spice. For me, growing up in the projects with my grandparents is my spice.

Judging by the way my college friends were acting once we all got back in the car, it seemed like they enjoyed their first trip to the projects. I didn't feel any sense of judgment from them whatsoever. In fact, as soon as we pulled off from in front of my grandparents' house, some of the guys immediately started bragging and joking about how they now had officially established their "street credit." These guys were awesome. We hadn't even picked up beer or gotten to the party yet and we were already having a blast.

The warehouse party was roughly a forty minute drive from my grandparents' house. We didn't want to get there too late, so we decided not to stop for beer on the way. This was a bad idea. Having no beer in the car, made the drive seem even longer. By the time we got to the party, we were ready to knock people down to get to the keg. I wanted a beer so badly that I didn't even stop to say hello to my high school friends who told me about the party. Finally, once we all had our red cups full, we did a lap around the room. It was great seeing a lot of my old high school friends and having the chance to introduce them to my new college friends. It was such a cool feeling to finally bring my two party worlds together.

As my college friends and I made the rounds, we were all blown away by the size of this party. It was being thrown in a two-story warehouse that someone, quote unquote, rented out. The whole time we were partying, my college friends kept asking me, "How is this legal? How is this legal?" They couldn't understand for the life of them how someone was allowed to throw a party in a commercial storage warehouse. I had to explain to them that my old school friends had a different definition of the word "legal." In the "Clinton, Maryland" dictionary, "legal" usually meant "ok until the cops show up."

Inviting my college friends to a party in my old stomping grounds was not only an opportunity for me to share my old world, but also a chance to fully embrace my new world. The time spent catching up with old friends gave me a better perspective of my new friends. On one side of me was the past, my high school friends and on the other side, the present, my college friends. Having these two different worlds side by side, painted a clearer picture of both. My old school friends represented a world of non-stop fun, whereas my new friends, who also represented fun, but fun with certain limits. If the only thing I cared about was having a good time, my old school friends were there for me, no questions. If I wanted to have a good time, but also get pushed to be responsible, I had to lean more on my college friends.

The perspective that I formed by bringing those two worlds together wasn't about judging or picking one group of friends over the other. It was about recognizing my own weaknesses and susceptibilities. No one ever puts a gun to our head and makes us party.

If we want more out of life than a "good time," it is important to surround ourselves with friends who share a similar outlook. Sure, my college friends could party hard just like my old school friends, if not harder, but they also made it a priority to crack open the books and keep their eye on the prize —graduating college. Maintaining balance and boundaries when it came to partying is something I battled with all throughout college. The fight to discern between the positive and negative influences was constant. I learned back then that, when it comes to partying versus being responsible, our friends will often switch teams.

- Chapter 13 -

Music

"Music washes away from the soul the dust of everyday life."
—Berthold Auerbach

OLD SCHOOL

Ever since I was a child sitting on my grandparents' living room floor, watching my mom, aunts, and uncles sing and dance to Earth, Wind & Fire's "Reasons" in front of the family record player, music has been a part of my life. It is my "go-to" source for good feelings and instant inspiration.

Growing up in the 70's, music was the heartbeat of our home. At a very young age, I was surrounded by sounds from big-name funk and R&B artists like Earth, Wind & Fire, Rufus and Chaka Khan, The O'Jays, The Ohio Players, L.T.D., The New Birth, and Cameo just to name a few. As a family, we had a pretty solid collection of music. Most of this music was kept at my grandparents' house, which is where I grew up. At the time, they were the only ones in the family with a decent record player. It just made sense for all of my aunts and uncles to keep their albums and records there.

Whenever my family got together, it was pretty much always at grandma and grandad's house. And there was never a time when we did get together that we didn't listen to music. I can still remember how excited all of my cousins and I would get when one of my uncles would go down into the living room to play records. There was nothing better than hearing that crackling sound from the record needle, letting you know that a song was about to come on. That popping noise would instantly change the entire mood of the house. It didn't matter what you were doing, the second that record player came on, it would put a big smile on your face. There were "Happy feelin's in the air, touching people everywhere!" as the band "Maze featuring Frankie Beverly" would say.

So many great memories come to mind when I think about the good old days of playing records. There was something uniquely beautiful about the imperfect, crackling sounds of an album playing on a turntable. Compared to the flawless sounds of digital music today, albums and 45's gave music character and provoked nostalgia. I just don't get those extras from Alexa or my iPhone. This is not to say that, today, I don't enjoy being able to play a song at the command of my voice, but that there is something irreplaceably special about listening to music on vinyl.

Another priceless extra that albums brought to music was the "album cover." Unfortunately, ever since CDs' hit the shelves, album covers have lost their significance. Back in the day, an album cover was considered an inseparable piece of art to go along with the music. As a kid, I used to love flipping through the albums in the record cabinet, just to see the covers. I can still remember the really good ones. It was obvious back then that a lot of artists believed that having a cool album cover was just as important as having cool music. Their idea of cool, however, often times ended up being scary, especially for young eyes. George Clinton's band "Funkadelic" was famous for their wild and scary album covers. The band's 1975 album, "Let's Take It to the Stage," has one of the craziest album covers I have ever seen. It has psychedelic pictures of skulls, monsters, and a green zombie girl who looks like the devil possessed Linda Blair in the movie the Exorcist. This album cover scared me so badly when I was a kid that I would only look at it during the daytime.

Thankfully, I didn't allow that crazy "Funkadelic" album cover to rob me of my beautiful, old school music experience. Instead, my childhood memories of music at grandma's house are filled with love, laughter, and joy. They also, of course, are filled with a whole lot of singing and dancing. That old school record player treated my family to some good music. It also blessed us with memories to cherish for a life time.

INTRODUCING: THE "BOOMBOX"

In my opinion, there is only one way to listen to good music —LOUD! Hearing a good song being played with the volume turned down low, for me, is a cruel form of torture. It's like letting someone smell their dinner cooking, but not letting them sit down to enjoy the meal. I like to feel my music. That's one of the great things about listening to music on a home or nice car stereo system. The powerful speakers allow you to feel the music.

During the old days of my grandparents' record player, enjoying loud music was pretty much limited to the home or car. There were no loud, portable music devices yet on the market. Fortunately, this all changed by the time the 80's rolled around. In 1981, the year of my tenth birthday, my mom bought me something called a Hitachi TRK-8110 E. This was a state-of-the-art portable radio and cassette player with two large round loud-speakers and a handle for carrying. Otherwise known on the streets as a "Boombox." It was a portable music system that gave you access to "loud" music at anyplace and at any time. All you needed to be in business was eight D-size batteries. For my generation, the Boombox was the hottest thing since Atari.

    I felt like the luckiest kid in the world when my mom told me that she was going to let me pick out a Boombox for my birthday. It was a dream come true. I can still remember the day she took me to Circuit City and let me pick out the one I wanted. Of course, I ended up picking out one of the most expensive ones. But it was kind of okay with my mom because she was going to put it on lay-a-way anyways. They set it up so that she could make a minimum of two payments a month until it was paid off. I knew right then that the next few months were going to be the longest few months of my life.

    Two and a half months and several emotional breakdowns later, I was finally on my way to Circuit City with my mom to make the last payment and pick up my Boombox. I thought that day would never come and it almost didn't. There were several times that I got upset and impatient with my mom because it was taking too long to get it out of lay-a-way. But my mom reminded me real quick about the price for being impatient. Back then, mothers didn't play the "I understand your frustration" or "Let's talk about it" game with their kids. For my mom, it was very simple —"Shut your mouth or you won't see a Boombox or anything else for your birthday." As soon as I heard that, my impatience would disappear instantly.

And thankfully it did. Instead of losing out on a cool birthday present, I was now walking out of Circuit City with it.

As soon as we got home, before even letting me take it out the box, my mom laid down some Boombox ground rules: Rule #1: I had to take extra care of it; Rule #2: I could only play it on my grandparents' front or back porch. This was an expensive birthday present and my mom expected me to treat it as such. Between the two rules, I considered Rule #1 the easiest to follow. Throughout my childhood, I always took pride in taking care of my toys. Expensive or not, this one would be no different. Rule #2 would be a lot tougher to follow. Like any other kid, there was nothing I enjoyed more than showing off my new toys. Having a brand new Boombox and not being able to walk around the neighborhood with it, in my opinion, kind of defeated the purpose. Especially since the thing had a handle on it. Naturally, my mom could care less about a handle or me wanting to show it off to the neighborhood. Her only concern was my safety. She didn't want her ten-year-old son walking around the projects with a brand new, expensive radio-cassette player. That would have been just asking for trouble. Boy…where would we be without moms?

In the early 80's, if you were from New York City, the Boombox was an iconic symbol of "Rap" music. For me, being from D.C., it was the perfect device to play "Go-Go" music. For anyone unfamiliar with the D.C. music scene, "Go-Go" is a type of live music that originated in Washington, D.C. during the 1970's. The high-energy dance music is a combination of funk, rhythm and blues, with a heavy emphasis on percussion instruments like the conga drums, timbales and cowbells. But at its heart is the live audience participation with the vocals. Therefore, unlike most other music genres, Go-Go music is fundamentally linked to its audience. The sound of the live crowd is just as important as the sound of the beating drums.

In the early days of Go-Go music, studio recordings were neither practical, nor required by its fans. The most important thing back then was maintaining that "live music" sound. As a result, most Go-Go music was distributed on cassette tapes. Recorded copies of live weekly shows would circulate all over the D.C. metro area. Getting your hands on one, especially a good copy, depended on who you knew. The best cassette copies were called "PA" tapes. These were recordings made directly from the band's PA (public address) system sound control board during a show. A "PA" tape was the "clearest" cassette copy you could get of a live Go-Go band performance and therefore the most sought after. If you were lucky enough to own one, it was like owning gold. I had the privilege of blessing my Boombox with a few.

80'S MUSIC

Music history tells us that the early 80's didn't just give birth to the Boombox, but to the modern "music video" as well. This was the era in which artists began to embrace the idea of expressing their music visually using short films. Music fans were no longer being won over just through an artist's songs, but also through their music videos. As a result, artists were able to break through a lot of cultural and racial barriers that previously existed in music. Being able to "see" a song proved to be a lot more powerful in bringing people together than just being able to "hear" it.

One of my favorite bands in the early 80's was Duran Duran. I didn't know any other black kids from the projects at that time who would even think about blasting Duran Duran out of their Boombox, except for me. It was all because of their cool music videos that I became a fan of their cool sound. "The Reflex" and "The Wild boys" were two of my favorite 80's songs and still are. I used to blast Duran Duran music so much as a kid, that my family and friends had no choice but to become fans themselves.

From "rock ballads" to rap songs —What better time to experience the full spectrum of music than during the 80's! Who could have ever imagined that a kid raised in the projects, like me, would one day find himself jamming out to "I Wanna Rock" by Twisted Sister? I surely couldn't, but life obviously could. For me, the 80's marked the beginning of a wild musical ride. A ride that would eventually lead me to a broad appreciation of all types of music. Rock, Rap, R&B, Heavy Metal or Pop, it didn't matter to me. As long as it made me feel good, I loved it. Let's face it, there are certain emotions that a "Quiet Riot" song can bring out that a "Culture Club" song cannot. Similarly, most would agree that attending a "Grateful Dead" concert produces a completely different life experience than, let's say, attending a "New Edition" concert. All four of these bands mentioned are great musicians, but the emotions and experiences they create are quite different. I'm grateful to have an appreciation for all of it.

As we embrace life, allowing ourselves to have access to musical differences, inevitably, allows us to have access to different life experiences. There's a lot more to be gained than just variety when we decide to step out of our music comfort zones. Diversifying our musical interests opens the door to diversity in our attitudes, emotions and experiences. In my own life, this was never more obvious than during the wild musical ride of the 80's.

THE COLLEGE YEARS

My appreciation for good music followed me throughout high school, all the way to college. In 1989, as a college freshman, I was turned onto something that was a lot better than just "good music." I was turned onto "Classic Rock!" It was "timeless" music. The artist list included bands like Led Zeppelin, Boston, Queen, Steve Miller Band, Meat Loaf and Bad Company to name a few. During my college years, at least within my circle of friends, developing an appreciation for Classic Rock was considered "a rite of passage." It was the foundation for recognizing good music.

Around the same time that I really started to get into Classic Rock, "Grunge" music came on the scene. In the early 90's, the Seattle based rock sound took off like a rocket. It was led by ground breaking artists like Nirvana, Sound Garden, Pearl Jam, and Alice in Chains. The new sound was perfect for the rebellious college scene. It even came with its own fashion and look —the "Grunge look." All you needed to pull it off was an old flannel shirt, jeans with holes in the knees, and a knitted hat and you were officially "Grunge." This may have been the first time in history that flannel shirts and ripped up jeans were almost unaffordable —all thanks to "Grunge."

During the 90's Grunge reign, other artist from different genres fought hard to jump into the spotlight. One of the bands that led that charge was "Metallica." They brought about the rebirth of "Heavy Metal" during the supposed era of "Grunge."

In 1991, "Enter Sandman," their first single released from the "Black" album was a smash hit. Heavy Metal was finally awoken from its deep sleep. I remember being blown away the first time I heard "Enter Sandman." The sound was so powerful and confident —it was American. With all of the Grunge and 90's R&B music everywhere, it was so damn refreshing to hear and feel the power of American Heavy Metal. There is nothing like it.

I heard a funny quote once that said: *"All you need to take over a small country is a few drunk high school friends and two Metallica albums."* Unfortunately, at the time I heard this quote, I didn't quite get it. Once I became a Metallica fan, it made all the sense in the world.

MUSIC EMPOWERS

There is no denying music's ability to empower us. It is one of the most effective tools available to stir up your passion to fulfill your purpose. Whether you're a boxer marching towards the ring for a big title fight, a football team rushing the field before a big game, or a potential presidential candidate announcing that you're running for office —music has the undeniable ability to set the stage.

Boxers tend to know this more than anybody. Take for example, the former heavyweight boxing champion of the world, Larry Holmes. Before his big fights, he had a tradition of playing the famous soul song "Ain't No Stopping Us Now" by McFadden & Whitehead. It is a song about succeeding despite the odds and obstacles —a "push through it" song. It became Larry Holmes' theme song.

The sport of boxing is known for turning ordinary songs into so called "theme songs." In fact, one of the most famous theme songs of all time, "Eye of the Tiger" by Survivor, came from one of the greatest boxing movies of all time —Rocky III. "Eye of the Tiger" was and still is one of the most empowering songs ever recorded. During a random event one day, I got to personally witness the power of that song.

The year was 2012 and a big presidential campaign was going on. I just so happened to be attending a speaking event in which former Speaker of the House and presidential candidate, Newt Gingrich was scheduled to speak. I can vividly remember hearing "Eye of the Tiger" suddenly come on before the Speaker entered the jam packed room. The crowd was instantly energized and pumped before he could even take the stage. That song, combined with a stage draped with American flags, created a sense of pride and patriotism all throughout the room. Newt used the "Eye of the Tiger" fight anthem to empower the crowd. To let them know that his candidacy stood for American resilience and strength. Regardless, if Newt was your guy or not, you couldn't help but to jump to your feet when "Eye of the Tiger" came on. I did.

Listening to the lyrics, it's easy to understand why "Eye of the Tiger" was chosen as the "Rocky" theme song. The entire film series is based on an all American "rags to riches" story centered on the main character, "Rocky Balboa." In each of the films, Rocky, played by the actor Sylvester Stallone, is faced with what seems like an insurmountable challenge. His courage, commitment, and endurance is ultimately put to test. Despite the odds, he finds a way to push through, to overcome the challenge. Emerging once again as an American hero.

Out of all of the Rocky films, Rocky III is my favorite. It teaches us a valuable lesson about the cost of complacency. In this episode of the film series, the character Rocky becomes comfortable in his newly found riches and glory. Through tragedy and defeat at the hands of "Mr. T," he quickly realizes that he must never forget the lessons learned during his time at the bottom and that the passion that propelled him from the bottom must remain if he is to stay on top.

As summed up so eloquently in the song verse:

"So many times, it happens too fast...You trade your passion for glory... Don't lose your grip on the dreams of the past...You must fight just to keep them alive..."
—"Eye of the Tiger," Survivor

The iconic Rocky film series represents so much about the American spirit and our determination to remain on top. We weren't born for second place and we never quit —NEVER.

MUSIC: AN ESCAPE

Anyone who has ever struggled will tell you that listening to music is a powerful means of escape from the worries and grind of everyday life. No doubt, in my own life, music has played a critical role in getting me through some really tough times. Some of the toughest were during my last stretch of high school and college. Most of these tough times revolved around my living situation. Before calling the student dorms at the University of Maryland "home," I bounced around between family and friends, looking for "happy" places to stay. After my parents got divorced, I didn't think that I would ever call another place "home." Sure, I always had a good time crashing with friends and I definitely appreciated my aunt opening up her home to me, but there was no place like "home" in Clinton. Every other place I laid my head ended up being just a "house."

Surprisingly, when I got the chance to live in a college dorm, it turned out to be the closest thing to "home" since my parents' divorce. It was hard for me to understand it at first. These were tiny rooms, and they usually came with roommates. Why in the world did I feel so at home living in a center-block box? I eventually realized that the "peace" that I felt while living in the dorms had nothing to do with size or appearance. It was all about "stability." Having my own space in a dorm, allowed me to be surrounded by my own stuff. I had my own closet to hang my clothes, my own drawers for my socks and underwear, and my own walls to hang the things that I liked. I could do whatever I wanted —it was my little "home." No more sleeping at friends' houses, living out of bags and boxes. No more beds with sheets that smelled like someone else. I had once again found my "little piece of the world" that I could call my own.

With all of its wonderful amenities, there was one catch to building my "home" life around living in a dorm —they typically close down during the summer and winter breaks. When the end of the semester rolled around, it was always depressing packing my things up to go stay at my aunts' or grandparents' house. I would have to once again get used to living out of bags and boxes. This was the routine. That was until I found out that I had the option of staying on campus during the summer and winter breaks! All I needed to do was apply for financial aid to cover my living costs. And that's exactly what I did. Somehow, I had successfully found a way to stay on campus during the breaks —to stay in my "home."

Unfortunately, my newly discovered, happy living situation would soon hit a huge bump in the road at the end of one of my spring semesters. For some reason, the financial aid I had received was not anywhere close to being enough to cover my summer housing costs. And there was no way my mom could afford to make up the difference. I was devastated, so was my mom. She knew that living on campus brought me a sense of peace and security. Something that I had been yearning for since her and my stepdad split up.

With little to no options, I unfortunately had to move myself and my things into my grandparents' house at the end of that spring semester. For reasons I can't recall, moving back in with my aunt during the break was no longer an option. The sadness I felt having to leave campus had nothing to do with who I would be staying with. This was all about instability and feeling displaced. Leaving the dorms meant once again living out of bags and boxes.

I was forced to accept that college was not my "home." The reality was, I would have to finish college and start my own life and family if I ever wanted to feel the love and happiness of a home again. Until then, I would have to fight for and create my own happiness.

A willingness to fight for my happiness is one of the few positive things that I took away from my parents' painful divorce. Even today, I will do my best to approach tough situations or difficult circumstances with the intention of not sacrificing my happiness. It's often tough though. Anger tends to find a way to creep in, especially when we are under negative pressure. Being human, anger is a part of us. When it presents itself, it has a tendency to make us feel strong. But the truth is, fighting for and controlling our happiness makes us stronger than any amount of anger ever could.

Sleeping in my grandparents' spare bedroom over summer break and being surrounded by bags and boxes full of my stuff, brought back ugly memories that I fought so hard to move on from. Those bags and boxes were a painful reminder of my unstable past. All I kept thinking about was finding a way to make them disappear —to escape the pain that was surrounding me.

Over the years, I have learned how to use certain weapons to help me fight the battles for my happiness. Laying in my grandparents' spare bedroom one night, looking around at those painful bags and boxes, I decided to break out my most powerful weapon —my music. Just when the pain seemed inescapable, I grabbed my earphones and started blasting Metallica's Black album. It was the perfect music to escape my pain. Those songs, those sounds —they took me away. They instilled in me the power and strength to look beyond what was surrounding me. From the moment I put those earphones on, my mindset instantly changed from feeling sad and trapped, to strong and determined. Determined to do what I had to do to never live out of bags and boxes again. As it turned out, Metallica didn't just provide me an escape, it strengthened me for the fight.

- Chapter 14 -

Not Without "His" Approval

It was spring semester, 1996, my last semester of college. After nearly five years of non-stop partying and somehow finding the strength and brains to get through every single calculus, physics, and engineering class offered at the University of Maryland, the time had finally come to put the college chapter behind me. Even though college was crazy fun and an experience of a lifetime, being an engineering major, I was relieved that the "crazy fun" was finally almost over.

Unlike some of my classmates during that last semester, I was fortunate enough to have a full-time job lined up and waiting for me after graduation. This was all because of an engineering internship I participated in two years before graduation. The experience and relationship that I established with this particular engineering firm opened the door for a solid opportunity after graduation. Ironically, at the time when I was offered the internship, my decision to accept it was based mostly on how much money I could make during the program. A future employment opportunity was the last thing on my mind. I can now clearly see why someone came up with the phrase "young and dumb." Unfortunately, without the guidance of peers, parents or other adults, sometimes the only thing that a college-age, male brain can intelligently and dependably decide on, is which party will have the most beer and the most girls. Thankfully, God is sometimes willing to look beyond the ignorance and frivolousness of our youth.

DESERVING

With my last semester in college quickly coming to an end and a solid career opportunity lined up, I had already decided on how I was going to reward myself for the five plus years of painful studying and non-stop partying that I had to endure. I figured, "What could be a better reward than buying myself a brand new $35,000 SUV!" Still "young and dumb," I obviously wasn't too worried about my $20,000 plus in student loan debt. The financial aid office made the mistake of telling me that I would have twenty years to pay it back.

Debt or no debt, this was about something I deserved. Everyone needed to see how hard I worked. What better way to show off and show the world that I was a smart, successful college graduate than to go $60,000 plus in debt in less than a month after graduating college? Unfortunately, I wouldn't be able to answer such an obviously sarcastic question until I became a bit wiser and a bit older. But at a time, when all I wanted to do was show off and impress other people, making sound financial decisions wasn't even on my radar. I was clueless when it came to the constraints that bills and a hefty car payment could place on my ability to invest and grow financially.

With age and maturity, I now realize that the ease at which I was prepared to make poor financial decisions back then, even after receiving a college education, had a lot to do with my personal definition of success. I didn't realize until entering my professional career, that "success" or "being successful" is a relative term or phrase. People's definitions of success weigh heavily on their personal values and sometimes the socio-economic status of the family from which they come. Let's take for example, if you are the first one in your family to complete high school, you and your family may have a strikingly different view of success compared to that of a family whose son or daughter is a 3rd generation graduate from Harvard or Yale. For the family whose idea of success is their son or daughter receiving a high school diploma, landing a full-time job and being able to rent a one-bedroom apartment, that might be more than success, it may be a dream come true. For the family whose daughter just graduated from Harvard business school, securing a six figure executive position with stock options and being able to rent a penthouse on the eastside of Manhattan might be considered just the first step of a successful career.

As far as my family goes, there haven't been any Harvard graduation invitations mailed out, or at least not yet. But there, undoubtedly, have been other achievements we can point to for markers of family success. The crazy idea that I needed to purchase an expensive SUV right after college to show off to my family and friends as proof of my success was ridiculous. Considering where I came from, just the fact that I completed college and had a stable career lined up, should have been all the proof I needed. But being the hard-headed, college graduate that I was, it wasn't.

My mind was made up. Nothing was going to stop me from getting that brand new SUV! Any of my smart friends or family members who tried to persuade me otherwise got immediately brushed off. My decision was final. The only thing left to decide on was whether to go black with black leather interior or forest green with tan leather interior. I really couldn't go wrong with either option. Both were guaranteed to turn heads.

SOLD, BUT NO SALE

It took about a month of going around to different dealerships to finally find the model with all of the options I wanted. As soon as I spotted it, those car salesmen spotted me. They can spot an "easy close" from a mile away. I must have looked like a desperate bunny rabbit walking into a fox den, looking for food. Before I could even do a full walk-around of the shiny new SUV, I was approached by a salesman, who asked me if I wanted to take it out for a test drive. I barely even got a chance to answer before he was handing me the car keys. Of course, with a huge grin on my face, I said "sure!" He suddenly then walked away and nonchalantly told me to "take my time." This salesman was already lining up his chess pieces on the board.

Being young and clueless, I just thought the salesman was being nice. I had no idea that he was just reeling me in. As soon as he walked away and joined back up with his sales buddies, I'm sure they all probably laughed and high-fived each other as they plotted their next move. It must have been fun for all of them, seeing such a predictable sale unfold.

The "test drive" is a car salesman's most powerful weapon. I found that out the hard way. Between the smooth ride, wood-grain dashboard, and the smell of the new leather seats, I was hooked. Any doubt about moving forward with this big purchase had been erased from my mind. Within ten minutes of taking the truck out for a test drive, I was hitting a u-turn and headed back to the dealership to make a deal.

When I parked the truck to go back inside the dealership, I couldn't help but turn around for one more glance. It was a thing of beauty. "I gotta have it!" is all I kept saying to myself. Unsurprisingly, there were other people staring at it too. Before I could make it inside to meet back up with the salesman, I noticed another customer checking out "my" truck. He had the same "I gotta have it!" look as I did. I thought, "There is no way I can let this dude take my truck!" Being hip to and a little wiser today with regards to sales tricks and techniques, I would bet money that this dude was a dealership employee or salesman himself. He was probably working in cahoots with my salesman to create extra pressure on me. Whoever he was, it worked. I had already convinced myself that I was prepared to do whatever it takes to make a deal.

As soon as I walked back into the dealership, my salesman had the nerve to ask me, "How did you like the truck?" Even for a salesman, it was such a silly rhetorical question to ask someone who was obviously in love with the truck. Besides, I had been showing my hand ever since pulling into the dealership parking lot. But I guess he wanted to remove all doubt before going in for the kill. So far, I had taken every bit of his bait. The only thing left to do was talk numbers.

When we walked into the finance office, the first thing the salesman asked was how much I wanted to pay monthly for the truck. Being inexperienced at the time with the whole car financing and purchasing process, I started blurting out a monthly payment range that I thought I could afford. Not only was I showing my hand again, this time I was lifting up my entire skirt! Back then, I wasn't smart enough to know that I should have started out with negotiating a final purchase price.

Once that deal was made, then it would have been okay to dive into a discussion about financing and monthly payment options. Agreeing on a final purchase price ties the hands of the dealership and forces the negotiation to center on interest rates and the length of the loan. The lower the amount financed, the lower the amount of interest paid and thus, a lower monthly payment can be negotiated. By negotiating monthly payments first, this allows the salesman to structure a finance package based on maximizing his profit in the sale.

Unfortunately, none of these car financing skills were with me in the sales office that day. The only thing standing in the way of the salesman taking me for everything I had was the bank. Being fresh out of college, I barely had any credit history. The banks would be qualifying me based on my limited credit history and current salary. This, to my benefit, tied the hands of the salesman in terms of the total sale price he could charge and possibly get approved. The bank, naturally, wasn't going to let me borrow more than they thought I could afford.

In a surprise turn of events, it was determined after running my credit report, that in order for me to finance a vehicle in that price range, I would have to have a co-signer. I sure didn't see that coming. Angry and upset, I asked the salesman if there were any other options. He told me that my only other option was to put more money down —a lot more. In my fairytale world, I was planning to put only $2,000 down on a $35,000 truck. This was all I had in savings and I naively thought it would be enough. In my world, $2000 was a lot of money. For a bank being asked to lend out $35,000 plus to a kid with zero credit history, to purchase something that depreciates the moment it's driven off the lot, a good faith down payment of $2000 was a joke. The bank would be taking all of the risks. With no more money to put down, the only option I had left was to get a co-signer. Sadly, I would have to leave the dealership that day with no deal and no truck.

On the way home, angry and upset, all I could think about was that dude I saw in the parking lot after taking my test-drive. That dude with the "I gotta have it!" look on his face. I kept envisioning him walking into the finance office after me, getting approved, my salesman handing him the keys and then him driving away in my truck. It was a painful thought, but even more painful leaving that dealership empty handed. But I told myself, "I would be back to get that truck."

The next day, I called my aunt, who was always supportive and there for me. I told her about my experience at the car dealership and the financing situation. She could hear it in my voice on the phone that I was really upset and down. Without even asking for her help, my aunt offered to co-sign and do whatever she could to help me get the truck. Like always, she didn't blink when given the chance to show her love and support for me. My aunt would be taking a huge chance on me by co-signing on a car loan. She and I both knew that this could potentially have an impact on her credit now and in the future. I was extremely humbled that my aunt was willing to put her credit on the line for me.

Two days after my aunt told me that she would co-sign for me, we drove up to the dealership to get my truck. As soon as we pulled into the lot, there it was —the same truck I took out for a test drive. I couldn't believe it! Right away, I walked my aunt over to see it up close and of course, she loved it. It was the hottest truck on the lot. As we both were checking it out, I suddenly noticed my salesman from a few days ago looking over at us. I could tell he recognized me. Casually, he walked over and joked about me being back again. In a confident voice, I said, "I'm back to buy this truck." Less than two hours later, my aunt and I were signing paperwork in the finance office.

In no uncertain terms, we were told that the deal was done. We signed all of the papers that were required, but because it was late in the evening, the finance office couldn't give us copies of the final financing documents from the lender. We were told that we had to pick them up the next day. Our salesman told us it wasn't a big deal and proceeded to hand me the keys and owner's manual to my new truck. He told me I was "good to go" and to enjoy my new Toyota 4Runner.

The dream had finally come true. My family was proud and my friends couldn't believe it, especially my coworkers. The first day I drove it to work, I invited all of them outside during lunch to see it. They were blown away and immediately started fighting over who would go for a ride first. I felt like a rock star. Amongst all of the excitement at work that day, I was still on the lookout for a call from the dealership about picking up my final paperwork. But the call never came. No big deal, I thought. Besides, I wasn't really concerned about last minute copies of paperwork when I already had the keys and the truck. This was just last minute sloppiness on their part, at least that's what I thought.

Three days had gone by and still no call from the dealership. "Oh well," I thought. I just assumed they were busy and hadn't had the chance to call. At this point, I had gotten really comfortable with my truck. I had even read through the entire manual and learned how to use all of the features and functions. More importantly, I even figured out how to set my favorite radio stations and adjust the EQ settings. Day by day, the truck was becoming a part of me.

Four days into feeling like I was on top of the world, I decided to take some of my coworkers out to lunch in my new ride. We ended up getting back to the office around 1:30pm. That's when I got the four-day late, suspicious call from the dealership saying that they needed me to come by that afternoon because there was some additional paperwork that needed to be signed before moving forward. Confused by the call and thinking that they must have mistakenly contacted the wrong customer, I told the salesman on the phone that I was supposed to be contacted about picking up paperwork, not signing any. He proceeded to tell me that I urgently needed to come in that afternoon to sign some additional papers. Feeling uneasy after the call, I immediately called my aunt and asked if she could meet me at the dealership that afternoon. I figured, if they needed me to sign additional documents, they would be needing my aunt as well. She was the co-signer. In my gut, I knew something was wrong. The salesman on the phone didn't sound right and he wouldn't give me any details about what needed to be signed.

Once we arrived at the dealership that afternoon, my aunt and I went straight into the finance office. We were joined by the salesman who sold me the car, the finance manager, and the general manager of the dealership. This all smelled of trouble. The first person to speak was the general manager. He proceeded to tell us that, unfortunately, the dealership was unable to get final approval for financing the vehicle. The reason being my limited credit and employment history. Even with a co-signer, banks still were not willing to take a chance on what they perceived as a risky first time buyer. There were a couple of banks that were willing, but not at an interest rate I would be able to afford.

My aunt and I couldn't believe what was happening. We both sat there in shock. How could a dealership let a customer sign the papers for a purchase and then allow them to drive the new car for three days without financing being approved? This was beyond making any sense, it was crooked as hell. Wasn't the whole point of me getting a co-signer so that I would get approved?

Me being me, I was determined to find a solution to the situation. There was no way that I was leaving that dealership without my truck. I asked myself, "How could this be happening and why?" It took everything in me to hold back my tears as I asked everyone in the finance office if they could leave the room so that I could speak with my aunt in private. As soon as they politely walked out, I broke down in tears. My aunt told me that everything would be okay and that sometimes GOD allows things to happen for a reason. She told me to be patient and that my time would come. As supportive as she was, being a mature adult, I'm sure deep down inside she had some reservations about me taking on such a huge financial responsibility so early on in life. I would have never admitted it, but deep down inside, I felt the same way. Maybe I was being given a second chance not to dig myself into a hole. Maybe those guardian angels who always show up at critical moments in my life where making a visit to the Toyota dealership that day.

Everyone can admit that it is tough being responsible when it comes to the things we really want and life's simple pleasures. We hope and pray for the strength to make wise decisions in our life, especially when it comes to deciding on things that can potentially have a negative impact on our future. In the case of me buying that truck, it was obvious, not to me, but to anyone who knew me, that I was not operating in the realm of wisdom. My choice to buy an expensive truck was based solely on my wants and definitely not my needs. The only thing that stopped me from making that choice was the bank. When it comes to buying expensive things, banks will often remind us that life's biggest choices are often not our own.

When I left the dealership that day without that truck, it was one of the saddest days of my life. But in my heart, I knew that one day I would be back at that dealership or some other. This time, I would be prepared, capable, and without a co-signer.

EARNING MY CREDIT

It took me a week to really get over the pain and embarrassment of having to return my new truck. Some of my friends felt bad for me and others laughed their asses off. Oddly, I got more comfort and confidence from the friends who laughed. Humor has a funny way of helping us put life's little and even big tragedies into perspective. There were so many other, more serious things that I had overcome in my young life, I couldn't let a stupid truck be the end of the world. Eventually, I picked myself up and moved on. I decided work would be my main focus. I figured, if I excelled in my career, everything else, at least financially, would fall into place.

For the next few months, I barely even thought about that "stupid" truck. Life was sailing along just fine. I was working, partying, and doing whatever else I could to enjoy life. For some odd reason, the smooth sailing was interrupted one night after a long evening of partying and heavy drinking. Out of nowhere, I suddenly became emotional and started thinking about that damn truck. It was the most random thing. Usually, I am all about the laughs and the good times when I have been drinking. But on this particular night, I lost it. My spirit became filled with sadness. I began thinking about how hard I worked in school and college, but had "nothing" to show for it. I started thinking about having to give that truck back and wondering why GOD decided that I didn't deserve it. Sitting on the side of my bed, I cried in front of my girlfriend like a baby, asking her why GOD had taken something I wanted so badly away from me. I told her that this was the first time in my life that I worked really hard for something and I felt like GOD had let me down. "Why?" —is all I kept asking, until I eventually cried myself to sleep.

Waking up that next morning, surprisingly, I felt no embarrassment or shame in the fact that I allowed myself to become emotional the night before. There was an acceptance on my part that sometimes we just aren't strong enough to move on without GOD. I realized that morning that I wasn't crying for a truck after all. I was crying for answers and peace. And in the morning, He delivered both.

GOD doesn't do anything to hurt or harm us. As painful and challenging as life can be, it all works together for good and according to His perfect plan. Sometimes it's tough to grasp this truth and live in faith, especially when we feel doubt or deserving of certain outcomes. There was no doubt in my mind that I deserved that truck, but GOD decided that I deserved much more.

When I woke up that morning, all sadness and desire for that truck had left my spirit. I felt a renewed sense of patience and control over my life. GOD heard me cry out to Him and let me know that He was still by my side. He removed all doubt that I had in His goodness and presence in my life. I once again had faith, which gave me peace.

A few months after my emotional breakdown and awakening, I got a call from my girlfriend's uncle who had recently bought a new pickup truck and was selling his old one. He joked with me about how his old pickup truck wouldn't turn as many heads as a Toyota 4Runner, but that it was a good, reliable truck that would get me from point A to B. He offered to sell it to me for half of what he was going to charge a stranger. Immediately, I told him that I was interested and wanted to come and take a look at it.

At first glance, I had a hard time picturing myself driving this pickup truck. Even though it was in great condition, it was just about as generic and plain as you can get in a pickup truck. Going from a brand new Toyota 4Runner, to a used Ford Ranger is like going from a brand new Ferrari, to a used Ford Pinto. Well, maybe not that extreme, but a big difference none the less.

Any person in the market for a pickup truck would have known right away that the price that I was being offered for this truck was a steal. Initially, my ego was blocking my ability to see this tremendous opportunity that was being presented to me. Still worried about impressing other people, I was almost willing to let this opportunity slip by because the truck wasn't flashy enough or cool enough for my "taste." Thankfully, I was surrounded by people who could share sound advice and cared enough about me to not allow me to let this opportunity slip away.

The person selling the pickup, my girlfriend's uncle, actually gave the best advice out of anybody. He told me to consider this purchase a stepping stone for something better down the road. Since my lack of credit history had been my biggest hurdle in buying a new car, he mentioned that borrowing a small amount for a used car would allow me to establish a good, solid credit history. This was all I needed to hear. I was sold! That following Monday, I was at my bank applying for a used car loan. It was approved that same day. This was all a sign of, once again, being on the right path. By that Friday, I was the only twenty-two year old, preppy black man in Washington, D.C. to be driving around in a "plain-Jane" Ford Ranger pickup truck.

That truck took me to and from work for two years. It was a true blessing in disguise. Sure, my friends made fun of me wearing J. Crew polo shirts and Banana Republic khakis, driving around in a used pickup truck, but I didn't care. I had my eye on the prize.

Two years after buying that pickup truck and paying the used car loan off, not only did I, without a co-signer, get approved for a new car loan, but I ended up selling that pickup truck for twice what I paid for it! Through all of my initial pains and struggles, I finally got that Toyota 4runner. But this time, it was with "His" approval.

- CHAPTER 15 -

A GOOD GUY WITH A GUN

You never really know how much you value your life until someone or something threatens to take it away. Having someone push the barrel of a silver, .45 caliber semiautomatic pistol into your stomach and threaten to pull the trigger if you don't do what they say will cause you to know how much real quick. That is exactly what happened to me late one night, at around 2:30 in the morning, walking home from bar hopping in Adams Morgan, Washington, D.C.

For anyone who doesn't know, Adams Morgan is a popular hot spot in N.W., Washington, D.C., known for its trendy bars, clubs, and restaurants. Back in the day when I used to party there, it was also known as an easy target for late night "stick-up" crews. My friends and I, we all knew this, but figured nothing would ever happen to any of us. We had been going to these bars for years. Plus, a few of my friends were police officers, so that comforted us quite a bit. Adams Morgan was such a convenient spot for us to bar hop. One of my good friends even owned a condo only a few blocks from the bars. His place became the "crash spot" whenever we all would go out. This was where I was headed to crash on the night I got robbed.

It was a typical Saturday night in Adams Morgan just like any other. My friends and I closed down the bars and then hit the "Big Slice" pizza joint. This was a "hole in the wall" pizza place that sold huge slices of cheese or pepperoni pizza to go. It was always jammed packed with a line out the door. For some reason that night, I was the last one, out of all of my friends, to get a slice order in. Slices of pepperoni ended up running out, so I had to wait for a new round of pizzas to get out of the oven. I didn't want my friends waiting around for me, so I told them to go on and that I would catch up. After about ten minutes of waiting for my pizza in the crazy crowd of drunks, I finally got my box of slices and headed out the door to catch up with my friends.

Once I got outside, I assumed that I would see my friends walking a few bars up the road. But instead, I didn't see anybody. I thought, either they were walking super-fast or they all jumped in a cab. It wasn't a big deal, I figured I would just keep walking and see everybody back at the condo. With my pizza box in one hand and a slice in the other, I headed north up 18th Street. After passing all of the drunks and the bars, I then took a left onto Calvert Street, which was very dark compared to 18th Street. It was a residential street lined with brick row homes on both sides, which continued up until the Calvert Street Bridge. I got about halfway past the row homes before I noticed a small red car that was stopped in the street a short distance ahead of me. Even though I was inhaling a slice of pizza and still pretty drunk, I could sense that there was something not quite right about the red car stopped up ahead. It was just sitting in the middle of the dark road for no reason. There was no one attempting to cross the street, no cars in front of it, and no one except for me in sight. My instincts were telling me that the red car had stopped because of me.

For a split second, I thought maybe it was a friend or someone who knew me and saw me walking, but my gut was telling me it was something else. As I continued walking, getting closer and closer to the suspicious red car, all of a sudden, the passenger side door opened up. When the overhead light came on inside the car, I could see the driver, front passenger and three people in the back seat. Everyone, except for the driver, jumped out of the car and ran towards the sidewalk on my side of the street. Somehow without me noticing, they split up before reaching the sidewalk. I lost sight of two of them, but locked focus on the two that were now standing about forty feet in front of me. By it being so dark, I couldn't see their faces to try to discern their intentions. My hope still was that I was just being paranoid, but my common sense just couldn't be overruled. These guys didn't look like or were dressed like anyone who would live, visit or know someone in that Adams Morgan neighborhood. At two o'clock in the morning, walking down a dark street, stereotyping is just what you do. That's if you're smart.

By the time I got within twenty feet of the two out of place guys standing on the sidewalk in front of me, one of them all of a sudden rushed towards me. My instincts instantly told me to turn around and run the other direction, but I was stopped in my tracks by the other two guys who I had lost sight of a minute earlier. There was nowhere for me to run. Right away, I knew that I was going to have to think my way out of this scary situation.

The problem was, these guys had no intention of letting me think. Within a split second, one of them suddenly raised a gun from his side and put it up to my stomach. He then said in a low, nervous voice —"Give me all of your shit." It was at this moment that I saw my entire life flash in front of my eyes. I had often heard other people talk about this happening when faced with life threatening situations, but I usually had a difficult time believing them. Well, this was the moment I became a believer.

With that gun pressed to my stomach, I saw visual images of my family, friends, and most cherished memories. This caused my fear to turn into anger. In my mind, all I could think was —"I dare you to threaten my life over a few dollars. As hard as I have worked over my lifetime, as much as I have overcome, as many things that I have yet to accomplish —Who the fuck are you to take all of that away from me!" I was filled with anger, but there was really nothing I could do about it. There was a guy pointing a gun into my stomach with his finger on the trigger. My options were zero. Defenseless and surrounded, I had no choice but to hide my anger and focus on getting myself out of this situation as quickly as possible.

Everything about the four thugs who cornered me that night scared me. But the nervousness in the voice of the one thug holding the gun is what scared me the most. My life was potentially in the hands of a nervous hoodlum, who could accidentally or intentionally pull the trigger at any time. With so many scary thoughts swirling around in my head, the one thing I knew for certain was that I had to find a way to get these guys away from me. The faster I could get them to flee my presence, the less chance there would be for something really bad to happen.

As soon as the thug with the gun told me to give him all of "my shit," I put both hands in my front pockets and pulled out everything, including the pocket linings. Pulling the pocket linings out of my jeans was my way of letting them know that I wasn't trying to hide or keep anything from them. Again, my goal was to get them out of my presence as quickly as possible.

After I pulled everything out of my front pockets, the guy holding the gun to my stomach used his free hand to grab my wallet and keys out my hands. At the same time, one of the guys blocking me in from behind began patting my back pockets to make sure that I didn't have anything else. With nothing else left in my pockets to hand over, the guy with the gun and now my car keys, suddenly asked me, "Where your car at!" In that moment, I knew one hundred percent that these guys were not playing around. Instead of my cooperation de-escalating the situation, it appeared that things were about to escalate.

Taking a big risk, I told them that I didn't have my car and that's why I was walking to a friend's house. The scary truth was that my car was parked only a block away, but I knew better than to tell them that. If I would have told them my car was close by, not only would they have forced me to take them to my car so that they could steal it, but they probably would have killed me because I would have clearly seen their faces. According to some statistics, they say your chances of being seriously hurt or killed at the hands of a criminal increases once you leave the initial location of the crime. Knowing this, I couldn't let them know about my car. And thank GOD I didn't. They ended up running off, settling for just my keys and wallet. My nightmare had finally ended.

Relieved, but overwhelmed with emotions, I burst into tears. I wanted to run off right away, but I thought it was safer for me to stand there for a few minutes to make sure the guys who had just robbed me were gone. I intentionally wanted to give them time to get away. If I took off running too quickly, they might have seen where I was going or felt threatened. This was the last thing I wanted to happen.

As I stood there on the sidewalk all alone, I could see the red get-away car with the driver a little further up the road, waiting for the rest of the thugs. A few seconds later, I saw them all jump in the car, then speeding off towards Connecticut Avenue. The car was too far away for me to see the tag number, but I was confident about the make and model. It was tough for me to grasp what had just happened, but somehow, I finally pulled myself together. Right away, I thanked GOD for getting me through this without a scratch.

Once I was one hundred percent sure that the red car was headed up Connecticut Avenue, I took off running towards my friend's condo. While I was running, all I could think about was that gun against my stomach and what would have happened if he had pulled the trigger. Having some of my own family members who have been shot and some even killed by a gun, I knew firsthand the devastation that can be caused by a criminal with a gun. Fresh in my mind were images of one of my cousins who had been shot, but survived. I thought of him lying in a hospital bed, nearly skin and bones, with tubes coming out and going into every opening in his body. Remembering the pain that he went through and how it was so unbearable at times that he prayed and wished to die. All of this played out in my mind as I ran.

After running nonstop as fast as I could, I finally made it to my friend's condo. I was completely out of breath when I stepped off the elevator and rang his doorbell. As soon as he opened the door and saw me, he knew that something bad had happened. I nearly collapsed towards him as he reached out to help me into the apartment. Right away, I told him that I had been robbed at gun point. Shocked, he looks straight at me and says —"No fucking way!" I tried to tell my friend what happened, but he kept saying, "Let's call the police!" He then grabbed the phone and dialed 911. When the operator answered, my friend told them what happened to me and then passed me the phone. I gave them brief details of what happened and a description of the guys. In less than five minutes on the phone, the operator told me that the police were downstairs in the lobby and to go down to meet them right away.

The first thing the responding officers asked me is what type of car the guys were driving. When I told them, they got on their radio right away to give the description of the car to the dispatcher. The robbery happened only about thirty minutes before the police arrived, so there was a good chance that these guys could still be driving around in the area and could be spotted. Also, the fact that they didn't get anything of real value from me, there was a good chance that they could still be driving around in the area looking for someone else to stick-up. I had no cash on me —only my license, credit cards and a set of keys. All of which could be replaced.

After the cops put out a "Be on the lookout" for the suspects' vehicle, they told me to jump in the passenger seat of one of the two police cars and take them to the location where the robbery occurred. I was a little nervous to get in the police car because I had been drinking Long Island Ice Teas and Bud Lights all night and I was sure I reeked of alcohol. As I nervously sat down in the passenger seat, I asked the cop driving if I would get in trouble for still being a little drunk. He laughed out loud and asked me if I was twenty-one. I told him "yes" and he said, "Well then, you have nothing to worry about. We are not worried about you being drunk right now—We want to catch these 'motherfuckers' that robbed you!" As direct as they were, these words were like sweet music to my ears. It was the best feeling in the world knowing that the "good-guys" with the guns had showed up. It was at that moment that I made a promise to never take for granted those who protect us and put their lives on the line every day to do so. You don't realize how much you need "good-guys" with guns until you find yourself in a tight spot. On Calvert Street in Adams Morgan that night, I found myself in a tight spot.

The first thing the police did when we got to the spot where I got robbed, was search the area for anything the robbers may have dropped or thrown as they fled the scene. One of the officers told me that it was common for robbers to toss a wallet or purse immediately after they go through it looking for cash. The reason being, they don't want to get caught with stolen items that could link them directly to a particular crime. I was hoping that my wallet and keys were tossed, but after searching up and down the sidewalk for about thirty minutes, the cops were unable to find anything.

Having to replace my credit cards wasn't a big deal. But these thugs knowing my address from my license and having the keys to my house and car was a huge deal. I thought, "What if they were on the way to my house right now? With my house key, they could walk right in on my roommates or even do something to my dog." All of these crazy thoughts were swirling around in my head.

The officers tried to assure me that the chances were slim to none that these guys would drive all the way to Maryland and try to go into my house. Even for dumb criminals, it would be too much work and too big of a risk, the cops said. Robbing a defenseless person on the street is completely different than entering a home in an unfamiliar neighborhood. The risks to the criminal are enormous.

Feeling somewhat reassured that these hoodlums were not headed to my house in Maryland, I began to relax and provide the police with details of the robbery and a description of the guys who did it. Not too surprising, all of them were wearing either an oversized t-shirt or a "wife-beater" tank top and pants that were hanging halfway down their ass. Sadly, I could have probably given that description being blind. These thugs fit every hoodlum stereotype imaginable.

Unfortunately, I remembered more about what they were wearing than what their faces looked like. The street was really dark, plus I tried to avoid making eye contact with any of them, especially the guy with the gun. My feeling was that if he, the guy holding the gun, felt threatened or challenged by me in any way, things could escalate for the worse. This was something I desperately didn't want to happen.

After I gave them all of the information I could remember from the robbery, they gave me a police contact number so that I could follow up on my case. They were confident in telling me that there was a good chance that they would catch the guys. Due to the fact that criminals are typically dumb and they usually keep doing wrong until they get caught. I wanted them caught that night.

My anger still raged as the officers drove me back to my friend's condo empty handed —no wallet, no keys, and no thugs. While driving, out of nowhere, I felt compelled to ask the officers if it was legal to shoot them if they broke into my house while I was there. The officer driving quickly looked over at me and said, "Damn right! If somebody walked into my house that didn't belong there, that's exactly what I would do!"

I couldn't have dreamed of a better group of cops to answer my call that night. These guys were blunt, down to earth, real American heroes who understood and defined clearly the difference between the good guys and the bad guys.

For the next two months, I slept with my dog and my gun by my side. The experience of having someone directly threaten your life is not something that instantly fades away. Maybe I was being paranoid and maybe the cops were right about the thugs not taking a chance coming to my home. But you know what, those cops weren't guarding my house every night and they damn sure weren't sleeping next to me. In my home, I'm the "good guy" with the gun. Until other "good guys" show up, I'm responsible for protecting the life of me and my family. There is nothing in the world like confidently knowing that you have the legal right to protect and defend yourself in your own home. It is a fundamental legal right that is guaranteed to us as Americans. Our freedoms are based on this right.

- CHAPTER 16 -

AWAKENING THE PATRIOT

Listening to the news one day, I heard an arrogant news anchor give his opinion when asked why he thought those who live in the "fly-over states" or Middle America are so patriotic and in love with their country. His short answer was, "That's all they have." In other words, Middle America isn't smart enough to know, like him, that there are more, so called, "enlightened" things to do rather than love your country. Appreciation for America's greatness, according to him, is an "option" when you consider or "crown" yourself to be an elite intellectual. Blinded by arrogance, what this news anchor failed to realize is that for a lot of folks, love and appreciation for your country is sometimes all you need.

SHOT DOWN

Ever since my middle school days, living right outside of Andrews Air Force Base and being part of a military family, I have always had a big heart for my country and those who serve. Even as a little kid, my affection for America came easy. All I had to do was pay attention and look around at the blessings that we have: freedom, opportunity, security, stability and the list goes on.

As I grew older, my affection for my country also grew and like anything that is loved, when that thing or part of it is hurt, pain is felt. One of the very first times I actually took something painful that happened to my country personally, was on Saturday, March 27, 1999. I was hanging out with friends in a bar having a great time that weekend, but on the other side of the world our U.S. military was involved in a conflict over the skies of Serbia, Yugoslavia. The U.S., alongside its NATO allies, were conducting bombing missions as part of the Kosovo War. The news was heavily covering the war and images of the destruction and fighting was being shown on TV twenty-four hours a day. On this particular night at the bar, for some reason, I found myself being glued to the TV that was hanging over top of the bar. The news was reporting that a U.S. F-117A Nighthawk stealth aircraft had been shot down over Serbia. While everyone else kept drinking and partying, I couldn't help but to fill up with anger and sadness. I took it personally.

All I could think about was the American pilot or pilots and if they survived. And if they did, what was going to happen to them if they got captured? Eventually, all of these questions circling around in my head caused me to get emotional. I didn't want anyone to see me upset, so I walked away from the bar and headed back into the restroom. Even I was shocked at how sad and angry I had become. The unexpected pain I felt in that moment was a clear sign of how much I truly respect and care for those who serve and protect this country.

911

It would only take a few years after that fateful night in March at the bar that I would once again see something on TV that would cause me to feel pain on behalf my country. This pain would strike me at my core, but not me alone. Millions of people all over the world would share in this pain. On September 11, 2001, the entire world came to a standstill as we all witnessed evil in its truest form. Pain and destruction had been inflicted on the United States on an unimaginable scale. If I ever had any doubts that real evil exists in this world, those doubts disappeared on that day.

The morning of September 11, 2001 was unusually beautiful on the east coast. I was living in the suburbs of Montgomery County, Maryland at that time and I remember how clear and blue the sky was on that day. Other than the weather, it was a typical weekday morning just like any other. I started my day by throwing on some sweat pants and a shirt and then taking Albert, my ninety pound Weimaraner out in the backyard for a walk. After he did what he had to do, we both came back inside and headed back downstairs to my room in the basement. Just like clockwork, once we got downstairs Albert wagged his tail and smiled as he waited for daddy to fill his dog bowl with food. This was our morning ritual. I miss my best friend Albert.

After getting Albert's morning started, it was then my turn. First, I hit the shower and then spent at least the next twenty minutes in the bathroom mirror getting ready for work. The way my room was setup, I could watch TV from the reflection in my bathroom mirror. It was perfect. I could get dressed for work and watch Good Morning America at the same time. On this particular morning, I saw something in the reflection that caused me to immediately stop everything I was doing. The image on the TV screen was showing smoke coming from the top of one of the World Trade Center Towers.

My first thought was that they were showing old footage of a previous terrorist attack on the towers. But then it hit me —all of those attacks occurred at the base of the buildings, never at the top. The next thing I thought was that it must be a fire on one of the upper floors. Nothing else was making any sense as to why smoke was coming from the top. As I looked on from the mirror in the bathroom, I could see that the smoke was getting heavier. That's when I decided to walk out of the bathroom to get a closer look at the TV screen. A reflection in the mirror was just not enough for me to figure out what was happening. When I turned up the volume, Charles Gibson from Good Morning America was reporting that a small plane might have accidently crashed into one of the World Trade Center Towers. There was no certainty about a plane crashing, but an early consensus was forming around that theory.

Between the smoke billowing out the top of the building and the panic on the air, there was no way I could go back in the bathroom until I knew what happened. As the minutes passed, the reporting became more and more chaotic. Some TV anchors on the air were still saying that it was a small plane and some were even suggesting that it could have been a missile of some sort. Meanwhile, concern was growing more and more for the people that were trapped by the fire, which was burning on such a high floor.

As I stood there in front of my TV, waiting to hear some sort of a confirmation of what really happened, suddenly a plane came from the corner of my TV screen and hit the other tower! "Holy Shit!!" I screamed. My immediate thought was that the smoke from the first fire must have caused the plane to lose sight and crash into the second Tower. I was still convinced that this all had to be a horrible accident, nothing else made any sense at this point. Charles Gibson thought otherwise.

Even with the limited information that was available at this point, Mr. Gibson and others on the air knew in their gut, after the second crash, that this was no accident. Within fifteen minutes, I too would find out that this was intentional and part of a planned attack on our country. All of the world would soon find out that these were no missiles or small plans that hit the Towers, but commercial airplanes full of passengers.

In shock from what I just heard and saw happen on live television, I quickly ran upstairs to tell my roommate what was going on. He hadn't turned on the living room TV yet, so he was clueless. As soon as I told him what was happening, he couldn't turn on the living room TV fast enough. All my roommate could do at first was just sit there, staring at the screen, in silence and disbelief.

At 9:15am on Tuesday, September 11, 2001, my roommate and I were witnessing the beginning of the worst attack on our country in our lifetime. Neither one of us was alive during the bombing of Pearl Harbor, but I get a sense that this is what it must have felt like. It didn't take long that morning before my feelings of shock and disbelief would be replaced by anger and the desire for revenge on whoever did this. I remember saying to my roommate in the living room that morning, "I'm not sure who did this, but whoever did it is going pay! This is the worst attack on the United States that we have ever seen. Somebody has to pay!"

With everything that had happened that morning, I forgot that I was supposed to be on my way to work. Part of me wasn't even sure if I should still go in. This was a major attack on our country that would have implications far beyond New York City. But to be on the safe side, I decided it was best to still make my way to the office. As soon as I jumped in my truck, headed for downtown D.C., I flipped through the news stations. By this time, all types of new news reports were coming in. There were reports that planes had hit the Washington Monument and the Capitol Building. Another report was saying that a plane was possibly headed towards the White House. It felt like we were in the beginning stages of World War III.

To get to work in downtown D.C., I always took 16th Street, which is a busy route that connects Maryland and D.C. On the morning of September 11th, I didn't know what to expect on my commute. The drive started off normally at first, but then something strange started to happen. Cars in front of me began stopping and making U-turns to head back northbound towards Maryland. Immediately, I started flipping the radio stations because I knew that those cars must have heard something frightening on the radio. Less than ten seconds later, that's when I heard it —the Pentagon had been hit.

As it turned out, the earlier attacks in New York were just the beginning. D.C. was now on the list. The first thing I did when I heard about the Pentagon attack was call my friend Derek, who worked in a printing shop a block away from my office. He always got to work before me, so I knew he could give me the scoop on what was going on downtown. Derek was a laid back guy, so when he told me on the phone that he was leaving work and getting the hell out of D.C., I knew things were bad.

I was still torn on whether or not I should keep driving towards downtown. I kept thinking, "Am I being careless or are those drivers who are turning around just being paranoid?" Not knowing what to do, I called my girlfriend, who worked with me at the office. She picked up on the first ring and told me that the office was closing and the buildings downtown were being slowly evacuated. This was all I needed to hear. At the next light, I hit the quickest u-turn of my life. I was headed straight back to my house in the safe, comfy suburbs of Montgomery County, Maryland.

While driving back to Maryland, my girlfriend and I talked on the phone about the planes hitting the buildings in New York and the Pentagon. Surprisingly, she didn't even think to ask me to pick her up from the office and neither did I bother to offer. I think with everything crazy that was happening, we just didn't even consider it to be an option. Sadly, I will admit, my chivalry was not up to par at this stage of my life. Our conversation on the phone lasted for about ten minutes before it was cut short by a lost signal. This would be the last cell phone call I would be able make or receive for at least the next 24 hours.

With no cell service and no work, like everyone else, I spent the rest of the morning glued to the news on TV. The images of smoke, fire, and destruction brought indescribable sadness, but it also stirred revengeful anger. Every single person on the planet wanted to know who did this, obviously, except for the motherfuckers that planned and did it. I have no apologies for my passionate language when referring to the animals that did this. Sometimes it takes passion and clarity to define evil.

The surprise attacks on September 11, 2001 definitely caught the U.S. off-guard. I had never seen my country put in such a "defensive" position —ever. As powerful as we are as a nation, we still bleed. Seeing my country bleed that morning, I couldn't help but to get angrily impatient, like so many others, waiting for answers as to who would be the target for our revenge. Until those answers would come, I would only have heartbreak and anger.

All I could think about were the people trapped in those burning Towers, "How scared must they be? How much pain must they be enduring? How hard must they be praying and how helpless must they feel?" The hell they must have gone through is unimaginable. As I watched this hell, I was waiting for GOD to step in at any moment. With this level of destruction and evil, only He would be strong enough to push back against it.

Before I would see GOD, I would see the Twin Towers fall, part of the Pentagon collapse, and a hijacked plane crashing in Pennsylvania, killing every single person onboard. I never in my life would have thought that I would get to see this level of evilness that human beings are capable of. Reading about the historical evilness of mankind is one thing, but seeing it unfold in front of your own eyes is another.

As the smoke began to clear and the bodies were being counted, I transitioned into a state of deep reflection: "What did we do as a nation to deserve this? What did the people in those Towers, the Pentagon, and in those planes do to deserve this?" Absolutely nothing is the answer. There is no rationale needed for evil, only a weak-minded excuse.

This was an attack so severe that it transcended the typical political arguments that divide us on a daily basis. As Americans, we became "one" in our hurt and anger. The entire world would realize that "anger" can be a powerful force for uniting people. Americans wanted blood and understandably so.

Even with the appetite for revenge raging in our hearts, we as a nation made it our priority to save lives and help our fellow countrymen in their most desperate time of need. Americans drove from every corner of this nation to offer help and assistance to those impacted by the terrorist attacks. There was no longer a "rural" or "big city" America, we were all one America. This was a moment of clarity for me, one of many that came out of the September 11th attacks.

I realized that the true strength and potential of this country, always reveals itself when we come together to protect our freedoms and way of life. It is no coincidence that these are also the moments when GOD reveals Himself. When we help our neighbors and help one another, that's when GOD shows up.

On September 11, 2001, when Americans braved through smoke and fire, hot ashes and steel to help their fellow countrymen —that's when GOD showed up.

- Chapter 17 -

The Power of Momentum

"A big part of successful living is doing what you do to the fullest extent of your abilities. Somewhere in that range lies "the zone;" the place where all the fulfillment of GOD's promise in you comes into broad relief. You are doing what you were built to do and in harmony with all that you've ever wanted to become."[2]

In physics, momentum is defined as "mass in motion." The greater the momentum, the greater the force required to stop it. Just like in physics, our "mental momentum" or "attitude in motion," takes a certain amount of force to stop. In life, we can use the power of momentum to repel negative forces that attempt to stop us from achieving our dreams, goals, and desires.

As we have all witnessed in sports, momentum can make the difference between winning and losing. A single athlete or

---

[2] Quoted in Chris Brady & Orrin Woodward, LEADERSHIP AND LIBERTY: PIECES OF THE PUZZLE (Flint, MI: Obstacles Press, Inc., 2009), 70.

team that builds and maintains positive momentum throughout a game can dramatically improve their path to victory. Momentum generates positive energy and builds confidence. As a team builds positive momentum, it becomes more difficult for the opposing team to stop them. For a team lacking momentum, the opposite is true. Just like an object standing still, a team without positive momentum lacks the energy needed to control the environment of the game. At least in a way that is favorable to them winning.

Just as in the case of a physical object experiencing momentum, our mental momentum is subject to external forces which effect the intensity and direction of this momentum. These forces can carry us in a positive or negative direction, depending on the nature of these forces and our reaction to them. Objects that have momentum in the physical world do not operate in a vacuum and neither do our thoughts and attitudes. Aside from a controlled environment in a science laboratory, there are rarely, if any, situations in life that aren't subject to external factors. In an imperfect world, negative forces will always attempt to impede our positive momentum. If the goal is to live a successful and productive life, we must reduce the impact of negative forces, while embracing positive forces. Similar to reducing air drag forces on a race car, we must shape our attitudes and minds in a way to deflect negative forces.

In the world of professional car racing, the goal is to design and build the most powerful and aerodynamic race car possible. The race car design team is charged with keeping the negative forces produced by air drag and friction to a minimum and positive forces produced by the engine to a maximum. Relying on engine design and power alone to combat the negative forces of drag and friction is not enough. Increasing engine power and capability can add more overall weight to the race car and therefore reduce overall performance. The designer strives for a balance between engine power and aerodynamics to win races. The same principles can hold true in our daily lives. The more successful and efficient we are at deflecting negative forces, the less mental power (weight) we must dedicate to overcoming negative forces.

IT STARTS WITH A PUSH

As a child growing up, I had to find a way to make it around a pretty challenging and bumpy race track of my own. On this track, I was constantly bombarded by negative forces. Forces that were impeding my momentum. But, I was fortunate enough to have a strong pit crew (family) in my corner, who could help me overcome those negative forces. Like any pit crew forced to run a race with limited resources, my family made the best with what they had. Sometimes all they could give was a push. But that push was always enough to start.

At the age of five, I was just starting elementary school and didn't know the first thing about life, let alone positive momentum. All I cared about were toys, my friends, and McDonald's Happy Meals. Just like most kids my age, my actions and behavior were guided more by my mom's belt than anything else. This all changed the day I brought home my first graded homework assignments. My grades were a mixture of smiley and sad faces, marked in bright red marker. Considering that they were my first graded assignments, my mother let me off with a warning about the sad faces. Without going into too much detail about this warning, there was no way I was getting any more of those sad faces if I could help it. It would be smiley faces from here on out.

    Once I was "persuaded" by my mother that getting good grades was my only option, I quickly learned to comply. To my mom's delight, my second round of graded homework assignments were filled with all red happy faces! It was a huge relief for me and my butt. For my mom, it was a special achievement that needed to be recognized and celebrated. Unlike some parents, who would give more attention to failures than successes, my mom never took my successes for granted. Raising a child and getting that child to succeed takes more than just strict discipline. It's also about recognition and focusing on good behavior just as much, if not more, than bad behavior. Even though my mom was confident that her discipline and expectations of me would achieve a certain outcome, she never took my ability to live up to her expectations for granted. She knew that eventually, it would take more than the threat of taking a toy away or a hit from a belt to keep me on a straight path. Someday, I would have to find the desire within myself to succeed.

    With happy faces now covering all of my homework assignments, not only was I in good with my mom, but with my kindergarten teacher as well. Life was good. The perks that came along with getting good grades and doing the right things were awesome. Not doing well in school became less and less attractive. For a kid who loved getting the latest toys as soon as they hit the Toys "R" Us shelves, this was a life I wanted to definitely get used to.

TEACHER'S PET

The academic momentum that started in kindergarten would eventually carry over to my next grades. As the positive momentum began to grow, so did my relationships with my teachers. I began to notice that teachers, just like parents, took pride in their kids who were vested in learning. For the committed teachers in my elementary school, knowing that a child was working just as hard as they were, was all the motivation they needed.

Even with a strong commitment to their students, a teacher's time and resources are limited. As a result, I've learned that a lot of teachers tend to focus their resources where they feel that they can make the biggest impact. Because I was pushed by my mother to do well in school, my behavior in the classroom sent out a positive signal to the teachers. They looked at me as one of those kids worthy of their time and resources. Help with assignments, more responsibility, being called on first and class leadership roles were just some of the benefits for showing the teacher that I was there to learn.

As I moved on to higher grades, the opportunities continued to grow. Being chosen for lead roles in school plays, extracurricular activities, and even second chances for acting up in class —all were the perks that came along with the desire to learn. Doors opened and opportunities became available that otherwise might not have been. All because I had shown a desire to achieve when given the chance. Staying committed to learning and maintaining positive momentum were attracting the people and resources in my life that I needed to go further. All of it was propelling me forward. Something as simple as the desire to learn had changed my reality.

NATIONAL CATHEDRAL SCHOOL

When we think of achieving our goals and dreams, it is easy to focus only on our current circumstances or doing it alone. This is sometimes referred to as thinking in the "natural." Having this mindset can make our goals and dreams seem almost impossible. For a kid who attended public school in the heart of a public housing project in S.E., Washington, D.C., I had to build the momentum that would change my thinking from the "natural" to the "supernatural." This momentum would be multiplied by those around me, who noticed my efforts and wanted to help in any way they could to nurture these efforts. Constantly building on positive momentum, I began to shatter any preconceived notions that I had of a limited reality because of my circumstances.

I can recall the day when my eyes really began to open to my new, unlimited reality. It was the day when I was told by my fifth grade teacher that I was one of a hand-full of kids from the inner city chosen to attend an exclusive summer camp program at the National Cathedral School of Washington D.C. Located in one of the most affluent neighborhoods in upper, northwest Washington, D.C., this is one of the country's most prestigious private schools. An opportunity like this would have been unimaginable if I had continued to live in a perceived "limited reality."

The summer camp program was created for kids who had maintained a high level of academic success and shown a strong desire to excel. Through hard work and the support of my school and teachers, I was one of a chosen few kids who could participate in this special program. For a kid from the projects, this was an opportunity of a lifetime. Getting a chance to be surrounded by other kids, from all different types of backgrounds, would help mold my perspective on life for years to come.

On my first day of summer camp, one of my most vivid memories was riding on the school bus on the way to the National Cathedral and passing by the beautiful wall mural painting of Marilyn Monroe. Someone had painted a large close up of Marilyn Monroe's face, mole and all, on the side of a four story brick building. The building was located on the busy corner of Connecticut Avenue and Calvert Street, not far from the National Cathedral. As a kid, I had seen the painting before. Driving by it with my family, always reminded me that we were in the wealthy part of D.C. My grandmother would refer to it as "Uptown." The difference this time when I saw Marilyn's face, was that I felt like I belonged here. I had done something to deserve to be in this upscale part of D.C. It wasn't money that brought me to this fancy new neighborhood, it was brains. Doors were opening because I did the best I could with what I had and someone took notice.

The camp consisted of kids from all over the D.C. metropolitan area. This summer program would be the first time I would actually get to be in a learning environment with kids outside of my race. It was awesome! As crazy as it may sound, I felt like I had gone to another planet to meet some new friends. Most of the teachers and camp volunteers were white, which was another new experience. Except for the people running the program, most of the volunteer camp instructors appeared to be college age. Even though they were young, these volunteers were some to the most dedicated and caring individuals I had ever met. Their positive perspective on life and love for kids, regardless of race, planted positive seeds in me. This camp showed me that there was a whole other world to see outside of my little neighborhood in S.E.,

Washington, D.C. I just had to maintain my momentum to get there.

One of the first things we did at the summer camp was climb the stairs to the top of the National Cathedral. From the roof, we got to see Washington, D.C. from the tallest point in the city. Aside from taking the long climb up the narrow, dark, spiral staircase, it was an experience of a lifetime. Not only did we get to see all of the detailed, hand chiseled stone gargoyles and sculptures that aren't visible with the naked eye from ground level, but we got to see a bird's eye view of the entire Washington, D.C., Maryland and Virginia skyline. It was breathtaking!

My Pastor, Dale O'Shields once said, "Our perspective on life is based on our position in life." Just like what we see through the lens of a camera, perspective is a function of position. The view changes depending on where we focus and aim the lens of the camera. The same holds true in our "view" of life. The times in which we develop a negative perspective on life, the solution can sometimes be something as simple as changing our position or our view of things.

Education allowed me to change my position early in life. Like a view through a camera, as my position changed, my perspective changed. Similarly, being blessed with the opportunity to attend summer camp at The National Cathedral School, put me in a position to see things that were impossible to see standing on a corner in the projects.

- Chapter 18 -

Stuck: The Comfort Zone

"A body at rest will remain at rest unless an outside force acts on it, and a body in motion at a constant velocity will remain in motion in a straight line unless acted upon by an outside force." —Newton's 1st Law of Motion

Throughout every stage of our lives, we will undoubtedly encounter challenges. This is just as sure as the sun will rise and set. Our pain, struggles, and fears are just a part of life and there ain't no way to get around it! The question is, "How do we handle and deal with these challenges?" We can either grow from them or allow them to control our lives. In order to grow, we must first be willing to change. By definition, for anything to grow, it first has to change. For us as humans, this means that if we are going to grow through our challenges, we have to first be willing to change our behavior and response to our challenges.

"All of us are self-made, but only the successful will admit it." —Earl Nightingale.

One of the worst outcomes that can result from not growing through our challenges is the tendency to get "stuck." This refers to the situation in which we allow our challenges to define who we are or limit who we can become. In my own life, it has been a constant battle to avoid getting "stuck." Sometimes, I have been a strong enough force on my own to get unstuck and other times, it has required support or even a push from a close friend or family member. It's easy to see that Newton's 1st Law of Motion pertaining to a body at rest or in motion also applies to human behavior as well. As we face challenges and adopt certain behaviors, we can become stuck (at rest) unless we apply a force to change our situation or the direction of it.

OLD FEARS, NEW CITY

"Unchallenged means unchanged."

The year was 2006, life was great for those of us living in or near the Nation's Capital. Contrary to the years under the leadership of Mayor Marion Barry, businesses and investments were pouring into the city. Anthony Williams had been mayor of Washington, D.C. for seven years and there was a new tone resonating throughout the city —one of rebirth and revitalization. No matter where you looked across the Washington, D.C. skyline, you could spot a towering cement crane hovering above a new construction site. It had been almost ten years since the MCI arena (now the Verizon Center) had opened in the Chinatown neighborhood, right smack in the heart of the city. Ever since the arena opened, the city seemed to be moving in a new and positive direction.

As D.C. started to become a cool place to live and work, young professionals from all over were landing jobs in the city and buying up properties. As properties in the nicer parts of the city, which were in the N.W. neighborhoods, became scarce and unaffordable, folks started buying up condos and townhomes in the poorer, rundown neighborhoods of D.C. Eventually, these "shady" properties would turn out to be the biggest jackpots for those who knew how to ride the D.C. real estate wave and knew when to get off.

Even though I was one of those young professionals working in the city during this booming time, I was living in the suburbs of Silver Spring, Maryland. I lived there with two roommates, who also worked in and around D.C. At the time, we considered it to be a great living arrangement. The rent was fairly cheap and the commute to the city wasn't that bad. Getting to work was a straight shot down 16th Street, which connected Montgomery County, Maryland and northwest, D.C. Living this close to the city, we felt like we could have the best of both worlds —access to city life, but without the cost and parking headaches associated with the city. As much as we tried to convince ourselves that living in the suburbs wasn't that bad, actually living in and experiencing the city life was something everyone our age wanted to experience.

For those of us who grew up in and were familiar with the poor neighborhoods of D.C. during the 70's and early 80's, such as myself, to see how these neighborhoods were being renovated and transformed into swanky, modern urban neighborhoods was unbelievable. Neighborhoods where you couldn't spot a white person for miles, were now becoming hubs of diversity. Having lived in the suburbs and gone to college, I was used to diverse environments. But for some of my black relatives and friends, it was a different story. Seeing a white person jogging on 14th Street early in the morning or strolling down U Street late in the evening was something they never thought they would see. D.C. was changing and it was just the beginning.

As the idea of living in D.C. became more and more enticing, some of my friends started to get in the game and buy property in the city. For me, the idea of buying property seemed too scary to even consider. Aside from the beauty of paying cheap rent, admittedly, I was afraid to even think about buying a house. Fear of change, fear of taking risks, and lack of knowledge were causing me to remain stuck in a rented room in the basement of a Silver Spring townhouse. In my mind, I justified my complacency by fact that I had a good job, making good money. I thought, "Why would I want to take on a mortgage payment and have to tighten my budget?" It boiled down to fear and an unwillingness to grow up. The idea of taking on more responsibility scared me. I feared change.

10 Negative Effects of FEAR[3]:

1. Dominates
2. Paralyzes
3. Torments
4. Deceives
5. Wastes
6. Weakens
7. Clouds
8. Fatigues
9. Hijacks
10. Alters

---

[3] Pastor Dale O'Shields, Church of the Redeemer (Gaithersburg, MD) Sermon: January 9-10, 2016.

Fear can be one of the worst enemies you will ever face in life. It robs you of your potential. There I was, blessed with a good job, but still afraid to stretch my wings and grow beyond my youthful ways. I was stuck in a living situation that was unbecoming of any responsible adult. So worried about having enough money to spend on partying, that I was putting my future on hold. Fortunately, I had people in my life that cared enough about me to call me out on my fears.

My fear of buying my own place was directly challenged one day when a good friend came over to my place to pick me up to go out. As I was getting dressed downstairs in my basement bedroom, my good friend Rick waited for me in the upstairs living room. I noticed that he wasn't saying much while he was waiting. "Maybe he was in the bathroom or just tired from going out the night before," I thought. After I was done getting dressed, I walked upstairs and noticed that he was just sitting there on the couch, in thought. Right away, I started wondering, "Did something happen? Did I take too long getting ready?" I was clueless as to what was on his mind. Before I could ask him what was wrong, he turned and looked me right in the eye and said —"You got to get the hell out of this townhouse! You are living like you are still in a college dorm. You are better than this, get your shit together."

Up until I heard those words, it never really hit me as to how immature and despicable my living situation was. The upstairs living room was cluttered with boxes, the kitchen counter was lined with dirty dishes, and the carpeting throughout the upstairs was filthy and covered in stains. It was nothing short of what can be described as an adult version of a frat house. Because I lived in the basement and kept my portion of the house clean, I chose to ignore the upstairs as much as possible. The only time I would get self-conscious of my house was when new guests would come over and they would have to walk over the filth to get to my room.

Rick was the first person to actually call me out on how I was living, but I soon found out that he wasn't the only one who thought about doing it. My mom eventually opened up about my living situation, after I told her what Rick said to me. Never mentioning it before, she shared with me a time that she came to visit me and made the mistake of using the upstairs hallway bathroom. Not knowing what she was getting herself into, she walked into the bathroom and turned on the light, only to be met with dirt and disgust. She described to me how the tub looked like it hadn't been washed in a year and the inside of the toilet was almost black. Also, she told me that the shower curtain was completely covered in mold. Hearing this from my mom for the first time, I was floored. "How could I let my mom be exposed to something like that?" I asked myself. I was embarrassed that she had been keeping this to herself for months. I was even more embarrassed that I didn't even have a clue.

Tolerating filth isn't a matter of cleanliness, it's a matter of character. It's about having enough self-respect to hold yourself and your surroundings to a certain standard. My best friend Rick's criticism and tough love helped to ignite a fire under my butt. His blunt honesty caused me to reflect on my standards and priorities as they related to how I lived. The momentum to make a change had begun. This momentum would eventually get me to a better place. But there was still more pushing and influence that would be required. Old habits die hard.

BEST BUY

The idea of moving out and buying a place remained on my mind. The seed had been planted, I just had to find a way. My girlfriend at the time, now my wife, was renting an apartment in D.C., but wanted to buy something soon herself. A lot of her friends were buying condos and it just seemed like the smart thing to do. Whenever she and I would hang out with any of her friends that bought or were in the process of buying, they would always talk about how easy it was to get pre-approved for a mortgage. They made it seem like the banks were just handing out loans. (They essentially were, but I'll save that conversation for later on.) Even my best friend Rick had managed to buy a condo and even one in a great, upscale neighborhood. Everyone was telling me that I could do it too, but I just kept making excuses. Even after spending months of condo shopping with my girlfriend, getting educated on the process and even watching her go to closing, I was still too chicken to start the process. Just like many situations in life, where we may fall short or are afraid to move forward, GOD can always step in to show us the way. In my quest to be a homeowner, I would need Him to show me the way. And that's exactly what He did.

    It was a Saturday morning and I was at the office working overtime on a project deadline. That's when I got a random phone call from my good friend Tim. He and I used to work together at the same architecture firm, but he had taken a job at a firm in Georgetown. Thinking that he was calling to catch up or pick a day to grab lunch, he randomly asked me if I was still interested in buying a place in D.C. I told him that I was still looking, which really meant that I was still coming up with excuses. He knew me very well and could tell that I was blowing smoke as usual. He also knew that I was making a decent salary and there was no excuse for me not to be a homeowner.

The architectural firm that he was working for, Shalom Baranes Associates, was involved in a lot of really nice residential and commercial projects all over the city. He told me that if I was serious about trying to buy something nice and in the city, he knew of a perfect opportunity. Now that he had my full attention, my next question was "Where?" "It's a brand new condominium on Wisconsin Avenue that my firm designed," he said. I couldn't help but laugh and asked him if he was crazy. I'm thinking to myself, "If it's on Wisconsin Avenue and brand new, there is no way I can afford it." Tim said that the new condominium would have small, one-bedroom units that should be in my price range. This still all sounded too good to be true. Finally, Tim said, "Jermaine, I know you don't believe me, but just go up there to the sales office and see for yourself. What do you have to lose?" He was right —what did I have to lose?

Tim mentioned that the only issue with buying one of these condos was that I had to put down a deposit and wait for the construction to be complete. The developer had just opened the sales office and they would be pre-selling units starting that up-coming weekend. Having already bought a condo himself and knowledgeable of the D.C. condo market, Tim knew that this would be the chance of a lifetime and that I should do everything I could to seize this opportunity.

The weekend couldn't come soon enough. I couldn't help but wonder, "Was this the opportunity I had been praying for?" It was a bright and sunny Saturday morning, a perfect day to look for a new home. Driving down Wisconsin Avenue on the way to the sales office, something just felt right. When I pulled into the small parking lot on the side of a gray trailer that was converted into a fancy portable sales office, people were already lining up to go inside. Even though I was extremely nervous and somewhat doubtful, I was still very much looking forward to asking questions and getting information. Immediately when I walked in, I was greeted by one of two extremely nice and charming women who ran the sales office. Their energy was like nothing I had ever experienced from a sales person. These ladies could sell water to a well, they were just that good.

    The sales lady who greeted me at the door invited me into her office and asked me right away, with a huge smile on her face, "What brings you here to see us!" Smiling back at her, I told her that I was referred by a friend who works at the firm that designed the condos that they were selling. Next, I mentioned that I am possibly in the market to buy one. She smiled brightly again and asked me, "How many bedrooms do you want?" I couldn't help but laugh at her flirty nature. Just like any good sales person, she was already putting in my head the vision of me buying a condo. Now she was making our conversation all about choices and details. She was very smooth.

    Because the sales office was getting really crowded, she switched gears and we started discussing the different price ranges of the units and the pre-qualification requirements. Knowing what my girlfriend paid for her condo and her monthly mortgage amount, I knew that the only units in my price range were the one-bedroom units. She had me fill out a quick, one-page financial assessment and based on that, told me that I would have no problem getting pre-approved for a one-bedroom unit. The next step would be to pick a specific unit for purchase and put down a deposit based on the purchase price to hold the unit until closing. This all sounded too easy to be true.

The sales lady could tell that I still had concerns because of the confused look on my face. She asked me what was wrong and I told her that I had always been too afraid to try and buy a home. With a sincere smile, she told me that she understood my anxiety and that everyone is nervous the first time they buy. I'm not sure if her sincerity was genuine, but it sure was what I needed to hear. There is something about getting a push or advice from a stranger that can be really inspiring. Coming from a close friend or family member, the same advice can be interpreted as a judgement. Whatever the reason, I was motivated leaving that sales office. I was on a mission to be a homeowner.

"How was I going to come up with the six percent deposit?" I thought. This was my next task to overcome. I had roughly a third of the amount I needed to hold the condo. I was pretty sure I could find a way to come up with the rest. Even if I had to use my credit cards, I was going to come up with that deposit. It's funny how our perspectives change once we set a goal. Before going to that sales office and seeing what I could potentially own a home, I was using every excuse in the book to talk myself out of why I wasn't ready to buy a home. Now that I knew what I would be missing out on if I didn't try to make this happen, I was determined to make it happen.

Owning a condo on Wisconsin Avenue, a brand new one at that, was something I never dreamed of. The fact that this could possibly become a reality, created the determination to make it happen. I was now focused on what I wanted. The word "focused" is very important to point out regarding this experience. Before, I really wasn't sure what I wanted. I knew that I wanted to own a home, but I had no idea where or what type of home. Without actually going out and taking a look at homes, I was denying myself the opportunity of choosing something to strive for, a specific home —a goal. Just knowing that you want to buy something, typically does not provide enough motivation to actually make it happen. For someone like myself, who was stuck in the debilitating world of "fear of the unknown," I needed to know, specifically, what I could have, before I could make a move. I needed a clear goal and a pathway to achieve that goal. And that's exactly what this amazing sales lady provided. She opened up my eyes to the value of clarity and focus when striving to achieve your goals. My hurdles were no longer intangible. In order to own my own place, all I had to do was to get pre-approved and come up with the down payment. The tasks necessary to achieve my goal were clear. No amount of fear in the world was going to stop me at this point.

  The D.C. housing market was hot and getting even hotter with each passing month. Now with the opportunity to own something of my own in this hot market being a real possibility, I leaned on every resource I knew to bring this thing across the finish line. The condominium sales office worked patiently with me in allowing me a few extra weeks to come up with the total deposit required to hold the property. Not wanting to use my credit cards because I knew it would have a negative impact on my credit, I started asking friends and co-workers how they came up with down payments on their homes. I wasn't embarrassed to ask them because I felt confident that most of them were in the same or similar financial situation as myself. Something that I was taught at a young age was never to be ashamed of who you are or think that someone is better than you just because they appear to have money. We all struggle with something at some point in our lives and if we haven't, we will. Asking for help or advice is a sign of confidence, not weakness. Losing out on this condo because I was too afraid to ask for help would have been weakness.

The first person I asked about down payment options told me that their parents gave them their down payment as a wedding gift. I thought, "Wow!" I'm all for hard work and making your own way, but I must say, who wouldn't love a wedding present like that! Some people do have it good. The next person I asked told me that they lived with their parents until they could save enough for a down payment. GOD knows how badly I wanted to own my own place, but there was no way I was moving back in with my mom. It wasn't even an option for me anyway.

The options that I heard so far, were not even close to being viable options in my situation. Still not giving up, I asked a third friend who told me about the option of borrowing against your 401K retirement account as a first-time home buyer. My eyes lit up! She told me to go down to the HR office and ask for information about borrowing from your 401K account. I immediately walked down to the HR office and told them about my situation and asked if borrowing from your 401K was even an option. Up until then, I had never even heard about such an option. It can be a startling revelation when you realize that there are so many things, especially involving financial matters, that we can be completely clueless about, unless they are brought up or shared by others. How was I supposed to know about borrowing from my 401K?

The HR director ended up informing me that my friend was indeed correct, I could borrow from my 401K! This was amazing news. Even though the amount I had in the account wasn't enough for the entire deposit, it was just enough to close the gap that needed to be closed to make the full deposit. Again, GOD was showing me how he expects us to work with what we have "in our hands" and let Him take care of the rest.

Determination to find a way, allowing ourselves to be teachable, and staying positive while operating under faith can lead us to paths that we are unable to see using our own sight. Relying on my own limited vision, I thought the only options I had were to either rack up my credit cards for the deposit or ask my mom for the money, which I was pretty sure she didn't have. It's truly amazing to think that I had everything I needed to buy a home right within my reach. But without going through the process to overcome my fears and demonstrating a certain level of faith, I would have never seen any of it.

Now that I had enough for the deposit, the next step was to get pre-approved for the loan. Surprisingly, this was the easiest step in the entire process. Fortunately, I had good credit at the time and was pre-approved right away. I had done it! My two major hurdles were now behind me. The stress of securing a condo unit was now over. But the next few months brought a different type of stress —waiting for construction to be complete so that I could move in.

I thought I was never going to move into that condo. My basement bedroom had turned into a storage room for all of the new stuff I had already went out and bought for my future new home. There were boxes and bags of new things piled up in every corner. Most of it was from Crate & Barrel and Pottery Barn. The vision I had for my new place was one of peace and happiness, something that I was missing since my parents got divorced. I had always loved the way I felt when I walked into a Crate & Barrel or Pottery Barn store. Everything had a contemporary style, but a cabin-in-the-woods like feel at the same time. I hadn't even gone to closing yet, but I had already gone out and bought furniture, pictures and anything else that I thought would look good in my new condo. This was how sure I was that I was moving out of that townhouse. Without even realizing it, I was giving GOD the highest honor —living in faith.

Roughly six months after my first visit to that condo sales trailer on Wisconsin Avenue, I finally got the big call from the title & settlement company. The waiting and anticipation was coming to an end. It was closing time! I couldn't believe it. It was my turn to be really happy!

The first thing I did when I hung up the phone with the title & settlement company was get on my knees and thank GOD. It was no coincidence that all of the things that I needed to hear, see, experience and go through were perfectly orchestrated to get to this moment.

THE CALM BEFORE THE STORM

As 2007 rolled in, my life was looking on the up and up. I was living in a brand new condominium in one of the most upscale neighborhoods in Washington, D.C. A neighborhood that I used to dream about living in as a kid. My new home was just several blocks from the National Cathedral, the place where I was chosen to attend summer camp as a child. It seemed like my dreams were finally coming true. I was even dating the girl of my dreams and had just gotten engaged. Life appeared to be moving in the right direction.

Along with everything else, my career also seemed to be on the move. I was attending graduate school part-time and working for an architecture firm. All of which lined up perfectly with the real estate and economic boom that was taking place in D.C. at that time. My fiancé and I enrolled in graduate school at the same time. Both of us were getting our MBA's. It was a goal of mine to go back to school to learn about business. With a bachelor's degree in Mechanical Engineering, I was pretty comfortable with my mathematics and technical skills, but I always longed for an education in business. No one in my family owned a business or worked for themselves, so I dreamed of breaking that chain. Business was an area of expertise that I knew very little, if anything about. The confidence that my engineering program gave me removed all doubt that I could complete an MBA program. "Nothing is tougher than engineering school" is the motto that I live by. With an engineering degree under my belt and then going on to get my MBA, I felt like my opportunities would be endless.

With the incredible growth and development that was taking place in Washington, D.C., architectural, construction and development firms were booming with business. Within my circle of friends and colleagues, there was a naïve sense that this real estate boom would go on forever. Friends of mine were quitting their jobs and jumping into the real estate and development business. At the time, it seemed like the smart thing to do and an easy path to wealth. I knew friends that were taking out equity loans on their homes that they had lived in for only a couple of months to invest in new properties or start businesses. At one point, even I —"Mr. Non-Risk-Taker Himself," considered taking out an equity loan on my new condo to buy an investment property. For whatever reason, I ended up backing out. But as time would soon tell, I would be glad I did.

With so many milestones achieved and life changes taking place, 2007 seemed to fly by in the blink of an eye. Getting engaged, steady job, new home, and all of my friends doing well —life seemed to be humming along perfectly. I had even successfully completed my MBA program and was considering new career options. Several of my friends had gone into commercial and residential real estate development and had made out quite well. The itch to do something new was increasing with each passing day.

With an engineering degree, MBA, and ten years of experience in the architecture visualization field, I was considering a transition into real estate development. My goal was to get on the "business side" of building buildings. Financially, being on the business end of things seems to win every time. I was thinking about my future and the lifestyle that I had envisioned for myself. But more importantly, I was getting married in a year and it was time for me to step up my game.

I knew that my inexperience in real estate development would be an obstacle, but that wasn't going to stop me from trying. If I could get my foot in the door, I was confident that I could learn the ropes. With all of my weaknesses, confidence in my learning abilities was not one of them. I have always valued my skill of being extremely teachable and showing an eagerness to learn. To get into real estate development, I would just have to get this skill to shine above my others.

Before sending out a single resume, I reached out to my contacts, both professional and personal. I knew that there was a good chance that someone in my network was either in real estate development or knew someone who was. If you ask anyone they will tell you, the easiest way to land a new job or at least get your foot in the door is through a referral. Who you know carries a lot of weight. This is something that should not be overlooked during a job hunt or career change.
Unfortunately, sometimes in our eagerness to seek something

new, we mistakenly ignore the valuable resources we already have in front of us —"what's in our hands."

Ironically, by the time I started making some solid connections in the real estate development world, the market was starting to drastically simmer down. Owners and buyers were starting to operate more and more under a sense of caution. The mood had drastically shifted compared to only a few years ago, when people were buying anything they could get their hands on. Development firms, at least the smart ones, were tightening their belts because they could see the clouds coming before the storm.

None of this bode well for my chances of getting into real estate development. By firms tightening their belts, this meant a slowdown in hiring, especially for those with no experience —like me. Without any new career leads, I decided to focus harder on my current career. "Maybe I could continue with my current job, but operate a small business on the side," I thought. "This way, I would maintain job security, but also increase my financial opportunities." With my years in the design industry, I was confident that I had enough contacts in my field to build a side business or at a minimum, be a part-time freelancer. Sometimes we have to crawl first before we can run. It looked like I had more crawling to do before that big career jump.

THE STORM: THE RECESSION

One thing that I have learned during my short time so far on Earth is that principles and laws established by GOD do not change with the times. If I throw a ball up in the air on

Wednesday, it will come back down just like it would if I threw it up on Tuesday. The reason being —the law of gravity. It is timeless. And just like the fundamental principles and laws of gravity, there are fundamental principles and laws of economics that are timeless. Throughout history, there have always been those that have tried to convince the masses otherwise. Those masses that have followed them, predictably, seemed to always come up short.

One of the most fundamental sources of America's strength and greatness comes from our belief in the principles of free enterprise economics. As a young nation, we have been able to rise to the pinnacle of economic prosperity due to our adherence to these principles. In 2008, a loud alarm went off, letting us know that somehow we had strayed from these principles.

The market crash of 2008 marked the beginning of the worst economic recession so far in my lifetime. Home values plummeted, new commercial and residential construction came to a grinding halt, and financial institutions began operating in full-blown panic mode. With the country spiraling in economic freefall, I had to ask myself, "What fundamental principles of free enterprise economics did we ignore or violate to cause this?"

Me and a lot of other folks who lived in Washington, D.C. during the recession of 2008 naively thought that we were impervious to the declining market situation. Being home to the federal government and some of nation's most valuable real estate, I never envisioned it getting as bad as it did. As it turned out, no part of the country would be able to run from this storm.

During the beginning of the recession, the architecture firm that I worked for was fairly large, so we were able to ride the waves a little longer than most. This still didn't prevent the weekly panics. As we all started hearing about our friends and family members getting laid off, we couldn't help but to assume that it was just a matter of time before it was our turn. Staying positive, I continued to pray that we could ride this thing out, and we did for almost another year. Just long enough for me to get married and still have a job to help pay for the wedding.

With all of the excitement of being newly married, I stopped focusing on the disastrous economy. Instead, I chose to remain positive and focus on a new future with my bride. She encouraged me to keep looking for new career opportunities, despite the economy. From the moment we got engaged, she had always been a big supporter of me going after my dreams. Her encouragement stemmed from the early conversations in our relationship and me expressing an interest in doing something that I was really passionate about. I liked my current job, but she and I both knew that my heart was crying out for a change. A change that I thought would come easy with getting an MBA, but the economy, unfortunately, had other plans for me.

As 2009 rolled around, having ridden the wave for as long as we could, my firm started laying off people and cutting salaries. The layoffs took place in waves. The first round was the saddest of all. I had to watch some of my closest colleagues cry uncontrollably, as they boxed up their personal items from their desks. Chills rang out all throughout the office. I thought, "Can this really be happening? Am I next in line?" Every day after that first round of layoffs, there was a somber mood throughout the office. People worked with their heads down, keeping a low profile —staying off-the-radar. No one spoke unless spoken to. There was a great fear of not "looking busy."

Everyone wanted to appear productive and essential. It could be anyone's turn next.

The second round of layoffs occurred a few weeks later and were just as painful to watch. The total staff was now cut down to nearly one-third of what it had been at the time I was hired. Things were starting to get a bit too close for comfort for me at this point. Even though I was using every fiber in my being to remain positive, there is a point at which everyone panics. I kept telling myself that they would keep me on board because my computer graphics skills were crucial to their marketing efforts. The only problem with my argument though, was that there were two of us at the firm that had this specific skill and the other guy had been there longer than me. I was pretty sure that if anyone was going to get cut, it was going to be me.

Surprisingly, a few more weeks went by without any more layoffs. Those of us who somehow were still able to dodge the bullet, remained hopeful. The mood in the office had even improved slightly over those few weeks. I think this had more to do with the fact that people had made peace with the situation and accepted whatever fate was headed their way. A few of my colleagues even joked about being the next one laid off, if and when the next round came.

Well a next round did come, but not in the form of layoffs, but salary cuts. The entire staff, including myself, received a formal letter informing us of the necessary changes to our salary due to the current financial constraints of the firm. As thankful as I had been about not getting laid-off in those first two rounds of layoffs, reading this letter was just as painful as any layoff I could have imagined. When I saw what my salary had been reduced to, it hurt me to my core. I had to turn my head so that no one could see my face as the tears fell.

All I could feel was hurt in my heart as I saw eighteen years of salary growth get snatched away in a second.

The hurt stung for a while, but it eventually turned into anger. Not the type of anger that would make me hit or slam something, but the type that would birth determination. All within a matter of seconds from the time I was handed that letter, my attitude of disappointment changed to an attitude of opportunity. I asked myself, "Other than making less money, what is there to be upset about? For years I had been talking about changing careers and doing something that I was more passionate about. Maybe a salary cut is just what I needed to force me to make a change?" As much as I tried to put a positive spin on it, it still stung a bit. Regardless of whether or not you are tired of your current profession, no one likes to have their salary cut.

Over the course of the next few weeks, I remained positive, sending out resumes and searching for freelance work to make up for the salary cut. But unfortunately, with the economy contracting as fast as I could send resumes out, it was like throwing straws against the wind. With all of the fight I had in me, eventually, I would meet my match. My number came up during that next round of lay-offs. In some weird way, I felt relief. In my spirit, I knew that is was time to let GOD take the wheel.

GOD CLOSING DOORS: GETTING LAID-OFF

Of all of the things to be most worried about when you lose your job, I never imagined it would be telling your wife. For me, it wasn't money, paying my bills or even buying food, it was picking up the phone and telling my other half that I was laid-off. Fear was not the reason I was dreading the call, it was pride. I wasn't even two years into my marriage and now this happened. My field, architecture and design, was one of the hardest hit during the recession. As the money dried up for development and construction, so did the demand for architectural design services. My wife and I had been riding along on this downhill slope for quite a number of months and anticipated that this day would come. We were just hoping that I could get into something new, before getting cut.

The most brutal part of the layoff process was that there was no heads-up or advance notice. Your official last day was the same day you received your termination letter. It was like a random sucker punch —one moment you're sitting at your desk and the next, you're "politely" asked to leave and to never come back. To lessen the pain of the punch, I made my exit as uneventful as possible. After I cleared my desk, I briefly said my goodbyes to those I was closest to and headed out the door. I didn't have too many personal things to take with me, so luckily, I could fit everything into my book bag. The last thing I wanted to do was be seen carrying the infamous "I just got laid-off work" brown box out to my car.

Truthfully, book bag or box, it hurt like hell carrying my stuff to my car that day. But I tried everything in my power to remain positive. For ten minutes, I sat in my car in silence and somewhat disbelief. Not knowing what else to do at this point, I decided to make the call. As soon as I called my wife to give her the news, shockingly, the call didn't turn out like anything I expected. She was actually happy for me! She even laughed and told me that she was tired of hearing about "that damn job." "Jermaine, you've been wanting to do something else and now this is your chance to do just that —do something else!" she said. After all, I was "stuck" in a career that I was bored with and clueless how to get out of.

Having someone special in your life who believes in you is one of the most valuable blessings in the world. Just like a boxing coach in the corner who believes in his fighter —sometimes more than the fighter believes in himself, everyone needs someone in their corner that believes in them. My wife told me that she believed in me. Now it was up to me to finish the fight. This was an opportunity to see what I was made of and how well I could handle pressure.

BIGGER, BETTER, STRONGER

I would eventually come to realize that the challenges that I had previously faced in my life, would turn out to be the source of my strength and confidence moving forward. No matter what, I had to remind myself that I was still that kid who: despite the odds —made it out of the projects, finished high school through a painful family divorce, completed college, and graduated from graduate school while working full time. I was not going to allow a downturn in my career to defeat or define me.

There was no doubt in my mind that this was going to be a tough battle, but I was determined to grow from this experience, both professionally and mentally. I heard a saying once that "Adversity introduces a man to himself." Looking back throughout our lives, most of us can probably say that we have been introduced to "ourselves" quite a number of times. No matter how positive or optimistic a person strives to be, losing your job will undoubtedly bring some pain and a certain sense of vulnerability. After all, your financial security is impacted as tough choices and adjustments have to be made.

With the new challenges before me, all I could do was hold my head up and expect things to turn around. Even though I found the strength to remain optimistic, I couldn't help but to occasionally feel frustrated with my current career situation. I sometimes felt like it was never going to end. One of the toughest challenges we face when coming up against a temporary hardship is remembering that it is temporary. Unfortunately, sometimes we can lose hope when we allow ourselves to form a permanent perspective based on a temporary hardship. In my battle to find a new job, my mind was constantly trying to form a negative perspective, distracting me with negative thoughts, and giving me every reason in the world that I was not going to win. But I never lost sight of the fact that this battle, just like all of the others I had faced, was temporary. As long as I stayed the course, I would win the battle.

I've learned that the first thing you must do if you expect to overcome any battle is to accept the fact that you are not above having a bad day —no one is. In my personal experience, I find that the trick is to try to keep that "bad day" from carrying over to the next day. Even the most successful and positive people hit a snag in the road from time to time. Bad days are just a part of life. It is a huge mistake to take on the naïve attitude that "life owes you a good day" or that you deserve a "smooth ride" because of who you are. Life doesn't owe us anything. As much as we want it to be, life is never going to be fair or a "smooth ride." Life is just going to be life —a journey of peaks and valleys. We can either choose to waste time beating ourselves up when things don't go the way we want them to or learn from the hard times and see them as opportunities to become bigger, better, and stronger.

One of the most important things to avoid when we are going through a tough time is taking our personal failures and frustrations out on other people. Sometimes, albeit unintentionally, we shift the negative feelings that we are feeling onto other people, basically blaming them for what we are going through. This only makes matters worse because some of those people that you are taking your frustrations out on, can help you move on. There is a natural tendency to get stuck in playing the "blame-game," blaming ourselves and others when things don't work out the way we planned. In some instances, we may even be justified in blaming others for our problems, but finger pointing is not the way to solve our problems. It fills up our spirit with negativity. Also, by focusing on "who did what and why?" we tend to use up our valuable time and resources. This time can be used more productively by focusing on getting unstuck and working positively through our problems.

FINDING A NEW JOB

Getting back on your feet after any loss requires discipline and focus. Our ability to maintain both is heavily dependent on our actions as well as our environment. An unproductive and unstable environment tends to produce unproductive and unstable results. Knowing that I wanted to get out of my current unemployment situation as quickly as possible, it was important that I do my job search in a productive environment. Initially, I assumed that conducting my job search at home would be a good idea. With Wi-Fi and food in the refrigerator, I thought, "What could be a better place?" Unfortunately, I realized right away that sending out resumes from home was a bad idea. The environment was too comfortable and the distractions were too numerous. During my brief attempt to work at home, my initial routine started with crawling out of bed, then turning on the TV, and making a pot of coffee. After catching up on the news for at least thirty minutes, while enjoying a cup of coffee, I would then finally start browsing the online job sites looking for something to jump out at me. The process of getting out of bed and making my way over to the front of my computer screen, should have taken no more than fifteen minutes to complete, but somehow this process ended up consuming nearly half of the morning. By the time I actually began searching and applying for jobs, it was already time to decide what to eat for lunch.

There I was, sitting in my pajamas, with no job, thinking to myself—this is how it all starts. Even though I was only in the beginning phases of getting my career back on track, I was already getting distracted by false comforts and a lack of motivation. Even something as simple as not getting dressed and walking around in your pajamas has an effect on your mindset. My thought was, there was no need to take a shower and get dressed just to sit in front of a computer all day. Would I have this same attitude in a professional work environment? I don't think so. Why wouldn't it be just as important to shower and get dressed if you are working for yourself as it is if you are working for someone else? Try showing up to work in pajamas and telling your boss that it didn't make any sense for you to spend time getting dressed because all you do is sit in front of your computer all day. Something tells me that you would have a really short work day and probably be asked not to come back tomorrow. Appearance matters and the way you feel about your appearance matters even more.

Not even a week had gone by and I knew I had to switch things up with my job search and get out of my unproductive and uninspiring environment. I needed to be out and about around other people in order to feel like life was moving forward. Going to a Starbucks or Dunkin Donuts seemed like a much more inspiring environment than sitting in front of the computer in the kitchen of my condo listening to the news or the hum of the refrigerator in the background. These early on distractions going on around me were nothing short of a "test." A test to see how well I could eliminate the things that were clouding my focus. Eliminating distractions had to be a priority in my "come-back" plan.

I decided to designate Dunkin Donuts as my new "coffee shop office." It was a lot cheaper than Starbucks and they had better sandwich choices. Located in the parking lot of a strip mall in Alexandria, Virginia, this Dunkin Donuts would become my headquarters for the greater part of my job and career search. It would also become the place where I became inspired to write this book.

During the first couple of weeks at my new "coffee shop office," I decided to "go big" in my career search. With nothing to lose and no reason to hold back, I started applying for executive level positons. I thought, "Why not? I had years of professional experience and an MBA —why not go big?" This was supposed to be a time for risk taking, something I was never good at. With no new job opportunities lined up, now was the time to explore a different career path and test new waters. The fact that I felt like I was taking a risk by applying for an executive level positions was pretty ridiculous. I didn't even have a job —there were no risks!

My mindset was still stuck on thinking small and doing the same old thing. I finally realized that I was excellent at doing the business of an employer, but not very good at doing the business of "myself." Since I had never held a company leadership role, I felt undeserving of a leadership position. The problem with that way of thinking was that I was always relying on someone else to "give me' that position instead of expecting it.

ENERGY AND PERSISTENCE

> **"Energy and persistence conquer all things."**
> —Benjamin Franklin

Regardless of how frustrated I became with the ups and downs of my job search, I never lost hope —ever. I hung my faith on GOD and the power of persistence. I knew that one way or the other, my breakthrough would come. It may not be in a way that I predicted, but a breakthrough was undoubtedly coming. Quite naturally, there were times that I wanted to scream, but I held the course. I would send out at least ten to fifteen resumes a day only to get an email reply two days later —"Thank you for your application and interest in the position, but the position has been filled. We will keep your application on file for future opportunities." But I held the course.

To keep my spirits up, I kept repeating the word "persistence" over and over again in my head. The principle of "persistence" is something that I learned from going to the gym. Instead of working out at the gym and focusing on "if" my body will to change, it's more motivating to focus on "when" my body will change. The idea of "when" something will happen is tangible, it gives you a moment in time to look forward to and therefore, encourages optimism. "Persistence" brings us closer to the "when" and further from the "if." We can all agree that it's a matter of "when" and not a matter of "if" our biceps become toned if we are persistent in doing arm curls three times a week.

    Another valuable behavioral asset that works alongside "persistence" is "variability." You can be relentless in your efforts, but it's also important to try different things and be open to the possible. Any good gym trainer will tell you that adding variety or "switching-up" your exercises is just as important as persistence. Being the remarkable machine that it is, your body will adapt to your routine exercises, with minimum muscle growth. By switching up your exercises, it keeps the muscles in a growth mode as they are, in a sense, unable to predict the next form of strain to be placed upon them. As a result, the muscles will grow to overcompensate for this unpredictability. Just think about that —even the muscles in our body know the importance of being prepared for the unknown.

    The undeniable benefits of persistence and variability that play out in the gym in terms of muscle growth, undoubtedly can play out in our life in terms of growing through our challenges. In my search for a job, I had to be persistent in sending out resumes. I had to maintain the attitude of "when" I would get an opportunity to grow in my career and not "if." But just like growing muscle in the gym, I had to combine persistence with variety in order to grow through the challenges of my job search. That variety came in the form of delegating a certain number of hours to sending out resumes and a certain number of hours to figuring out how to become an entrepreneur. I had to make the decision that following my dreams was just as, if not more important than getting a job. All I knew was that outside of getting a job, I wanted to empower and inspire people to go after their dreams. This was what I wanted to do with the rest of my life. Now was the time for me to find a way.

A NEW STUDENT OF ECONOMICS

"Free enterprise is designed to separate the wheat from the chaff. If you are not good enough you will fail; until you either get good enough or go into another field better suited for your gifts. No stimulus package will change that! This is a non-negotiable economic law." [4]

When I wasn't sending out resumes, I spent a lot of time reading and educating myself on free market economics. Since I had gotten laid-off because of the economy, it seemed like a good idea to better understand the economy. Even with its imperfections, no other system in the world has lifted more people out of poverty than the American free enterprise economic system. Under our free enterprise economic system, "the sky is the limit" for those who are willing to work hard, hustle, and achieve. As Americans, we have high expectations when it comes to our economy and its ability to produce jobs

---

[4] Quoted in Chris Brady & Orrin Woodward, LEADERSHIP AND LIBERTY: PIECES OF THE PUZZLE (Flint, MI: Obstacles Press, Inc., 2009), 81.

and create opportunities for ourselves and our family. These expectations are understandable if you look at the fact that the United States is not even 250 years old and we have managed to create one of the strongest economic engines in the world. Achievement and success is in our DNA. Of course, just like any nation, we have had trying times in our history, both socially and economically, but we have managed to come out stronger each and every time. This current recession and downturn of the economy would be no different.

Admittedly, I had been clueless for most of my life as to why the American free enterprise economic system is looked upon by people from all over the world as offering and creating the most opportunities for themselves and their family. There is no denying the fact that people from all over the world are willing to risk it all to come to the United States in hope of a better life under our free enterprise economic system. I often asked, "What is so bad about other countries and their economic systems that would make so many people leave their own countries to come here?" The current recession had me reflecting on the fact that I knew so very little about the economic system that is the beacon of hope for so many in the world. By not taking the time to understand and appreciate something, how can we expect to keep it?

One of the most positive things that came out of the recession and losing my job was the desire to understand and learn more about economics. After all, all of us depend on the economy for our well-being now and in the future. Considering that I lost my job, it wasn't enough for me to just sit back and expect someone else to do all of the understanding for me. I wanted to know what caused this economic slowdown and why it happened in the first place. In my attempt to better understand the current state of the economy, I first began by looking at myself and then looking at society as to reasons why I we had entered a recession. From an individual standpoint, certain questions came to mind immediately: "What role did I personally play, if any, in causing this recession?" and "What financial decisions, investments, or risks did I take part in that could have contributed to this downturn in the economy?" It is a mistake to underestimate the role that we all personally play in maintaining a healthy and growing economy. Because all of us play a part, it's not unreasonable to assume that our individual actions or inactions contributed to this new and dismal economic reality. I have often heard the phrase, "We get the government we deserve." Well, it can also be said that, "We get the economy we deserve."

Even though our economy is not run by the government, there are policies, however, put forth by leaders in our government that can have a positive or negative impact on the economy. Fortunately, as Americans —free people, we are blessed with the right to choose the leaders in our government and therefore the direction of our country. This is not something that should be taken for granted by any means, as many have sacrificed and died to secure these rights and freedoms. The moment we cast a vote to choose our representatives and leaders, we are essentially choosing policies that will impact and influence the economy and the direction of our country. The general question to ask is, "Are we elected leaders that advocate for policies that will help or hurt our economy?" It is also worth asking ourselves, "Are these leaders promoting economic policies based on the intentions of the policy or actual proven results?" The great economist Milton Friedman once said —"One of the great mistakes is to judge policies and programs by their intentions rather than their results."

In today's political world, there are definitely no shortages of lofty intentions, but achieving actual, positive results seems to go missing. It would be unfair to suggest that a person or politician wakes up in the morning and says to him or herself, "What can I do today to screw up the economy?" The reason that a lot of economic ideas, though well-intended, yield inferior results is due to the disregard for fundamental, proven economic principles. Any realistic economic program has to start with the premise that there is no such thing as a "free lunch." Our parents have always told us that nothing in this world is for free —Why should we stop believing them now?

As I began educating myself on free market economics and looking at the current American economic policies and culture as a whole, I started to wonder what we could have collectively done, if anything, to avoid such a disastrous recession. Being an engineer, I wanted to understand this mess and know what it would take to prevent it from happening in the future. It's funny how quickly we become interested in a subject that normally doesn't concern us, when that subject effects how much money we get to keep in our pockets. For me, the subject of economics all of a sudden became extremely interesting. Like any other subject, I decided to first begin with the basics and look at the history and foundations of the American economic system and how it compares to the rest of the world.

With a bit more free time on my hands, thanks to being unemployed, I decided to educate myself on free-market economics and its principles as laid out by the Scottish philosopher, Adam Smith, the father of free-market economics. *Born in 1723 in Scotland, Adam Smith is considered the father of modern economics. He is best known for his work, An Inquiry into the Nature and Causes of the Wealth of Nations*

(The Wealth of Nations), published in 1776. In this work and other publications, Smith explains how rational self-interest and competition can lead to economic prosperity. The American free-market economic system was built upon these principles espoused by Adam Smith.

Whether you are selling lemonade on the corner or working for an investment bank on Wall Street, you play a part in the overall economy. If you are selling something or providing a service willingly and for an agreed upon price, by definition, you are a player in the free-market economy. Under our free market economic system, people are free to take part in any enterprise of their choosing, if they are willing to put in the work, take the necessary risks and endure the costs that come along with that enterprise. At the heart of America's free market system is competition, which pushes innovation and encourages efficiency in the production and provision of goods and services. The end result is a market place where the demand for services, products, and labor promote a prosperous society. As everyone in society pursues their own individual economic self-interest, society benefits as a whole. These free market principles have led to the most powerful economic engine that the world has ever known —The American economy.

Throughout history, there have always been those that argue for more government involvement and regulation over the economy. Most of these arguments have been made under the guise of "equality" or leveling the playing field as some like to call it. Even though the intentions of such arguments and policies may appear noble, the results they produce typically prove otherwise. Heavy handed governmental economic policies usually lead to less economic freedom for the individual and more power in the hands of the government.

I heard a wise man once say, "No one spends your money better than you do!" It goes against all common sense to think that somehow someone in Washington, D.C. knows how best to spend your hard earned money better than you do. The argument and naïve belief that central planning of the economy through an all knowing and all powerful government can lead to "equality" for all has been crushed to the point of embarrassment. Relying on someone who works on Capitol Hill or even in the White House to make the best decisions when it comes to your personal economic self-interest is like relying on your neighbor down the street to run your home or personal finances better than you.

"We do not help industry by artificially keeping people in the game who have not earned the favor of the customers!" [5]

There are two very simple factors that are at the heart of the failures and waste that result from a centralized or planned economy: lack of efficiency and lack of accountability. There is a popular phrase in the world of economics that says —"When everybody owns something, nobody owns it." This phrase refers to the fact that accountability is all but removed as ownership and responsibility is left to the masses. To illustrate the point, take the example of a rental car that you may rent for travel or business. When the guy at the Enterprise counter gives you instructions on returning the car and informs you that the car must be returned clean and with the same amount of gas, the last thing in the world you are considering is personally handwashing the car and putting in the 93 octane,

---

[5] Quoted in Chris Brady & Orrin Woodward, LEADERSHIP AND LIBERTY: PIECES OF THE PUZZLE (Flint, MI: Obstacles Press, Inc., 2009), 81.

expensive gas. In your mind, you are hoping that it rains on the way to drop off the car and that they won't notice the engine knocking from the 87 octane, cheap gas that you pumped at the QuikMart. The point to be made is that nothing gets taken better care of than the things we own or have a personal commitment to. In the case of a rental car, we justify our lack of accountability by what we perceive as shared unaccountability. That rental car gets used by hundreds of people —Why should I get on my hands and knees washing it and filling it with the good gas just to have the next guy renting it dirty it up and fill it with the cheap stuff? The choice ends up being to do the minimum —what is minimally accepted or what we can get away with. As a result, the condition of the rental car eventually suffers due to this repeat negligence. From the standpoint of Enterprise, the car owner, it may appear that they will suffer losses from the vehicle neglect as well, but as a business, it is more than likely that these costs are passed along to us, the customers in the form of higher rental prices. This simple economic example of the rental car shows the significant role that accountability plays in overall costs. One of the major factors that has been attributed to government programs exceeding their budgets is the inherit lack of accountability within government agencies. As the government grows, it becomes more and more difficult to hold individuals or agencies responsible for their actions, thus resulting in a lack of accountability.

 The other extremely important factor that affects the performance of government or a private business is efficiency. Productivity, profits, and costs are directly linked to how efficiently operations of an organization are performed. In the private world, the incentive for efficiency is obvious. There are only so many hours in a day and only so many hands to do the work. It is in the self-interest of the individual or business to perform tasks in a timeframe that maximizes benefits, performance, and return. An individual or business has an incentive to run like a well-oiled machine due to the fact that they bear all of the costs and reap all of the benefits. In the case of the government, the costs associated with any lack of efficiency is passed down to the tax payer: you and me. As a result, we the people end of fitting the bill and more money gets taken from our paychecks.

As a modern society, of course there are important roles for the government to play and tasks that we, as citizens, have to pay for through our tax dollars. The fortunate thing for us is that we have the Constitution that clearly defines these tasks and we have the right to question any government activity that goes beyond these tasks. Everything that the government does has to be paid for…everything! There is no such thing as a free government program or benefit. It might appear to be free to the individual or business receiving the benefit, but society as a whole picks up the bill. Every subsidy, benefit, or program that the government provides has to be paid for through taxes or borrowing. As informed citizens, we just should be aware of the costs that come along with government programs and do everything in our power to make sure we are getting what "We the people" are paying for and at a cost that we as a nation can afford. Being informed and aware of the nation's financial commitments and economic health is vital to maintaining a robust free market economy.

For some Americans, including myself, this free market economic system that we have been fortunate enough to be born into, we often take for granted. This lack of appreciation or indifference isn't so much as a result of the lack of love for what America offers us, but more due to the lack of understanding as to why our system offers such opportunities. As much as some of us appear to take America's free market system for granted and the fruit that it bears, we are often quickly humbled at the moment its benefits come to a halt. This was the case in 2007, when the housing crisis brought the U.S. economy to its knees. It was then that a lot of us, especially the younger generation, realized for the first time how delicate our economic system can be and how much we all depended on it for prosperity.

As the disaster unfolded, the job market became brutally difficult for a vast majority of people. Even for those in the most specialized and sought after career fields, there was no escaping the wrath of this recession. Unemployment was skyrocketing and there was no immediate end in sight. Fear and uncertainty gripped every single American. To make things worse, the inescapable, 24-hour cable news networks were airing the collapse non-stop. If you were anywhere with a television, you got to witness the step-by-step, minute-by-minute, hour-by-hour and day-by-day collapse of the U.S. economy —in real-time.

It's hard to imagine anyone in this country that wasn't impacted in one way or another by the recession. Depending on age, experience, career industry, and geographic location, the level in which a person was personally impacted by the recession varied significantly. For younger, working age people, most of the pain came in the form of salary cuts, lay-offs, and shrinking job opportunities. For older employees approaching retirement age and seniors who were already retired, the blow to their financial security was devastating. They painfully witnessed the stock market tumble and their 401K and retirement savings disappear right before their eyes.

Retirement age undoubtedly increased and retirement spending undoubtedly decreased as a result of the market crash.

Things were spiraling uncontrollably downward according to every news outlet. There was even talk in the news about the idea of a potential depression! All of the negative news was just leading to more and more fear and uncertainty. At some point, too much fear and uncertainty can lead to a self-fulfilling prophecy. There was no doubt that we were experiencing a severe recession, but at what point does the news go from informing us to unintentionally misleading us. If all we are seeing on TV is our country falling apart —Are we to assume that this will have no impact on our actual reality? There is a great quote by Wayne Dyer that says —"If you change the way you look at things, the things you look at change." Since there was no way I could change what the news reported, I had to change "my news." Instead of watching and seeking out the latest negative headlines, I began studying economics and researching the causes of a recession. If I could have a better understanding of free-enterprise economics, I could possibly play a better role as an informed citizen to do my part in preventing a recession.

Like any tragedy, there is always an urge to seek out and blame a "bad guy." In this case and like many other financial collapses, those big banks and investors on Wall Street must be to blame. "Wall Street had screwed us again!" was the narrative being pumped out by most of the news media. All I kept thinking was, how could Wall Street be the sole blame for all of this destruction and chaos? The relationship between Wall Street and the everyday working man is not a forced relationship, so shouldn't some of the blame be shared? I thought long and hard about this recession and what could have been done to avoid it, if anything. What role did I personally play? What role did my employer play? What role did my neighbor play? All of these questions swirled around in my head and I wanted answers. Based on conversations with my friends and family, it quickly became apparent that I wasn't the only one who was unintentionally ignorant when it came to understanding the true causes of this recession. Because none of my friends and family members worked on Wall Street, they considered themselves innocent victims of the recession and having played no role whatsoever. Then it hit me. Sometimes "unintentional ignorance" plays just as critical of a role as any when it comes to preventing or causing a disaster.

The big question for nearly everyone was: How would we all adapt and overcome this economic collapse and feel the least pain? For me, only a few weeks had gone by since I had gotten laid-off, but it didn't take me long to realize that this was no bump in the road recession. The American economic engine had come to an abrupt halt. Regardless of the negative outlook, I made up my mind to remain positive and make the best out of the situation. This was supposed to be my opportunity to pursue my passion!

The idea of taking advantage of my "involuntary" free time to pursue my dreams was all good and dandy, but I needed some type of income to pay the bills. I sent resume after resume with no luck. Even applying to positions that were outside of my field, but presumably qualified for, based on my education and experience, turned up nothing. The message was loud and clear —most companies were not looking to hire and train someone who didn't already have experience in the position they were looking to fill. On the job training was a thing of the past. This new economic reality was the complete opposite of what I remember conditions being like in the late 1990's. Back then, it seemed like the only thing you needed to get a decent job was a degree and a professional resume. Employers were looking for "potential" more than anything in their candidates for hire. This is the beauty of having a healthy, robust economy —employers tend to focus more on whether or not they consider you to be "trainable" and if so, they are willing to invest in your potential. Boy, those were the good old days.

MILTON FRIEDMAN: THE GUY WITH THE GLASSES

One of my most valued treasures that I took from graduate school came from a simple homework assignment on economics. This was a subject that didn't really spark my interest at the time, probably due to the fact that I considered it an area of interest for people with real money. Watching those stock market numbers scroll across the screen on CNBC looked like a foreign language to me. Sure, I didn't consider myself an economic illiterate or broke, but I thought that those mainly interested in economics were the wealthy or people coming up on their retirement who needed to monitor their investments. Maturing with age, I have realized that it's a big mistake not to respect or be educated in matters concerning money. How can we expect to make money if we don't understand it? Believe me, if it meant making more money, I wanted to understand it!

As I got started on my simple economics homework assignment, I noticed that a requirement was to watch a short video of a debate on economics that was led by a bald man with "big square shaped" glasses. Although it was tough to pay attention to the issues being discussed because I couldn't help but stare at those "big-square glasses, the brilliance of this speaker broke through the distractions. His name was Milton Friedman, an American economist and one of the most logical and intelligent men I had ever heard speak. The topics of the video lecture and debate focused on free market economics and making the case for a limited role of government in a free market based society. Even with my apathy towards economics at the time, the sheer genius of his logic, the simplicity of his arguments, and his mastery of inescapable truth was so inspiring. His confidence of the subject matter was on another level. I would listen to his audience ask him questions or make statements that I just knew would back him into a corner or make it impossible for him to defend his positions. Without skipping a beat, not only would he win the argument, but he did it with a smile on his face. Always remaining a happy warrior, Milton Friedman's confidence was rooted in a solid understanding of the fundamental principles of the free market. He didn't speak in platitudes, but gave logical explanations and arguments to defend free market principles. His brilliance was his ability to debate an issue without offending or demeaning his opponents, but instead allowing his opponents to see the illogic in their arguments on their own. He accomplished this by asking questions that would push his opponents to argue from an "unprincipled" position, which would expose the inconsistencies in their arguments. It was at this moment that I realized there is difference between knowledge and truth —Truth is everlasting, knowledge changes.

After being blown away by watching this first video of Milton Friedman, I began to search for other videos of him making the case for freedom and a true American free enterprise system. I was amazed by the number of lectures and debates there are online of this brilliant economist who made understanding economics enjoyable and interesting. I wondered, why hadn't I heard of this great man until now? In my mind, this is a person that should be listened to and studied in every high school history class, every college economics class, and in every political movement that advocates for freedom. To strengthen my point, many of the debates that we are having in our country today regarding the appropriate role of government in our economy have been debated by Milton Friedman decades ago. Even more surprising, a lot of the arguments in favor of more government involvement in the economy have already been made decades ago and defeated soundly. Just by making a few searches and clicks on your computer you can easily see that the arguments on the side of freedom win easily against those who argue otherwise. History has unequivocally shown that it is not kind to societies that don't err on the side of freedom and place ultimate trust and faith in their governments.

Milton Friedman respected the laws of economics like an engineer respects the laws of physics. By definition, these laws are based on proven, unwavering principles —Nature's laws. He knew and understood that society benefits most economically when the people are free to make their own economic choices. This allows, what is often referred to as, the "Invisible Hand" to control and produce market forces that drive economic activity. Milton Friedman was awarded the Noble Memorial Prize in Economic Sciences in 1976 and the Presidential Medal of Freedom in 1988.

- Chapter 19 -

Unstuck: Time to Make the Donuts

REBUILDING THAT OLD MUSTANG

In order for something to be truly remade or reborn, it sometimes has to be stripped down to its core, exposing its true, basic components. Take for example, an old classic Ford Mustang that an owner wants to restore. He dreams of bringing it back to its original beauty and glory. The first thing that owner does before starting the restoration process and spraying a single drop of paint on that aged and damaged body is to sand it down to the metal. This removes all of the old paint and imperfections that have built up on the body over time. He doesn't want the old coats of paint, dents and dings to interfere with the new coat of paint. Once the body is sanded and smoothed, a primer coat is applied and then it is finally painted. The reason that the owner goes through the tedious process of sanding and stripping the car body down to its core is to insure that when painted, its true beauty shines through. He knows without a doubt the true beauty of that car and the way it will look when fully restored. The reason he knows this is because he has seen that car at its best. Either through pictures, on TV, or in person, he has been able to see what that car looked like at its best —the day it rolled off of the assembly line. Even though a car can be restored, it is never as good as the day it was new. Even with the best tools and restoration skills in the world, a car is only new once. Sure, every component of a car can be replaced with a new one, but at what point does that car go from being restored to being replaced? Our life as human beings is much more exciting than the life of a car. We grow and adapt with age, always looking forward to being better than we were yesterday. That classic restored Mustang has already seen its best day. The only thing it has to look forward to for the rest of its life is to hopefully get restored as close as possible to its original condition by its owner. Fortunately for a car, it is unaware of its limited life.

As human beings, we don't roll off of an assembly line, polished and in tip-top shape. No one knows what he or she will look like or how they should perform at their best. We are born to learn, grow, and become wiser and stronger with life and age. Unlike a car, when we are created we don't come with manuals, photographs, or specs that show how we should look and perform at optimum capacity. We have to live and experience life in order for that to be revealed. As of today, no one has been able to conclusively predict what we are capable of becoming as humans. GOD likes to keep this inside information all to himself it seems.

Getting covered in rust over time has never been a problem for humans, but our spirit and potential to shine can get tarnished just the same. Setbacks, negative experiences and life itself can start to affect our attitudes and our ability to live to our fullest potential. Whether or not you allow these "setbacks" to define you is key. Just like rust, if we allow negativity to remain, it will eat away at our core and eventually consume us. This ultimately ends up effecting the way we are seen by others and the way we see ourselves. As human beings, we have to constantly do our own unique type of "sanding and "painting" in order to put on and keep our best shine. Like the guy that takes the time to fix up that classic car because he knows it's worth it, we have to know that it's worth it to do whatever it takes to maintain our shine, our true beauty, and our potential. The good news is, unlike a car that is at its best when it is "born" on the assembly line, the scrapes, bumps, and bruises we encounter as human beings along the road of life are actually a necessary part of our journey in order for us to become our best. Most successful people will tell you that those scrapes, bumps, and bruises were critical in developing the strength and attitude to become successful. It is pretty fair to say that we have to get knocked down a few times in order to realize our true beauty and capabilities.

STARTING THE ENGINE: SETBACK FOR A SETUP

Sitting in front of a computer every day at Dunkin Donuts, sending out resumes and hoping that someone or some company would come along and make my dreams come true was taking entirely too long. It was frustrating and disheartening to think about all of my education and sacrifice and there I was, unemployed and practically begging for someone to give me chance at a job. Believing in myself and trusting in GOD, I knew that there had to be another way to support myself and at the same time achieve happiness. I should have realized years before I got laid-off and put in this frustrating situation that fulfilling my dreams and following my passion would require me to completely switch my life around. Coming out on top was going to require me to do things that I had never done before. I was going to have to stretch myself and let go of fear and limiting comforts. Most importantly, I was going to have to take full responsibility for the current challenges in my life and take full responsibility to overcome them.

The education and experiences that I had acquired over the years were great at providing structure in my life, but that structure was also preventing me from growing. Up until this point, my life had seemed to always be following a path leading to comfort instead of a path leading to growth. This was a weakness that I carried with me ever since my parents got divorced. Ever since that painful event took place, my decisions and actions have always been based on "What would provide me the most security?" and "What would provide the most comfort?" Because of the pain, I was always making comfort a priority in my decision making process. Growing up after the divorce, there is no question that this worked as far as me not losing control of my own happiness. However, making "comfort" my goal was also impeding my ability to be all that GOD intended me to be.

I heard a speech one day by the famous motivational speaker, Les Brown, who said that "If you have something special to share and you don't act on it, life will move on you!" This is something I have grown to believe more and more each day. Life has an unpredictable and sometimes counterintuitive way of achieving the greater good. Looking at my personal situation, it took one of the worst recessions in our lifetime in order for me to get my act together and I still have a ways to go. GOD must have known that no matter how many times I heard it from my good friends and the people I loved that I needed to start taking more chances in life, it was never going to be enough to rid me of my fears. I can't help but smile when I think of the idea that GOD thought so highly of me that He was willing to crash the U.S. economy so that I could finally step into my greatness.

Quite naturally, I did a lot of self-reflection in between emailing resumes and developing ideas for pursuing my passion. Anyone who has ever found themselves having to aggressively find a job, knows exactly what it's like to have to look at yourself in the mirror and be honest in assessing your talents and abilities. Under the pressure of needing a job, your perceived weaknesses will often overshadow your obvious strengths. It is important to remember that these perceived weaknesses are only "your" thoughts and aren't necessarily perceived the same way by others. Of course, we all have weakness and it doesn't do us any good to not acknowledge that simple fact. I have learned that it makes for a smart strategy to focus on your strengths and use them to create your opportunities. Businesses often use this strategy when they are attempting to enter a market. Instead of spreading themselves thin, they will often allocate their resources to their core strengths and use those strengths as an effective way to enter a market. There is only but so much time and energy available in a day, so why waste them on the negative things.

It might come to a surprise to some, but every single one of us, in a sense, is a "business." Just like a business in the traditional sense, we have to establish a vision and a mission for ourselves. If we don't know where we want to go and what we want to accomplish, this makes it extremely difficult to reach any of our goals. Similarly, just as a business, we have to make investments in ourselves and develop our gifts and talents so that we can share them. All of us have unique talents, but we must make the time to hone those talents. This can be achieved through hard work, practice, education, and experience. Putting in the work, will allow you to become comfortable and eventually confident in your abilities and talents. Once we finally recognize that we have something special to share with the world, the only thing left is to share it. For me, getting laid-off, as stressful as it was, forced me to make time for myself, to invest in myself, to recognize my talents, and to develop the courage to share my talents with the world. Just as Les Browns said, "Life was moving on me." Losing the comforts of job security forced me to become stronger and more determined to make things happen. I heard a very powerful saying one time —"Some people will not become a 'diamond' because they avoid the pressure." This had been me for years up until this point. The pressure was now surely on and this time there was no way I could avoid it.

- CHAPTER 20 -

AWAKENING THE ENTREPRENEUR

"Entrepreneurs don't sit around and wait for opportunities, if they aren't there, they create them."

One of the most fascinating things about life is that we never know how a seemingly, random experience will change us for the rest of our lives —how a single event can awaken us to our purpose. For me, it happened over thirty-five years ago and I didn't even realize it in the moment. My life was forever shaped on the day I watched my stepfather return from sea after a long tour of duty overseas aboard a Navy aircraft carrier.

It all began on a beautiful and sunny Saturday afternoon in Norfolk, Virginia. I was 12 years old at the time, my parents were newly married and my stepdad was serving in the U.S. Navy. After a six month tour of duty out at sea, my stepdad was scheduled to return to port at the U.S. Naval base in Norfolk, Virginia. My mom, uncle, and I drove almost four hours to Norfolk from D.C. to watch his ship dock from its long journey. As we stood near the pier, the ship slowly approached the dock and families began to cheer. One of the first things I noticed was the continuous line of sailors standing at attention as they stood side-by-side along the top deck of the ship. It was as if they were guardians of this great symbol of American power.

As the ship got closer to the dock, I began to see their brave facial expressions as they stood at attention with their arms crossed behind their backs. Their uniforms blew rapidly in the wind as their bodies remained fixed to perimeter of the top deck. Even as a kid, I became overwhelmed with emotion. My chest tightened, and I felt a sense of fullness in my soul. I glanced over at my uncle and noticed tears streaming down his face. Even though this was a day of happiness and celebration for my stepfather returning from sea, I knew why my uncle cried. The sight of men serving something greater than themselves is a reason to cry. This is when I realized what it means and feels like to love your country.

Looking back, this was the moment that the seed of my passion was planted. This was my calling. A calling to find a way to share this awakening experience of patriotism and love for our country that I was blessed to experience. As the years passed and as I grew older, I finally came to realize that it was time and that I was capable of doing something big and bold to ignite the spirit of my country.

Passion and love for my country have been growing in my heart ever since that weekend trip down to Norfolk, Virginia. I always knew that I wanted to do something with this passion, but I didn't know how or what exactly. All I knew for certain was that if what I saw that weekend was able to make such a positive impact on me and how I feel about my country, then there isn't a doubt that it would have a similar effect on others as well. Before seeing that ship and those brave American marines and sailors returning home on that sunny weekend, I had no concept of patriotism, sacrifice, and duty. I was just a kid from the projects with no actual sense or understanding of America's greatness and how blessed we are to be born here.

It made a huge impression on me to see with my own eyes the guys and women who hold the line to protect what we have and cherish as Americans and to see the sacrifice on the part of the families they leave behind. All of this was leading me to my dream of one day finding a way to capture and share the same experience and awakening that I did. Appreciating and loving your country is empowering as well as unifying. There is no denying how great it feels when we are united as a country. Most of us get to experience the power of unity during events such as the Olympics, the Super Bowl, or during a fourth of July celebration. For me, this was never enough. In my mind, all of this was just a tease of what America could be. If I could only find a way to make every day feel like the fourth of July in each and every American's heart, then I would have achieved my dream.

In order to understand how to best awaken America's spirit and to inspire passion for our country, I had to first look at the things that inspired me. I have always been inspired and moved by imagery that celebrates winning. To be able to capture the experience of winning and what it takes to get there is a unique and special gift. Whether it is producing a commercial about a winning sports team or directing an ad that promotes our great armed forces, if it is well produced and from the heart, it will empower and inspire the audience. I can recall numerous commercials and ads throughout my lifetime that have personally touched my spirit or given me a sense of empowerment. One of my most memorable commercials that has stuck with me throughout the years is the famous U.S. Marine Corps commercial that depicts an infinite line of marines appearing to be standing on guard along the streets and shores at numerous locations throughout the United States. The narration and music, combined with the precision and fierceness of the U.S. marines, moved me as a proud American. The imagery and symbolism of this commercial, in my opinion, embodied everything that a marine stands and fights for, which is to protect and defend every inch of this great country.

Even though years had passed since I first saw that marine commercial, it was still ranked up there with one of the best. The reason it stuck out so much to me is because it showed me the power of imagery and sound in delivering a message. As I brainstormed ideas of how to bring more passion and love for our country, that marine commercial always came to mind. With so much movie and television producing talent in this country, I couldn't help but wonder why more projects weren't being developed with the intention of highlighting the greatness of American. Inspiration is so important to maintaining our identity and purpose as Americans. It is important that we see ourselves for who we are and who we want to become. As far as I knew, there wasn't any popular movement or dedicated media platform created with the purpose of inspiring passion for America and this saddened me greatly. Did those in the film and TV industry forget about their own country or have they grown so big that they now take America for granted? Something so basic, but yet so important, like being proud of your own country, is increasingly missing in our art and media culture.

As Americans, we have something truly special and hold a unique place in the history of the world. If you ever doubt

America's special place in this world, just ask the people from other countries who are willing to leave everything they have ever known behind to make a life for themselves and their family here. As for me, love and appreciation for this country becomes more and more a part of who I am with each passing day. Whether I am watching the fireworks down on the mall in Washington, D.C. or listening to someone sing the national anthem before the Super Bowl, I always find myself getting emotional and feeling proud to be an American. When I was younger, I typically tried to hide these emotions because I didn't think it was cool to express your feelings openly, especially patriotic sentiments.

Even at my grandfather's funeral and burial services, in which he received full military honors for his service in the army, I tried my hardest to hold back my emotions. At first, I tried to hide the hurt and sadness I felt by allowing myself to be distracted by conversations with family members and old friends who came to pay their respects. When the time came for the actual burial and hearing the sounds of the honor guard team firing three volleys from their rifles, no amount of strength in me could keep me from collapsing a few feet in front of the casket, overcome with emotions. This was the first time in my life that I ever experienced feelings so powerful that I literally collapsed to my knees. It was less about sadness, and more about love, and respect for this man, my grandfather, who served his country, even during a painful time in America's history in which he probably felt his country didn't serve him. Crying on my knees, I was honored and proud to be his grandson.

It's sad that anyone, at any age should ever feel like they have to hide their proudness and patriotism towards their country. Looking back on the emotions, the tears, the proudness, and the patriotism, I realized that they were all signs pointing me in the direction of my true passion. But, like most people who are blessed enough to discover their true passion, it's often quite difficult to actually pursue it. The two things that often cause the most difficulty or stand in the way the most are fear and a job. Up until this point in my life, I had both working against me, but now having been laid-off, I just had fear to overcome.

TAKING THE FIRST STEP

The most important thing to making anything happen is taking that first step. Just because you don't have the answers to all of your questions doesn't mean you shouldn't get started. For me, it was that constant battle with that internal voice that kept saying, "You're not prepared…you haven't thought this through enough…how is this going to pay your bills?" All of these self-imposed doubts were continuously trying to keep me off my game. It was tough, but I fought to resist every one of them. Building an empowering brand and inspiring people to love their country may have not been something that I ever done before, but my passion and sense of purpose was going to be enough to take me to where I needed to go.

The vision for what I wanted to create was much larger than anything that I had ever done or seen before. My goal was to inspire people to achieve their greatness and spark an awakening in this country. The first step was going to be building a website which would serve as my springboard. Having something for people to see and share would be the fastest way for me to get feedback, grab ideas, and build support. It wouldn't be enough to talk about what I wanted to create, I needed something to show. I have often heard that some million dollar ideas have been sketched on a napkin, I was sketching mine on a computer screen.

Like any entrepreneur, I was continuously looking for inspiration to fuel my creativity and passion. The one source that I could always count on was music. To take my passion to next level, I would sometimes put on headphones and blast some Metallica, Creed or Three Doors Down. The strength projected in their music would put me in a mood of invincibility, especially cranked up. This is exactly what I needed to push through the voices in my head telling me to stop pursuing my dreams and to wake up and get back to sending out resumes. There were even times when I would be listening to music while thinking of ideas and would tear up because the song that I was listening to would provide the perfect spark to a new idea. It was as if GOD was using the music to talk to me and tell me to keep pushing forward. Considering what I was attempting to do, how could I not get emotional? This was my passion, and I was going to make it happen. I was following my dream, which was to build a movement and a brand that celebrates the country I love.

Through this entire creative process, I was realizing more and more that releasing your emotions is a good thing. Emotions are the language of the heart. There was one day in particular that my emotions were really getting the best of me. I was working on a developing some ideas for a section of my website that would be dedicated to the history of the U.S. Marine Corps. All of a sudden, Daughtry's song "What About Now" comes on and it just hit me to my core. "Look at what I am creating." I whispered to myself. Tears began to pour down my face as I began to feel so proud and thankful that life had brought me to this place.

My vision and purpose was becoming clearer and clearer. I was now ready to use everything I had in me to bring my vision of patriotism and love for this country to reality. If I felt such passion for this country, I'm sure there were others out there as well. There was no way that I could be the only one out there looking for a way to awaken the spirit of this country. Where were the voices that celebrate the brave men and women who protect this country? Where were the voices that celebrate freedom? Where were the voices that celebrate free-enterprise? Where were the voices that celebrate hard work and earning your success? Where were the voices that celebrate winning? Where were the voices celebrating leadership? These are just some of the questions that were constantly eating away at me and there were no answers in sight. I felt that America was crying out for a cheerleader. With the blessings and opportunities that this country provides us every single day, I was determined to do my part in giving back. It was all still a dream at this point, but I was confident that I was on my way to building that dream.

BUILDING A DREAM

"Imagination is everything. It is the preview of life's coming attractions." —Albert Einstein

When I decided to take the journey to follow my dreams, I decided to follow GOD's rules and release my faith. Now that I was unemployed and left without any excuses not to take more risks, it was the perfect time to put my entrepreneur hat on and put my faith to the test. The first thing I did was to take a look at some current and past endeavors that sought to inspire and shine light on sources of America's greatness. It was one of the most inspiring research projects that I had ever taken on. During the entire process, I learned so many great things about America and the principles in which it was founded. I felt like I was finally getting a better understanding of what makes America so special. As I continued my research and looked for as many sources of inspiration as I could find, one day I came across a new cable show called "Real American Stories" that aired on the Fox News Channel every weekend. The show was a series of video documentaries on the true life stories of random Americans from all walks of life. Everyone from Vietnam veterans to Hollywood actors were interviewed and asked to share their personal and unique American story. It was so inspiring to watch and listen to people from different experiences and backgrounds explain why they were proud to be an American.

    The weekly episode also had an online version of the show where you could watch the inspiring interviews online. This is where I got the idea to do my own version of Real American Stories. My vision was to create a complete online multimedia experience combining video interviews of everyday Americans sharing their unique and inspiring stories along with exciting figures and events in American history. The goal was to create the number one online resource and community for inspiration and empowerment.

Now with a vision and sort of an idea of what I wanted to create online, I needed to familiarize myself with the technology used to create online blogs and other social media platforms. In a weird coincidence, a day before I got laid-off, I just so happened to notice a co-worker, named Will, browsing the firm's blog site. The company had just recently launched the site and it was still in a testing phase. As far as I knew, not many people in the office knew it even existed. Being a bit curios, I asked Will if he knew who put the site together. Surprisingly, Will laughed and said that he had been put in charge of putting the site together. Without hesitation, I pulled up a chair right next to his desk and started asking him questions about how to create a blog site. He told me that the process was pretty simple and that there was a free online blog creation and hosting platform called WordPress. The site had thousands of free templates for creating personal and professional blog sites. These templates made the process of embedding videos, articles, postings, and links into a blog website simple and easy. Even though there were lots of really nice templates, none of them matched what I envisioned perfectly. I knew that I would either have to hire a web designer to build my custom site or do it myself. Call me crazy, but figuring out how to customize a blog website sounded pretty exciting to someone who was spending nearly every morning sending out resumes.

Because I chose the best Dunkin Donuts in the world as my office, there just so happened to be a Barnes & Noble right across the parking lot. I was in and out in five minutes with a beginners guide to building a WordPress blog. This engineer was smart enough to know that there had to be a "WordPress Websites for Dummies" out there somewhere that could help me get started on building a website. At first, the idea of learning code and developing my own site was a bit intimidating, but I knew without a doubt that I could figure it out and have fun doing it. It wasn't an option for me at the time to pay to have a website built, so I was forced to do it on my own. If I worked smart, I knew I could do it. Not allowing myself to get intimidated by what was unfamiliar to me at the time was key. I kept thinking about the famous quote by Robert Schuller "Inch by inch, it is a cinch; yard by yard, it's hard." By learning how to build a website by taking small steps would allow me to grow my confidence.

THE ENGINEERING PROFESSOR

Developing a confident approach to figuring things out is one of the most important things that I picked up as an engineering student in college. Making it through one of the toughest engineering programs in the country taught me that even if you don't know how to do something, have the confidence to know you can find out how to do it. Thanks to one of my strictest engineering professors, I was taught a valuable lesson on how to approach unfamiliar or complicated problems.

This lesson of a life time took place during my junior year in one of my toughest engineering classes. It involved a homework assignment where I was able to get through all of the problems except for one. I spent nearly two hours trying to solve this particular equation, but I finally gave up and decided I needed help. We had an exam coming up at the end of the week and I knew that there was a good chance that this type of problem would be on the exam. Not wanting to take any chances and screwing up on the exam, I decided to go to the professor's office and get help. The last thing I wanted to do was to go to the professor, but I had no choice at this point. As engineering students, we would get our asses chewed out if we went to a professor without showing some evidence that you at least tried to solve the homework problem. In my case, I was definitely headed for a good chewing.

Eventually, I got the nerve to walk across campus, over to the engineering building and knock on the professor's door. After three quick knocks, he opened the door and I asked him if he was available to help me with a problem on the homework assignment. He hesitantly invited me in and told me to take a seat in front of the chalk board in his office. I swear it seemed sometimes these professors had no heart. The next thing he did was ask me which problem I needed help with and to show him how far I had gotten. I said to myself, "Here comes the chewing!" I told him that I didn't have anything to show him because I couldn't do the problem. This was a big mistake. He looked at me like I was an idiot. Keep in mind that this was during the 1990's, when it was still okay to look at kids like idiots and not have to worry about the political correct BS that has become so much a part of college life today.

The professor asked me again to start the problem on the chalk board and again I told him that I didn't know how. He knew that I was frustrated, but he insisted that I start the problem before he would even think about helping me. Ready to walk out of his office at this point, I turned to him and said, "I need help." That's when the professor jumped up from behind his desk and asked me, "Do you know how to at least write the problem on the board?" Angrily, I replied, "Yes" and proceeded to write the problem on the chalk board. Once I had the problem written, he then asked me if I knew the next step to take. This time, I thought before I answered and I began to write what I thought was the next step. He replied, "Good, now what's after that?" Again, I wrote down what I thought was the next step and to my surprise I heard another "Good" from the professor. It was at this point where I became stuck.

No longer sounding frustrated with me, the professor jokingly said, "I thought that you didn't know how to do the problem." I replied, "I don't." "But you just did the first two steps without any help," the professor responded. Suddenly, before attempting to go any further with solving the problem, the professor explains to me the importance of not being afraid of trying. Also, he demonstrated how getting through the first steps in solving a problem can provide you with clues and the help you need in getting through the next steps. After a few more back and forth struggles, we eventually came to the solution.

At the end of my much needed "grilling," it became obvious that finding the answer was only a small part of the lesson. The professor's goal was never to embarrass me, but to get me to see how much my confidence grew with each step taken. As my confidence grew, so did my ideas on how to solve the problem. I began to actually use my brain instead of shutting down in frustration. That engineering problem no longer intimidated me. Also, this lesson taught me that by diving into a problem, you can began to ask the right questions that will put you closer to the solution. It all has to do with elevating your confidence, which allows you to work smart. I find this lesson also applicable to problems in everyday life. With each layer that we peel back on a problem or task, we expose clues on how to peel back the next layer. The perceived wall of complexity is weakened with each layer of doubt removed.

I never forgot the lesson I learned from that engineering professor over twenty years ago. Here I was now, twenty years later, and needing to solve another problem, but this time no professor around to help me. There I was with a vision, but feeling alone and like I lacked the knowledge and financial resources to create it.

THE BATTLE: VISION TO REALITY

Sometimes when we have a task or goal that appears too big to achieve, and we mistakenly look at it only from an intimidating distance, it often appears too difficult to attain. If I would have considered all at once, everything involved in bringing my vision to reality, the chances are that I would have become overwhelmed and even discouraged. In addition to learning to always take the first step, I also learned as an engineering student that the best way to approach a complicated task or to reach a difficult goal is to break that task or goal into smaller tasks or goals that become less intimidating to achieve. Now with a beginner's book on WordPress in my hand and a template to start with, I was confident that I could get started on building my own website. Even if it wasn't perfect in the beginning, my fear of trying was gone.

Within a matter of a few days, I had a basic blog website up and running. I started posting inspiring articles on American history and highlighting various leaders that played a significant part in building this nation. Learning about who we are as a nation and what we are capable of achieving has always fascinated me, so building this site was exciting. I chose the name "RealAmericanSpirit®.com" as the name of my website. The reason I used the word "Real" is because I wanted to dedicate all of my efforts to highlighting the "Real" things that make America great —the people and the principles in which it was founded.

Building RealAmericanSpirit®.com was like building a piece of a dream. The big difference was that it was real and I could actually see it coming to life on my computer screen next to my cup of coffee. The challenge was to keep pushing forward with creating "the dream" and not get stuck or caught up in doubting whether or not what I was doing would have value. It's amazing how our minds will sometimes play tricks on us or keep us from taking any action just because we aren't one hundred percent sure that we will be successful. When it comes to your dreams, your fears and doubts have to be controlled or they will control you.

A SOLDIER NEEDS A UNIFORM

Sitting in Dunkin Donuts one morning and doing my usual routine of sending out resumes, but trying to build a website, I began feeling a bit frustrated with my situation. Life was testing me that morning. Instead of letting my thoughts and emotions get the best of me, I left my cup of coffee and laptop for a few minutes and walked outside to get some air. I needed to reboot my thought process so that I could remember who I am and what I am capable of achieving. Instead of diving back into my routine that day, I decided to take the day off and figure out how to fight and win this battle.

The next morning I decided to spend the day focusing on ways in which I could maintain my strength and keep my focus. Strangely, the first thing that came to mind was the power of "teamwork." There is no denying the great things that can be accomplished through teamwork. When teams are formed to achieve a specific goal, the members of that team each bring certain talents and skills to the group. By combining these talents and skills, they work together as one to develop a capability that is far greater than the sum of each of their individual capabilities. As a result, the team can achieve a goal far greater than that which can be achieved through individual contributions of its team members. This multiplying effect is known as synergy. It is the power that fuels a winning team. Whether it's a sports team, a military unit, or a law enforcement agency, synergy is the energy behind the team's success.

In order to maximize synergy, it is essential that a team functions as one. This "cohesion" requires disciplined interaction between the individuals that comprise the team. There are many tools used to promote team cohesion, but there is one tool that is utilized more than any other —the uniform. The first part of the word uniform is *"uni,"* which means one or consisting of one and the second part is *"form,"* which means to bring together parts or combine. Aside from being a means to identity its members, the uniform more importantly establishes cohesion and common purpose within a team. Once an individual places on the uniform of his or her team, a mental transformation takes place. That individual acts, reacts, and performs under the conditions of knowing that their actions have a direct effect on the success of the team. Not only is the individual responsible for carrying their own weight, but the weight of the team as well. There is a greater demand for performance of the individual and therefore each individual delivers more for the team. As a result, the individual and the team grows in strength and capabilities.

The uniform establishes a mindset. Once an individual places on the uniform, they mentally prepare to bring their "A-game." Without even realizing it, putting on a uniform is like placing on a layer of armor. The uniform can block mental distractions as well as allow you to overcome certain fears and weaknesses. It establishes a focused and determined state of mind.

One of the things I would often struggle with the most when trying to achieve my goals was the ability to stay focused and relentless in my efforts. Sometimes, I would try to pretend that I was a soldier or warrior committed to winning a battle. By doing so, it often gave me the confidence I needed to fight my way through to reaching my goals. As a "dream warrior," the only thing I was missing was a uniform.

Make no mistake about it, whenever we are trying to make a major change in our life or do something that has never been done before, we are in a battle. It is a battle for our own happiness and a future that we can be proud of. The recession of 2008 marked the beginning of one of the toughest battles of my life. But it also marked the birth and beginning of new dreams. For me, one of those dreams was to become an entrepreneur. My very first steps towards becoming an entrepreneur came out the idea of designing my own entrepreneur uniform or "gear." This gear would act as armor to repel fear and maintain focus, which is often the toughest struggle for an entrepreneur. This gear that I would wear into battle would be called "Real American Sprit® Gear."

In designing my own gear, I started off with a jacket. This jacket would have two essential components that would provide the power for me to fight through my fears —GOD and the Flag. GOD would allow me to overcome my fears and the Flag of the United States of America would always remind me of my purpose. If these two powerful forces can carry a soldier through battle, there wasn't a doubt in my mind that they could carry me through as well.

Through prayer, a vision, and using the skills that I had acquired over the years, I was able to design a brand and gear that I would someday share with the world. Until then, this would become my uniform for battle as an entrepreneur.

PATIENCE IN BATTLE

In life, as well as in battle, it's imperative to have options and backup plans. You can never perfectly prepare for or predict all conditions that you may encounter along the way. One minute you can be moving along smoothly and then all of a sudden, you can be forced to change course.

I knew that getting on the path towards my dreams was going to be unpredictable as well as challenging. Even though I was making significant progress in building my vision and brand, I never stopped sending out resumes. Being confident that things would eventually turn around in the future is one thing, but being able to take care of your responsibilities today is another. No matter how badly you may want to achieve your larger goals in life, the bills have to be paid. The irony is, the more I remained positive about achieving my larger, future goals, the more positive and optimistic I became about my immediate goals, which was to acquire a consistent source of income. Without even realizing it, the positive momentum I gained from pursuing my passion carried over to my job search. Never underestimate the power in positivity.

With what appeared to be positive momentum working in my favor, I had even finally gotten a positive email response for a potential job opportunity. The position wasn't particularly in my field of expertise, but at least it was good news for a change. The opening was for a sales position at Xerox. I purposely started applying for sales positions, thanks to the suggestion of my wife. Always being the strong and smart person in my corner, she made the suggestion that I get sales experience during the market downturn. It would be good not only for my resume, but also for building confidence and relationship skills. As an engineer, I always considered myself pretty confident, but being confident at selling yourself is a completely different kind of confidence. Being able to handle rejection and getting a door slammed in your face is a special skill in and of itself.

After a series of interviews and with no other full-time opportunities lined up, I ended up accepted the sales position. Even though the base salary before any commissions was only barely a third of what I was making at my previous full-time position, I was eager to learn and seize this opportunity. I learned a long time ago, never to be above an opportunity that will allow you to gain experience and grow. Even during high school when I worked part-time as a dishwasher at a Chinese restaurant or as a cashier at Popeyes, it always proved to be a growing and educational opportunity. Professional sales was going to be different than anything that I had ever done before, but I was eager to avoid my natural instinct, which was to stay in my comfort zone. As I have come to learn more and more about life, "playing it safe" and succumbing to fear can be the biggest obstacle to our growth.

As we embark on the winding road in pursuit of our dreams, we often assume that an open door or clear path will be clearly visible or standing in front of us. Sometimes open doors and paths are hidden around corners. Jumping into a sales job, my immediate reaction was to ask myself, "How is this going to bring me closer to my dreams and goals?" Without any obvious open doors or clear paths at this point, all I could do was trust in GOD and remember what He had done for me in the past.

Immediately when I started, I knew that this was going to be an entirely new world for me. The good news was that I would be working for a sharp manager. This guy was a true sales professional who was a master at his craft. He had no problems cracking jokes about me right away, which I kind of liked. It demonstrated his humility and sense of humor, which I considered highly valuable and desirable in a manager. There I was, a rookie, but an engineer with an MBA, obviously capable of learning in his eyes, but who didn't know the first thing about sales. This was going to be a fun ride.

During my first few weeks in training, I quickly noticed how everyone put a lot of energy into their appearance and the way they dressed. I kind of knew that this was going to be the case, being that my wife was in sales. Even though I was new to the sales profession, I still knew that looking good when you stand in front of that mirror is just as important, if not more, as how you look standing in front of other people. Admittedly, I had slacked off a bit in the dress department ever since I got married. Shopping for clothes took a back seat to other fun things. Of course I still had nice things for going out or for celebrating special occasions, but not enough to sustain me for an everyday sales job.

Being new to the industry and wanting to make a good impression, I had to go shopping. For the first few weeks, it wasn't a big deal dressing the part, but I became a little worried with each passing week because I didn't know how long I could keep the GQ look going. Between picking up a new shirt and tie every few weeks and the weekly dry cleaning bill, this dressing up everyday thing was pretty expensive. Fortunately, I have a good wife by my side who suggested that I get a navy-blue sports jacket instead of trying to wear a suit every day. I only owned two suits, so there was only so many ways I could switch things up relying on shirts and ties. My Brooks Brothers, standard issue, navy-blue sports jacket allowed me to dress up any pair of dress paints or khakis and at the same time still look professional. I sure did have a lot to learn about the tricks of the trade in the business world.

In sales, I quickly learned that it's all about confidence and the image you have of yourself. This is the source of your strength. With each passing day, I was realizing that people skills can actually take you farther a lot faster than other professional skills in certain situations. I would see it first hand when guys, who were newly hired and didn't know the first thing about the copier industry but would go out in the field and grab strong leads or even close a deal. All because of their confidence and the belief in what they were doing. It was mind blowing to watch. This coming from a person who had spent all of his previous professional career in the design industry, where success depended mostly on technical skills as opposed to people skills. There was one funny situation at my sales job in which dressing sharply and looking confident almost got one of my sales partners beat-up. The incident happened during the whole "Occupy Wall street" drama. There were a large group of protestors who had been camped out at McPherson Square

Park in the heart of downtown D.C. for weeks. Our sales office was right around the corner from the camp sight and we would sometimes walk through the park on the way to make sales calls or to grab lunch at one of the nearby sandwich shops. There was one particular day that John, one of my sales partners was walking alone through the park like he would normally do any other day. For some reason on this particular day, the "Occupy" crowd started yelling at him and harassing him for being a "one percenter!" Fortunately, John made it back to the office without getting hurt or hit by anything. When he finally calmed down and told us what happened, we couldn't help but laugh at the fact that they called him a "one percenter." These "Occupy" folks weren't that smart after all. If they knew what John and the rest of us were actually making at that sales job, they would have probably invited us into one of their tents.

With all of new experience and education I was gaining in the sales industry, I grew tremendously in my people and relationship building skills. Also, my confidence level increased drastically with each rejection or slammed door in my face. Also, with each passing day being out in the field, I learned more and more about how to focus on goals and less and less on obstacles preventing me from getting there. The education that I was getting at my new sales job was turning out to be just as valuable, if not more, as any college degree. Never in a million years would I have thought that I would have been working in sales with a degree in mechanical engineering. Not attempting to be arrogant, but doing sales was not one of my career goals.

Looking back at this experience, it was all part of GOD's perfect plan. Just like other things that happened in my life that didn't necessarily make sense at the time, its purpose would come to light soon enough. I ended up staying in sales for roughly a year or so until I got a series nudges in my gut telling it was time to move on. The first nudge came one afternoon when our sales manager told the team that he had something scheduled at the office before noon and wanted us all in from the field and to make calls from the office until then. At around eleven o'clock, we were all told to come out into the showroom for a presentation. At first, I just thought it was just going to be another presentation on a new copier or some new scanning software. As we all got up from making calls and headed toward the showroom, we noticed an unfamiliar face standing next to our manager. He had a small suitcase strapped to a portable dolly as if he came to our office straight from the airport. Scott, our sales manager introduced us to the rather modestly dressed but very confident looking gentleman named Anthony with a tough to pronounce Italian last name. With a thick, unmistakable New York accent, he thanked us for inviting him and stated that he was an author and professional sales coach and that he was invited to do a brief presentation on cold calling and effective sales strategies. Right away, I noticed that some of the cocky sales reps on my team were sizing him up before he was even five minutes into his presentation. Arrogant "know-it-alls" are rarely in short supply in the sales business. Because I was still a rookie and eager to learn, my ears were at full attention.

  The first thing I admired about this guy was his obvious love for the sales business. He spoke with such confidence and at one point even bragged about making just as much money, if not more, as any doctor or lawyer. His respect for the sales profession was unwavering and suggested that if we wanted to be successful in this business we must regard ourselves as true professionals, never considering what we do as not a true profession. According to him, it was all about the mind and the attitude, not the product. He mentioned that he had a book coming out that was going to be titled something like "Put me in the middle of the desert and I can sell a copier!" We all laughed at the title, but knew that this guy should be taken seriously. No one can possibly have that much confidence and not be successful. Even though I didn't plan on being in sales for the long haul, that didn't stop me from respecting and admiring this person who was obviously a master at his craft. I dreamed of one day being as confident in what I do as this guy. I started asking myself, "Why wasn't I in a career that I could be passionate about like this guy?" With doubt and a million questions circling around in my head, I started feeling trapped. There I was, surrounded by passionate sales people, doing what they liked to do and all I kept feeling was out of place. It wasn't that I was questioning whether or not I could do something but rather, did I want to do it?

After the presentation, I left the office with mixed feelings. Part of me wanted to really put in the work to get good at sales and the other part wanted to put in the work to get really good at something that I was passionate about. The competitive side of me wanted to prove to the team and myself that I could become really good at sales. This was my ego talking big time. Whenever my ego tries to dominate my thoughts, I always seek out a second opinion from those close to me. I decided to call a friend who knew my career situation and also knew the things I was passionate about. The first thing he noticed when he answered the call was the frustration in my voice. Even though I was telling him how awesome of a sales presentation that guy gave, he could sense the edge and insecurity in my voice. As I was going on and on about how good this guy was at sales, my friend abruptly interrupted me and said, "Jermaine! That is his game, not yours. Stay focused on your game." He reminded me of why I took that sales job and what I was supposed to get out of it. My goal from the start was to learn how to sell and to understand and respect the psychology behind it. Being the number one copier salesman was not my goal. Being number one at empowering people and inspiring them to love and take pride in their country was my goal.

That guy that gave that sales presentation was undoubtedly good at what he did, but he couldn't hold a candle to the ideas and passion that I have for awaking the spirit of this country. Les Brown always talked about getting to the point in your profession where you can confidently say, "This is what I do." Well, I wasn't there yet, but GOD had already told me that one day soon I will be able to say, "Empowering people to achieve greatness and inspiring them to love their country is what I do."

Now with my head right and a clear perspective, I hung in there with my sales job, remaining focused on my goal —to learn. As months passed, I realized that being positive and open to learning provided a sense of peace and purpose. I took on the attitude of being thankful for the opportunity to learn sales as opposed to focusing on what I didn't like about sales. Although I had developed a better attitude about my sales job, the itch to pursue my passion remained. It wasn't going away anytime soon and it was foolish to try to convince myself otherwise. Trusting that one day I would see a sign, I kept grinding on and doing the best I could with what I had. This approach has always brought me out on top and I expected nothing less in this current situation.

With each passing month, I seemed to be getting more and more educated and confident with the process of selling. At this point, I had yet to win any awards, but I was confident that

I was on track to win some soon. As long as I remained persistent and kept making calls, the success would come. It was always at the end of the month where I would realize the true pressure of sales. From corporate leadership all the way down to the sales managers, the end of the month meant do what you have to do to hit your number. All of this pressure of course ended up being applied directly to the backs of the sales reps. As tough as this time of the month was, it was during this monthly crunch that I learned the most about how to produce under pressure. During those crazy pressure weeks, I would always drive into work listening to Journey or Pearl Jam to get me hyped up before I got into the office. One morning, I was switching CD's and I had the radio station set to CSPAN for some strange reason. Usually, I would pay no attention to what was being discussed and would go right back to pumping my music. But for some strange reason that morning, I paused before switching the radio back to CD. For the next twenty minutes, what I heard being discussed on CSPAN brought me back home to the thing that I am passionate about the most, this country. This was one of those "signs" or "nudges" that life was giving me that I spoke of earlier.

Sitting in traffic on the George Washington Memorial Parkway, I became glued to the conversation on the radio. They were discussing the fight over the newly proposed healthcare law being pushed and promoted by President Obama and the Democrats. CSPAN was taking callers on the topic and had separate call-in lines for Republicans and Democrats. I'm guessing that CSPAN created two different call in numbers to make sure that the time given to each side of the argument appeared equal, but I couldn't help but cringe at the fact that Americans were being forced to pick a political side in order to express their viewpoints. Considering how so many of us today put political party affiliation above all else, even common sense, it wasn't a surprise to me that the callers were supportive or unsupportive of the law based on party loyalty. Also, what I found most fascinating about the arguments was the lack of *"critical thinking"* used before taking positions. Instead of making arguments based on true and viable intelligence, some callers were calling in and giving arguments based on how they "feel" about the issue. Just saying that you "feel" like healthcare should be free or a right is not a logical argument compared to arguments based on individual rights, constitutionality, and economics. I might "feel" that my neighbor should take out my trash every other Friday, but that doesn't mean that he should or he has to.

As I continued to listen to the calls coming in on the radio, both sides were just digging in and talking past one another. It boiled down to one side arguing "feelings" and the other side arguing "principles." If I didn't know any better, my "feelings" might tell me one day that I should be able to jump out of a window and fly but the "principles" of gravity tells me otherwise. Fortunately, all of us don't have to be as smart as Albert Einstein to know that humans can't fly, just like all of us don't have to be a geniuses in economics to know that healthcare can't be free. In order for anything to be given away for "free," it has to be first paid for or produced by someone. The idea that a government can provide healthcare or medical insurance at zero cost is illogical in a free society. If eliminating the problems in our society associated with high costs are as easy as passing a bill or signing a law, why wouldn't we pass bills and sign laws to make military equipment free or food or water or even televisions? Feeling that something should be free is nothing more than expecting someone else to pay for it.

The United States of American is a republic and therefore our Constitution doesn't support the idea that citizens can just vote themselves "things" at the expense of their fellow citizens just because a politician thinks or feels that it's the right thing to do. History has shown us that ideas and policies implemented that allow people to, essentially, vote themselves "things" or what they consider personal necessities is a dangerous road to go down if we expect to remain a free society. Developing the attitude as a country that we can rely on a politician for our well-being is like relying on a king for scraps or what he deems you worthy of having. As Americans, it would be wise for us to always remember that those that came before us didn't sacrifice and give their lives so that we could be taken care of at the expense of our neighbor, but for us to be free to take care of ourselves and our neighbor.

As the calls kept pouring in about this hot topic of healthcare, I became more and more glued to the conversation. For me, it wasn't so much about the healthcare law, but more about the direction that our country was going. Growing up in the projects and having grandparents who relied on government assistance for income, I personally know how critical of a role government can play in people's daily lives. It would be an easy argument for me to make that my grandparents needed government assistance considering the racial disparities and lack of economic opportunities they faced being black and living through the 1930's, 40's, 50's and throughout the 60's. So for the callers who were basing their arguments on "feelings," I understood that impulse completely. But I also understood the argument coming from the other side. For very good historical reasons, a vast number of Americans fear that the growth of government and its ever increasing involvement and control over our lives is a direct threat to our freedom. History provides many examples of the danger associated with large, powerful governments. It would be wise for us, as informed citizens, to understand and be aware of these historical lessons.

Still sitting in traffic, but only a few blocks away from the office, I was just about to put my CD back in until a very passionate caller came on the air. She was calling in on the Republican line and was obviously very upset about the proposed healthcare law and what it would mean for the country. She sounded like she could have been in her sixties or seventies, and based on her slight accent, she probably was calling in from a rural part of the country. There was something about the sadness in her voice that really grabbed my attention. The way she expressed her love for this country and her concerns that this healthcare law would open the door to the government being able to strip away our freedoms. She mentioned how other countries have lost certain freedoms due to increased government control and involvement in people's lives and that she feared that happening to America. She referenced Europe and other parts of the world who have trended more and more towards government control and how that has impacted the freedoms, prosperity, and security of their people.

Becoming increasingly emotional as she expressed her fears and concerns, the caller eventually broke down and started crying on the air. She made a tearful plea that we, as Americans, not do this to our country. The CSPAN moderator tried to comfort the elderly woman as best as he could. I could tell that she was trying her best to control her emotions but unable to do so. Right as the moderator was getting ready to let her go and thank her for the call, she tearfully made one last statement that I will never forget. In a sad voice, she said,

"This is America...We love America so much...we love America." Hearing this and feeling this lady's obvious love for this country, I began to tear up. She was crying because she was afraid. This was someone who was putting the country first and who was truly concerned about the consequences that this law would have on our country.

As a kid, my grandfather always told me to listen and pay attention to what older people have to say because, in his words, "You don't get old being no fool." So I paid close attention to what this lady had to say and really thought deeply about why she was this upset about a particular law passing. To many, these are common sense concerns, but are too often mocked as crazy, extreme right-wing, uncompassionate or even racist positions. Call me crazy, but there is nothing racist about being distrustful that your government will be a good steward of your healthcare, but at the same time be almost twenty trillion dollars in debt. Compared to private industry, the government runs like an inefficient machine whose parts are rarely, if ever replaced, but oil to run it is in endless supply. As long as a government knows that it can take in tax dollars, there is very little incentive to strive for superior results. This is what I envisioned with regards to this new healthcare law, a program promising lofty goals, but no genuine concern with results.

The state of politics in our country is more divided than ever. You have one side of our political spectrum who wants to grow the power and size of government in order to implement their best-intentioned plans of "progress" on society. It's worth noting that history has shown us that the last place a growing, powerful government will take us is in the direction of "progress." On the other side of the political spectrum, there is a strong belief that progress and prosperity can be best achieved by maintaining a constitutionally limited government, which has a responsibility to protect individual rights. It's obvious that neither side is short on intentions, but history tends to be only interested in results and so should we.

I asked myself a simple question, "How would it be possible to provide health insurance to the uninsured for free or at an "affordable" cost without increasing cost to others?" The money either had to come from increasing taxes or increasing costs to the people who currently have insurance. Without doing either of these, the basic economics of the plan just didn't add up. The idea that a politician can even convince people of such economic fantasies says a lot about the state our country is in as far as being informed citizens. Promising people things that may help them individually, but hurt the country collectively is not a sustainable solution. Why would it be okay for my neighbor and his family to have to pay more for their health insurance just so that I can have health insurance? Wouldn't this breed resentment and envy in our society? Since when as a country do we justify pulling our neighbors down in order to push another up? Isn't the beauty of our free enterprise system is that it allows growth and prosperity without being at the expense of another? These are just some of the questions that we need to ask ourselves before we can truly move forward as a country.

With all of the thoughts and emotions running through my head after listening to CSPAN that one fateful morning, it was a clear wake up call for me to get more serious about making a positive difference in this country. More subtly, it was also a sign letting me know that the days of working in copier sales might quickly be coming to an end. For me, this wasn't about a healthcare law, this was about "truth." That entire healthcare discussion and argument reminded me of an assignment I was given in graduate school on critical thinking. The point of the assignment was to teach techniques on how to ask the right questions in pursuit of the truth. Before realizing the value and importance of critical thinking, I used to be like one of those self-righteous callers who would think that they were right about something just because they "felt" right. Thanks to a very valuable homework assignment and wise graduate school professor, I learned how to practice the skill of "critical thinking" before accepting or making so called simplistic arguments. This invaluable skill is key to not being just another source of noise in an argument, but rather a contributor of facts and the truth.

Something as simple as a talk radio conversation had lit a fire in me that I couldn't ignore. There are just times when GOD taps us on the shoulder and on this particular morning, I felt as if GOD was tapping on mine. There was a silent voice speaking to me and saying, "Don't stand on the sidelines any longer." This was a voice I could not ignore.

- CHAPTER 21 -

ASKING THE RIGHT QUESTIONS: CRITICAL THINKING

"The truth is incontrovertible, malice may attack it, ignorance may deride it, but in the end there it is."
—Winston Churchill

TRUTH

My Pastor Dale O'Shields once said during a sermon on truth —"Live for what lasts." Truth is the one thing on this earth that truly lasts. Living for it is living for knowledge and living for greatness. There are many things in this world that change with the times —"truth" is not one of them. As the world around us changes ever so rapidly and information is more accessible than ever before, you would think that "truth" would ring out louder than ever before. Unfortunately, the opposite is true. In fact, in this smartphone, 24-hour news cycle world, as "information" becomes more and more abundant, it becomes easier and easier to become distracted, deceived, misguided, and misinformed. The first step in preventing the possibility of being distracted or misguided is to first acknowledge that there is a big distinction between information and truth. Anyone or anything can crank out information, but the value of that information is determined by whether or not it is grounded in facts and truth.

As a society that once relied on the news media to serve as a check to our political leaders and those in power, we know find ourselves being "informed" by those who put political and self-interests above the country itself. To add fuel to this fire, the political arena in our country is becoming more and more ideological and combative in nature. Substantive issues facing our country are being ignored while trivial and selfish matters dominate the headlines. Trying to decipher what gets reported in the news can be frustrating for those of us who just want to be told the simple truth so that we can decide what's best for the country. There is a popular quote that says: "Better to be slapped with the truth than kissed with a lie." If we ever intend to be all we can be, both as individuals and as a country, these are wise words to live by.

In today's world, unfortunately, voices of truth and empowerment are increasingly getting drowned out by all of the politically correct noise being pumped out across the media and entertainment spectrum. The saddest part about this situation is that it is the weakest in society that gets hurt the most. Information without truth at its core does not empower and does not encourage growth. Although, it may be easy to blame the media for the downward trend in our country, there are others forces at work as well. We as a nation are straying more and more away from the very principles that made us a great nation in the first place. The beauty and benefits of freedom, self-reliance, hard work, and personal responsibility are unfortunately down-played by many in today's political and "wanna-be" elite class. In the real world, these ideals and principles matter.

COFFEE AND A CUP OF TRUTH

There was a very popular civil court case back in 1994, Liebeck vs. McDonald's Restaurants, also famously known as the McDonald's coffee case. The case involved a woman who accidentally spilled a hot cup of coffee in her lap that she purchased from a McDonald's drive thru. As a result, she received severe burns in her pelvic area and ended up suing McDonald's for medical and punitive damages.

Just like a lot of people, when I first heard about the case in the media, I thought it was crazy that someone could sue a restaurant and possibly think that they could win for spilling a cup of hot coffee in their own lap. As I latter found out that the woman, the plaintiff, actually won the case, I immediately asked myself, "How is this possible? Is common sense and personal responsibility no longer expected in this country?" I'm pretty certain that this was the first reaction of most people familiar with this highly publicized case.

It was almost impossible not to hear about and pass judgment on this case, it was all over TV and throughout talk radio. The opinion shared by most people I knew and the so called experts in the media, was that the woman was at fault. Some of the most common opinions I heard were: "She should have known better." "What was she thinking?" "She has no right to sue because of her own negligence." "It's her fault, why should McDonald's pay her anything?" Overwhelmingly, this was the side taken by most people I knew. It was also the side taken by a lot of folks on TV and radio talk shows. Even if it wasn't intentionally, the media was pushing the idea that it was beyond ridiculous that somehow a person who suffered severe burns as a result of spilling hot coffee in their own lap was somehow deserving of damages from the restaurant who sold them the coffee. Like a lot of information that is discussed and disseminated in the media, important details and facts are often omitted. Even with the limited information discussed and available to the public at that time regarding the case, most people, just like myself, accepted an emotionally based argument as the only possible truth.

By the time I was in graduate school, years had passed since I heard about the McDonald's hot coffee case. In fact, I had actually forgot about the case until it was brought up again by one of my graduate school professors. During one of our lectures, the professor asked if anyone in the class remembered the McDonald's hot coffee case. It was no surprise that everyone in the class raised their hand. Next she asked what we remembered about the case and what opinions we had formed about the decision of the court to award the plaintiff in the case such a large amount of money for damages, pain, and suffering. The entire class unanimously agreed that the lawsuit was frivolous and the amount awarded by the jury to the woman for damages was excessive and unjustified. The class even went so far as to criticize our legal system for encouraging irresponsibility and abuse.

After expressing our opinions openly, the professor gave us a homework assignment related to the case. The assignment was to read the legal text of the McDonald's case in full and then read a book from our assigned reading list titled *"Asking the Right Questions: A Guide to Critical Thinking" by M. Neil Browne & Stuart M. Keeley.* Included in the book, were a series of questions and assignments that we were instructed to complete once we were done reading the case and the book in its entirety. At the time I was given this assignment, I considered myself a fairly smart guy, but, admittedly, I had no idea what the term *"critical thinking"* meant. Of course I knew what the word "thinking" meant, at least I thought I did, and I knew that the word "critical" meant very important or dangerous, depending on the context. Based on how the opinions of my classmates drastically changed regarding the McDonald's hot coffee case after we read the case and completed the assignment, I quickly realized that I wasn't the only one in my class who didn't know what the term "critical thinking" meant.

In short, *"critical thinking"* can be described as a learned set of "thinking" skills that allow you to evaluate and process information in a disciplined and unbiased way. The goal being to identify and eliminate false information and ideas before forming opinions or conclusions. This can be achieved by acknowledging problems, weaknesses, and inconsistencies in an argument. Adopting such an intellectual behavioral pattern allows us to think and access information in a more comprehensive and intelligent way. The ability to think critically decreases the chances of being unintentionally and intentionally misguided. It also empowers the individual with the ability and confidence to approach and solve problems without relying on help from others. Watch out politicians.

From the very beginning of the assignment, I really wasn't sure what new information I would get from reading the case.

We had all heard about this sensationalized case for weeks on the television and radio. My initial thought was that the professor just wanted to refresh our memory of the case before reading the book on critical thinking and completing the assignment. All of these assumptions were eventually flipped on their head once I actually read the case and discovered all of the facts. Immediately, I realized that I did not know as much about the case as I originally thought. Also, there were a lot of facts about the case that were not discussed in the media or were simply ignored. "But why?" This was a question that I could not ignore and that I was hoping to answer.

After reading the case, which left me with more questions than answers, I proceeded to the second part of the assignment, which was to read the book on critical thinking. Compared to other required readings in my MBA program, this was a very thin book and a short read. I couldn't help but wonder, "How important could this book possibly be compared to our other required readings?" It was just too short to be of any real, significant value, I thought. Well, we all have heard the saying "Good things come in small packages." This book was definitely a "good thing." In fact, it was a complete game changer as far as the way I would process information moving forward. Despite its size, this tiny book contained some of the most useful tips and tools for empowering individuals in their abilities to seek truth and achieve intelligence. Because this book provided me with the tools to test the logic in my arguments and expose the biases in my opinions, what I assumed and thought I knew of the McDonald's case was completely flipped on its head.

As a class, our initial opinions and assumptions pertaining to the case were based on selected and limited information. Most of which came from the media or talk show hosts. The common mistake that we too often make is that we assume that if it comes from the news or is talked about on a talk show, it must be true, Right? We unfortunately buy into the idea that because a story is discussed on the news, there is an obligation to tell the whole story and all sides. Big mistake. It might come as a surprise, but sometimes there are actually three sides to a story —the right side, the wrong side, and the truth.

    Before actually reading this case, all I ever heard discussed was the huge amount awarded to the plaintiff in the law suit and how irresponsible this lady was for putting hot coffee in her lap in the first place. Never did I hear on TV or the radio about previous injuries and severe burns that resulted from the extremely hot temperatures of the coffee served at McDonald's restaurants. Never did I hear about the previous instances or cases in which McDonald's was legally warned and ordered to lower the temperature of the coffee they served, but yet refused to comply. With huge financial resources and power over public opinion, McDonald's was reluctant to modify its coffee temperature. In this particular case of Liebeck vs. McDonald's Restaurants, the amount awarded to the plaintiff by the jury was based more on repeat court order violations and correcting McDonald's behavior and less about putting money in the plaintiff's pockets. Of course, none of this background information on the case was popular in the media or on the talk shows and therefore public opinion formed as such. If more facts on the case or some historical context leading up to this case were allowed to play out in the court of public opinion, "Would the national dialogue regarding this case have been any different?" You bet it would.

    Even without background information on the McDonald's case, my entire class had formed an uninformed opinion on the merits of the case. After reading and learning how to think and evaluate the case "critically," we all realized that we were ignorantly guilty of making a ton of assumptions. By examining this very familiar and highly discussed McDonald's hot coffee case through the prism of "critical thinking," my classmates and I quickly saw how easy it was to be persuaded and even misguided in forming our opinions. In this case, our misguidance wasn't based on what we knew or what we were told, but rather on what we didn't know and what was untold. As a result, prior to becoming critical thinkers, our conclusions on the McDonald's hot coffee case were based almost entirely on partial information and emotions. With this valuable homework assignment, we were all taught the value of *Asking the Right Questions*.

EMOTIONS VS. TRUTH

"If we lose sight of seeking truth, we become distracted by intentions at the expense of results."

In everyday life, it's amazing how our emotions get ahead of our ability to think rationally and critically. Some of what should be the most obvious and basic things in life are so tough to grasp when we allow our emotions to get involved. Rational and fact-based decision making quite often takes a backseat to our emotional instincts. It's sad to say, but there are a lot of people that are in power and make a living off of emotionally based decision making and the inability to process and evaluate information critically.

This is commonly on full display when we turn on the TV or pick up a newspaper and are presented with sound bites or simple answers to complex questions. A lot of times, complex questions or issues are framed as simple questions or issues on purpose. The purpose being to persuade and encourage over simplification of the issue or problem. For example, if you ask the average high school or college student if he or she thinks that water should be free, you probably would get a resounding "yes" for an answer. If you ask that same student if he or she thinks that water companies shouldn't have to pay their employees, you probably would get a definite "no."

Immediately, we see the inconsistencies in these two positions. "How can we have clean water without paying someone to provide it?" Without considering the basic costs and economics associated with providing this so called "free" water, the students failed to think "critically" before forming their opinions. Two simple questions come to mind when considering whether or not water should be free: 1. "Who will pay for cleaning and purifying this 'free' water?" 2. "Who will pay for maintaining the infrastructure that delivers this 'free' water?" As you can see, by not asking ourselves critical and important questions pertaining to even the most straight forward and simple subjects, we can easily form illogical opinions and conclusions due to the traps that are put in place by our emotions and feelings. Simply "feeling" that water, healthcare, food or any other perceived life necessity should be free is not a position based in sound, consistent logic. Just because a position invokes a certain level of emotion or is highly supported in certain social circles does not qualify it as a logical or even realistic position. This "free" water argument is a simple and straightforward example of a scenario that demonstrates how quickly and easily we can be suckered by our emotions. After all, who wouldn't want free, clean, and safe drinking water for everyone?

As mentioned earlier, some people in our society start businesses and even run for public office based on their assumptions about our inability to think critically and ask the right questions. When it comes to having a heart for your fellow human being, I have come to realize that Americans are some of the most giving and charitable people in the world. Sadly, the feelings and emotions associated with giving and charity are sometimes viewed as a weakness and something to exploit by some among us. It is their assumption that feelings and emotions will dominate the decision making process, which allows for the opportunity to exploit and deceive. For a deceptive business, the target could be an uninformed customer or in the case of a savvy politician, a low information voter. To them, it's all about "how you feel," rather than truth and results. If we lose sight of seeking truth, we become distracted by intentions at the expense of results.

"Perception unchallenged becomes reality."

Masking the truth or omitting facts, especially by those who we rely on for information (i.e. news sources, elected leaders, scientists, educators, etc.) is a powerful means of manipulation. A good friend once said, "The most insidious power of the news media is the power to ignore." On a daily basis, we all hear hot and sometimes controversial topics being thrown around on the news, by politicians, celebrities, or even amongst our friends. It wasn't until I hit the age of thirty that I realized how many of my friends were smarter than Albert Einstein, Milton Friedman, and Thomas Jefferson all combined. Who would have known? It's amazing that some of us think we know everything we need to know when we graduate college or hit thirty. It's as if "history" started yesterday. Even though I am always tempted, the older I get, the more I try to stay away from discussing controversial topics with friends and family. I have learned that to have a productive debate and discussion about any issue, an environment of respect has to be established. All parties have to be genuinely interested in the opinions and thoughts of others. I learned very fast in my adult age that bringing up politics at the bar after seven Bud Lights is never a good idea.

It takes effort to think critically and to seek the truth in all matters, especially in a world where information surrounds us in every direction. Practicing critical thinking isn't so much about being the smartest person in the room. It's more about having a mindset that is trained to avoid making assumptions and forming opinions without first asking the right questions. At the root of most assumptions and opinions are personal biases. We all naturally have personal biases regarding particular issues or subjects. As critical thinkers, we must identify and minimize these personal biases to prevent unintentional influences on our thoughts and judgment. Our culture, environment, and upbringing can play a major role in how we feel about certain subjects. In order to think critically, it is important to disregard these extraneous personal influences and make it our goal to be guided by knowledge and facts that are in agreement with reality and truth, even if that means that we have to go against our own previously valued beliefs.

Individually and collectively, we have to be willing to take responsibility for our intellectual abilities and be prepared and confident enough to admit our intellectual weaknesses. It is only then that we become truly empowered and guided by truth. Critical thinking seeks to constrain our thought processes in truth and sound reasoning. Without such constraints, it becomes easy to neglect history, facts, and data to support our positions.

TRUTH AND THE FOUNDERS

The Founders of this great country looked to history for "truth" and guidance in developing a system of government that actually produced freedom and prosperity for the people. It's fair to say that the Founders thought "critically" as they debated and developed the outline for our free Republic. Throughout history, the good "intentions" of man had been highly overrated. The results of those good "intentions" have resulted in tyranny and suffering for the masses. They knew that even under the rule of the most well intentioned leader or king, the nature of man could not be trusted and therefore ultimate power had to stay in the hands of the people. A system of government had to be put in place that would result in maximum freedom and prosperity with minimum governance. Any form of government that was established had to be restrained to protect the rights of the people.

    The American experiment of freedom is actually based more on "what doesn't" work in a functioning, free society than "what does" work. At first, this might sound odd or ridiculous, but the Founders were well educated on historical and modern governing philosophies of their time. Suffering under the tyrannical principles of an English king and monarchy, the Founders knew firsthand what didn't work. The idea that a king four thousand miles away would know what's best for the people in the American colonies was a deep and growing source of contention. With tyranny and taxation ever increasing and freedoms decreasing, the move for independence was born. The men and women who bravely fled the so-called comfort of a king to start a life in America were once again faced with the question —Is man capable of self-government and thriving without a King? Even with doubt and tremendous fear of the unknown, the colonists were brave enough to question the status quo of having an all-powerful, "all-knowing" king. The process of "asking the right questions" had begun and the assumption of loyalty to a king was forever changed. Because of the rapid growth and success of the American colonies, it was only natural that those who started a life in America would want to keep the fruits of their labor. The notion that a king in a distant land had rights over their property and was entitled to a share of their profits that he saw fit, was unacceptable. The idea that man was incapable of self-government and that prosperity can only be given by a king was losing its grip.

The famous British historian, Lord Acton, once said, "All power tends to corrupt, absolute power corrupts absolutely." All we have to do, while standing in line at Starbucks, is look to the side and read any newspaper headline to realize the brilliance of Lord Acton. History had shown the Founders how the world's greatest empires and nations had collapsed due to the centralization and lack of restraint of power. At the time of the American colonies, Britain was a world superpower. Unfortunately for the colonies, they lived under the tyranny of this superpower until their independence. After successfully defeating the British and blessed with the opportunity to create something new, the Founders developed the frame work for self-government that we have today, where freedom is cherished and rights are secured.

- CHAPTER 22 -

UNSTOPPABLE

"It all comes down to faith and focus."

In the opening of the book, I quoted the famous Psalm from the Bible: "The righteous will flourish like a palm tree." —Psalm 92:12-14

These empowering words from scripture compare the strength of the human spirit that is in alignment with the Word of GOD, to the strength and perseverance of the palm tree. It is well known that palm trees in their natural habitat, can endure and persevere in some of the harshest climates and weather conditions throughout the world. In extremely hot and dry climates, it can flourish by having a root system that allows it to be able to tap into deep sources of water underground. During severe storms, the palm tree's deep root system also allows it to withstand torrential rains and hurricane force winds. To add to its ability to endure, the palm tree is also able to bend significantly with the winds. Unlike other species of trees that may break under similar conditions, the palm tree becomes stronger and taller with this bending, as its trunk grows larger due to the continuous stress and forces of the winds. Lastly, to add to all of its amazing qualities and strengths, the palm tree can also produce fruit regardless of changing seasons and weather conditions.

There are many lessons that we can take from the adaptability and strength of the palm tree. Similarly to the conditions and storms that are imposed upon the palm tree, life imposes its own storms on us. Our ability to weather these storms and grow from them is intrinsically connected to how well we heed GOD's Word and His instructions to navigate these storms. Through nature, the palm tree not only has adapted to the harshness of its environment, but it uses its environment as a source of growth and strength. This raises the question for each of us: Are we appreciating and embracing the storms that we are in? As we come face to face with the storms of life, we can choose to plant our roots deep in faith, which will allows us to bend and grow with the storm or we can break or snap as we succumb to the storm —the choice is ours.

A STRONG FOUNDATION

Just when you are cruising along and things finally seem like they are going your way is when life will come up with creative ways to knock you off of your game. It could be something as simple as an argument with a girlfriend, traffic, or someone talking on their cell phone next to you on the treadmill. Life sure can make life tough if we let it. Our ability to deal with life, to keep moving forward, to block out distractions, and to remain unstoppable —It all comes down to faith and focus. Faith in GOD and the ability to focus on the things that matter and not the things that don't. These are the keys that will unlock the doors to our goals and dreams.

Traveling this bumpy road that we call life, I have discovered along the way that one of the best ways to stay on your game is to develop a mental behavior pattern that allows you to push through life's challenges without allowing these challenges to have a negative impact on your overall attitude. This requires you to constantly work on yourself and developing that inside voice that says, "I am bigger than my challenges." Our confidence is born out of this voice. We have all heard the phrase that "We are sometimes our worst enemy." It is up to us to decide whether this holds true or not. Crushing that internal enemy means that you have to stand up to you! "It's not my fault," "This isn't fair," or "Why me?" are just some of the "spirit-destroying" conversations that will play out in your head over and over again if you let them. It's easy to get sucked into a negative back and forth dialogue with yourself. In some ways, it comforts us to have these conversations with ourselves because it removes the responsibility we have to ourselves. Make no mistake about it, being responsible for overcoming our challenges requires work. For most of us, the last thing we want to think about is work, when we are going through a tough situation. Unfortunately, there's no way around this work if we want to become strong in the face of our challenges. Like any task or job that we may despise, but choose to remain committed in hopes of a rewarding outcome, the same is true of working through our challenges. The pay and reward comes in the form of confidence, a stronger sense self, and even a certain level invincibility. None of which would have come without our willingness to push through our challenges on the way to achieving our goals.

In order to get to the point in our lives that we truly and confidently believe in ourselves, we have to be willing to be tested. We have to be willing to persevere through the pressures and the fights on the way to reaching our goals. Sometimes we bring these tests upon ourselves and other times they are presented to us as part of life. In either case, we have to convince ourselves that we are capable and ready for challenges. Throughout my own trials, something as simple as just "believing in myself" has been my strongest weapon in helping me battle some of my toughest challenges. Having studied engineering in college, one of the things I admire the most about having majored in engineering is the intensity and frequency in which I was tested. Making it through all of the calculus, physics, chemistry, and engineering classes is, by far, the toughest thing I have ever accomplished. As a result of that intensive and brutal program, there are quite a number of arrows I have been able to add to my quiver. For example, whenever I face a difficult challenge, I ask myself, "Will getting through this be harder than engineering school?" Every time the answer is no. Also, when attempting to solve a problem and coming up with the answer seems impossible, I remember the importance of stepping away and clearing your head. Sometimes coming back to a problem, with a fresh perspective is all it takes to come up with a workable solution. These are just some of the powerful lessons I picked up in engineering that I am able to apply to everyday life.

Being an engineer is my rock, my foundation. I have to sell myself every day on the idea that I am an engineer and therefore, I am mentally equipped to overcome any challenge and solve any problem that life throws at me. We all have a battle that we are proud of winning, a place of strength where we can spring from to face our challenges. This place should serve as the "foundational rock" for growth and propelling forward as we pursue our goals. It is up to us to sell ourselves every day on the strength of this "foundational rock," which we build our confidence and abilities upon. To acknowledge the existence of our "foundation rock" is the first step in building confidence in knowing what we are capable of achieving. It is evidence of our ability to overcome and make things happen.

ONE NATION UNDER GOD

"Blessed is the Nation
Whose GOD is the Lord." —Psalm 33:12

A rock solid foundation that I share will millions and millions of others is the fact that we were born in the greatest country on Earth, the United States of America. Just considering our history and the odds we faced to even come into existence as a nation is nothing short of a miracle. Relying on their faith, sense of purpose, and the sheer courage to fight for what they believed in, the early American colonist were able to defeat one of the world's greatest empires. At the time, there were many who doubted whether or not a bunch of ill-equipped and sometimes poorly trained colonist even had a chance at defeating the powerful British Empire. Thankfully, there were those who ignored the odds and were committed to the dream of freedom and willing to put it all on the line to achieve this dream. Being one of the millions blessed enough to call this country my home, I consider the opportunities we have in this country a true blessing and something that should never be taken for granted. We are literally standing on the shoulders of giants who built a nation from scratch. Not any nation, but a nation built on timeless principles of freedom, unlike anything in the history of humankind. Knowing the tremendous sacrifice that went into building this great country gives me every reason in the world to be thankful and no reason at all to ever make excuses.

There will be times that you will literally have to declare "all-out war" on the challenges that are standing in the way of your dreams. This is exactly what the founders did when they decided to go to war with Great Britain to win their independence. The founders of this nation had a vision for a country that was different than anything tried before in the modern world. They envisioned a nation of, by, and for the people. A nation free of tyranny and rule by any king, a nation where we, the people are sovereign. A line in the sand was drawn on July 4th, 1776, when the founders of this great nation signed the Declaration of Independence, declaring our independence from Great Britain.

> "We hold these truths to be self-evident, that all men are created equal, that they are endowed by their Creator with certain unalienable Rights, that among these are Life, Liberty and the pursuit of Happiness." - The Declaration of Independence, July 4, 1776

The above quote from the Declaration of Independence is probably the most familiar and quoted statement from this historic document. This is the statement which gave birth to this nation and who we are as people. It defines who we are and what we stand for as Americans. Unlike some other nations of the world, our rights do not come from man, a king or dictator. As an American, we consider all men to be born equal and with certain absolute rights that have been given to us by GOD, our Creator. The first being Life; the second being

Liberty —freedom; the third being the pursuit of Happiness —the right to live life as we see fit. Being free to follow our own destiny should be without force and coercion from the state. Our rights are bound in so much as they do not infringe on the rights of others.

The Founders expressed their grievances with British rule directly in the Declaration of Independence:

> "The history of the present King of Great Britain is a history of repeated injuries and usurpations, all having in direct object the establishment of an absolute Tyranny over these States." —The Declaration of Independence, July 4, 1776

As strongly as the founders and colonies believed in their cause, defeating British rule and achieving independence was unimaginable, even by the strongest supporters of independence. At that time in history, Britain was the world's sole super power. The idea or possibility that a rag tag army put together by thirteen colonies in a distant land could defeat the superior military might of the British Empire was a fantasy at best. As history would eventually prove, GOD had other plans.

In one of the most historical events in humankind, the American Revolutionary War between the thirteen colonies and Great Britain would eventually give birth to the United States of America. Our great nation would go on to grow in size, economic influence and power. Eventually, this new nation, founded on principles of freedom and equality for all, would become a beacon of freedom for people all over the world.

The time period between the colonies winning the war for independence and where we are today as a nation has been filled with challenges and pain as we continue to establish the nation in which the Founders envisioned. The United States of America is a great nation, but not a perfect nation. Men are not perfect and therefore, America is not perfect. As a black person, from a black community, what I have come across as one of the most common sources of resistance to the history and significance of America's founding is the issue of slavery and how it was accepted by the Founders. For some in the black community, it is difficult, if not impossible to look beyond this horrible period in American history. Understandably, the credibility and character of the Founders are put into question, as slavery was tolerated and accepted during our nation's founding. Seeing beyond the evil of slavery and the role the Founders played in its perpetuation tends to prevent the conversation and discussion of the actual vision of the Founders.

How could the Founders come up with a document so profound and liberating to humankind as the Declaration of Independence, but still own slaves and accept the institution of slavery? On the face of it, it doesn't make any sense. Were they just hypocrites? Is the statement "We hold these truths to be self-evident, that all men are created equal" intended only for white people? These are all questions that a cynical person can twirl around in their head for hours and days.

I personally consider the Declaration of Independence a sacred document, not just in the founding of this nation, but in charting the course of freedom for all of mankind. It is an empowering document in every sense of the word. A battle cry for any past or future society that finds itself living under a repressive dictatorship or government. Considering the uphill battle and political circumstances at the time the Declaration of Independence was written, the Founders clearly looked to a higher power for inspiration and guidance in drafting this historic document. The powerful words written by Thomas Jefferson and signed by our Founders, clearly rose above human imperfections. One can only wonder if the Creator himself guided such frail men in their destiny for our new nation.

As I kid, I once asked my mother a question while she was watching the news —"Why is it that all of these other countries all over the world seem to have it so bad and are so poor compared to America? Why are we so lucky?" The news was showing something about starvation and death in Africa. I was in high school at the time and was starting to pay more attention to the news and current events. As a black kid, I felt hurt seeing the sad and poor conditions of the African people on TV. Even though in America, we had all kinds of races of people and poor people among them all, I felt like Black people had it the worst in America. To make my world view at the time worst, I look at the TV and all I see is people of color having it bad. I really wanted to know what people of color did to deserve such pain throughout history and even today —"Why did it seem that the "white" countries had it so good compared to all of the other countries?"

My mother could tell that I wasn't her "only interested in video games" little boy any more. She was surprised by my question and interest in the news. After remaining silent for about thirty seconds, her answer really surprised me. At this time in my mother's life, she was going through a lot due to her divorce and was really into religion. Her life was centered on Jesus and church and everything was judged through that prism. She said that the reason that those countries suffer is because they don't worship Jesus Christ and accept him as their Lord and Savior. I was silent for a bit after her response. At first, it seemed possible that could be it. When I considered which countries where suffering and in chaos, Christianity was not the dominant religion. Then I thought, this could not be the cause. I might not have been an expert on religion or Christianity, but I knew in my heart that suffering and black mail are not the offerings of Jesus and GOD. Besides, in America we have people of all faiths and I didn't see the same type of suffering here. As faithful a Christian as my mother is, I concluded that her view was wrong and selfish at best. Without any answers to the suffering that I witnessed on the news, I eventually moved on from the subject and wouldn't find my answers until nearly twenty years later. It all started with me taking a close look at the phrase "One Nation Under GOD" and really thinking about what that phrase actually implies and means to us as a nation.

When it comes to faith and religion, I am a very private person. It is my opinion that people should be free to worship however and to whomever they see fit. For certain groups of Americans, the battles and arguments of whether the United States of America is "One Nation Under GOD" is a never ending one. As an engineer, I decided to go along with the presumption that the United States of America is "One Nation Under GOD" for the purposes of analyzing the benefits of such a presumption that is shared by so many.

First, let's ask the question: What does it mean to be "One Nation Under GOD?" The pivotal word in this phrase is the word "Under." The term "under" means beneath or below. The words "One Nation" and "GOD" are self-explanatory. If we consider the United States of America to be "One Nation Under GOD," that implies that our nation is "beneath or below" GOD. As for our system of governing, this implies the absence of an all wise king or dictator. Power rests in the hands of the people whose guidance and wisdom come from a higher power, hint the phrase "In GOD We Trust." As a nation, this implies a society where the respect for life, liberty, and property are valued. In practical terms, the United States of America has a constitutionally limited form of government. This ensures that our government remains limited in power and protects the rights of its citizens.

If we take a look at societies that don't operate on principles of human rights and freedom, conditions tend to be unfavorable to prosperity and peace within that society. The tendency for the abuse of power, human rights violations and suffering are common. Thus, I finally arrived at the answer to the question I posed to my mother twenty years ago. After considering what the motto "One Nation Under GOD" means from a practical sense, I can confidently conclude that what we have achieved as a country cannot be anything else but a blessing. As a nation, we have accepted the fact that man is not perfect and therefore he does not possess the wisdom to govern as such. This recognition and acceptance of man's frailties, has allowed us to develop a system that keeps his imperfections in check and allow the people of this great nation to remain free and prosper under their own free will. If we should ever be steered or be derailed from this course set forth by our Founders, we only have to look as far as the first paragraph of the Declaration of Independence to be reminded of what so many fought and died for in establishing this great nation.

> "When in the Course of human events it becomes necessary for one people to dissolve the political bands which have connected them with another and to assume among the powers of the earth, the separate and equal station to which the Laws of Nature and of Nature's GOD entitle them, a decent respect to the opinions of mankind requires that they should declare the causes which impel them to the separation." —The Declaration of Independence, July 4th, 1776

The reason the United States of America is an exceptional nation is because no man has or ever will be our king…GOD is.

RUN YOUR RACE

In a practical sense, it's quite normal to wonder exactly what GOD's grace or intervention looks like. Most of us can give examples in our own lives of how a dire or challenging situation has miraculously turned around in our favor regardless of our own doing. This is often referred to as GOD's grace. No matter how hard we try to explain or understand such miracles in our lives, we typically come up short. Our inability to come up with easy answers to such miracles is only fitting since miracles, by definition, are the handy work of GOD. Human understanding is not required or needed in His world.

If I had to come up with a great example that shows what happens when GOD places his hand on something to produce a miracle, I would have to use the example of the famous world champion racehorse Secretariat. The power, strength, and endurance of this Triple Crown winning racehorse were nothing short of supernatural in the world of horse racing. Many consider Secretariat to be the greatest racehorse to ever live. His build, proportions, muscularity, and size were as close as you can get to perfection in a racehorse. The best description I ever heard regarding this amazing horse was given in a book title. The book is called: *"The Horse GOD Built: The Untold Story of Secretariat, the World's Greatest Racehorse"* by the author Lawrence Scanlan. Based on a book title like this, it seems like I wasn't the only one touched by this very special horse.

I first learned about Secretariat when Disney put out the powerful film titled "Secretariat," which depicting the life and journey of this truly remarkable American thoroughbred racehorse. The film told the courageous story of the owner, Penny Chenery, a devoted wife and mother who sacrificed time with her own husband and children in order to look after her family horse farm. With her mother passing and her father too ill to take care of himself and the farm, Penny took responsibility for looking after her father and the success of the farm. Unfortunately, her aging father eventually passed away and the fate of the farm would completely rest in Penny's hands. It was at this point that Penny decided to take it upon herself to do whatever it took to get the farm back on its feet. Unwavering in her commitment and sense of purpose, Penny was determined to find a way to keep her father's legacy and the family farm alive.

At the start of Penny assuming full responsibility of the family horse farm, there seemed to be few options for resolving the farm's hefty financial burdens other than selling it. Looking for a sign or something to place her hope in, Penny took an interest in a pregnant mare that was expected to drop her foal very soon. According to the storyline in the movie, the future owner of the foal was yet to be determined due to an agreement her father made with the owner of the sire who mated with the mare. The sire was named "Bold Ruler" and was the leading sire in North America at the time. He was owned by a wealthy man by the name of Ogden Phipps. Before his decline in health and eventual death, her father made a deal with Phipps that they would decide who gets which foal by a simple coin toss. For Penny, to stand in her father's place at the coin toss was an honor and would serve as the spark she needed to begin rebuilding the proud legacy of her father's farm.

When that fateful day finally came and the coin was flipped, Penny ended up losing the coin toss, but winning the pick. The colt she received would one day prove itself to be the best second pick anyone could ever ask for. Her journey from this point on would unfold to let her know that she had actually won the toss in more ways than she could have imagined. As the result of fate and a simple coin toss, Penny would come to own one of the greatest racehorses of all times. On March 30, 1970, fate brought a bright-red chestnut colt into the world and into Penny Chenery's life. The baby colt went by the name "Big Red" but eventually was given the official racehorse name of "Secretariat." Those who witnessed the birth say that the baby colt stood up within forty-five minutes of being born! From that moment on, it should have been apparent that this horse was destined to be nothing short of a miracle. When Penny saw her miracle colt for the first time, it marked the beginning of a shared journey towards greatness. This special bond between horse and owner would reveal the undeniable power of faith, love, and commitment.

At the heart of Disney's fantastic portrayal of the life and journey of Secretariat is the role and importance of faith in our lives. It was faith that gave Penny Chenery the strength and courage to fight for the survival and legacy of her family horse farm. Even without the answers, Penny remained strong in her faith that she would find a way to turn things around. In life, it has been said that GOD doesn't always give us what we want but often gives us what we need. The miracle of Secretariat showing up in Penny Chenery's life demonstrates this point so beautifully. The horse that was a second pick in a coin toss gave her everything she needed and more to believe in herself and stay true to the values of a winner that where passed down to her by her father. In turn, she gave Secretariat everything he needed to become the champion he was meant to be. There was a powerful scene in the movie in which Penny first introduced "Big Red" to her father. As he slowly got up from his chair to admire and gently rub the horse's nose, he slowly turned to his daughter and whispered the words "Let him run his race." Incredibly, those few poignant words would spark the journey for the miraculous life of Secretariat. He was allowed to run his race, win or lose. For a true winner, the possibility of losing must never be allowed to be an excuse for not trying. Secretariat was raised, nurtured, and trained in the absence of "fear." As a result, fearlessness and faith unleashed the full potential of this miracle horse and its courageous owner.

 For those of us that were too young at the time Secretariat dominated the world of horse racing, such as myself, Disney does an amazing job creating a present day affection for this special animal. Anyone watching the movie for the first time and unfamiliar with the story of Secretariat like I was, the scene of the final lap of the Belmont in the race for the Triple Crown is a serious nail-biter. The way Disney builds the suspense of not knowing if Secretariat survives the final lap is done masterfully. The jockey that rode Secretariat during the Belmont and throughout the quest for the Triple Crown, Ron "Ronnie" Turcotte, was known in the world of horse racing for pushing a horse to its limit. In fact, he was known for pushing a horse so hard that it caused its heart to burst. Penny knew this when she chose him, but resisted her fears and picked him anyway. She wanted a jockey that would not hold back, that would bring out the champion racehorse that she knew

Secretariat was destined to be. During the final lap of the Belmont, Secretariat would indeed be pushed.

As the dramatic last lap unfolds with Secretariat increasing his tremendous lead, blowing past all of the other horses, the film pans back and forth between the race and the cheering crowd. Amongst the cheers, there were many gasping in disbelief. No one could believe what they were witnessing. Penny was torn between cheering Secretariat to victory and an overwhelming fear for the horse's well-being. The scene was shot perfectly as the movie audience witnesses Penny's internal battle between her faith and succumbing to fear. Faith would eventually win over as Penny's voice penetrates the voices and cheers of the crowd and yells out to Ronnie —"Let him run!" Faith immediately went to work. The result would be the unleashing of the most powerful racehorse the world had ever seen.

The race for the Triple Crown is the emotional high point of the movie. This is the critical moment in the journey in which Penny releases all of her fears and truly lets Secretariat "run his race." All the while knowing that her jockey will push a horse to potentially dangerous limits if that's what it took to win. Penny refused to be held back by fear and lays it all on the line. Secretariat continues at a ferocious pace and continues to increase his lead. As the suspense continues to build, the camera pans over the crowd, showing people cheering but at the same time gasping in disbelief. Suddenly, the camera switches to a view of the final bend of the last lap and stays there, keeping the audience in suspense. All of the racehorses are outside of the camera view. The movie audience is now unaware of who is in the lead. The music and the cheering comes to a complete halt, putting the viewer on the edge of their seat. As someone who didn't know the story of

Secretariat or whether or not he survived this final race for the Triple Crown, I was horrified of how this race and movie might end. My fear was that Secretariat wasn't coming around that bend. All I could think of was that jockey and his reputation for pushing horses to their limit. The suspense was killing me. My excitement of Secretariat winning quickly switched to fear of him not surviving. As soon as I was about to give up hope of him coming around the bend, that's when I saw something on the movie screen that I will never forget. What I saw was one of the most powerful movie scenes I had ever seen in a movie. Breaking the screen silence and suspense, Secretariat comes blasting around the bend in full speed! The thunderous pounding of his hooves hitting the mud, the sheer power and length of his strides, and the speed of this beautiful animal that only GOD could create are captured perfectly in true Disney Magic.

In real life, everything that this horse was meant to be was put on display for the world to see that day at the Belmont. It was as if GOD picked this horse for that day to show off what He can do when we push our faith. Thanks to Penny Chenery pushing her faith, Secretariat was not allowed to be held back in fear. He was allowed to run his race to victory. Just think, the world would never have known this miracle horse if Penny would have given in to fear. The greatness in "The Horse that GOD Built" had been unleashed because someone was willing to test their faith.

THE HUMAN SPIRIT

In terms of power and resilience, there's nothing that can hold a candle to the human spirit. It can experience death, destruction, and disappointment and will still find a way to persevere. We all collectively define the strength of the human spirit. It is our willingness as humans to push ourselves even when life aggressively pushes back. As individuals, the power of the human spirit is exuded most when we make our minds up to accomplish or achieve something and refuse to let anything stand in our way to get it. The famous motivational speaker *Les Brown* discusses in one of his early motivational speeches the power of the human spirit. He defines it as "The power to hold on in spite of everything, the power to endure, the hunger and ability to face defeat again and again without giving up." He goes on to call this "the winner's quality." Having this quality depends on two factors: how we react to life and how much we are willing to fight for the things we want out of life. It all comes down to how bad you want it and the mindset you maintain until you get it.

    Our very existence as country can all be attributed to the strength of the human spirit. The patriots and courageous warriors who gave everything in order to defeat British tyranny and establish this country knew that their cause was worth fighting and even dying for. They were willing to put it all on the line, including their lives, in order to secure freedom, independence, and a better life for themselves and future generations of Americans. Facing insurmountable odds and a superior enemy, the colonies had to be creative and adaptive in order to defeat, what they perceived as, a far superior opponent. The American forces had to constantly look for ways to outsmart or outmaneuver the much larger British forces. It was through winning small battles and achieving strategic victories that the Americans were able to demoralize and finally defeat the once powerful British Empire.

There are many life lessons that can be taken from the battles of the Revolutionary War. The American colonies who fought against the British had a clear sense of purpose —an unwavering commitment to victory and freedom. Because they were relentless in their cause, this served as a force multiplier, making up for any perceived disparities in strength and capabilities between them and the British. Even with doubt, fear, and uncertainty, the colonies pushed forward to achieve their once unimaginable dream —Independence. As individuals in pursuit of our dreams, we also have to be committed and relentless when it comes to our dreams. Maintaining a strong sense of purpose, while being adaptive and resourceful will eliminate doubt and any perceived lack of resources. It has been said that the toughest thing to do is to stay focused on your vision. We instead like to focus on the "when and how." Once the colonies decided to fight the British for their independence, just imagine if they had spent most of their time and efforts on the "when and how." At the time they made the decision to go to war, the answers to the "when and how" didn't exist. To focus on something that doesn't exist is a waste of time. Thankfully, they remained focused on the vision and as a result we have the United States of America. Imagine what you can do if you stay focused on the vision!

"Life will get tired of whipping you sometimes."
—Les Brown

Life has proven to us that with a clear vision, a noble purpose, and an unshakeable commitment to your goal, the universe will acquiesce. Life will step aside because it is no match for the human spirit. It is unstoppable.

NOTES

1. Outpatient Information Guide: Malcolm Grow Medical Clinic. 2012.

2. Quoted in Chris Brady & Orrin Woodward, LEADERSHIP AND LIBERTY: PIECES OF THE PUZZLE (Flint, MI: Obstacles Press, Inc., 2009), 70.

3. Pastor Dale O'Shields, Church of the Redeemer (Gaithersburg, MD) Sermon: January 9-10, 2016.

4. Quoted in Chris Brady & Orrin Woodward, LEADERSHIP AND LIBERTY: PIECES OF THE PUZZLE (Flint, MI: Obstacles Press, Inc., 2009), 81.

5. Quoted in Chris Brady & Orrin Woodward, LEADERSHIP AND LIBERTY: PIECES OF THE PUZZLE (Flint, MI: Obstacles Press, Inc., 2009), 81.

Made in the USA
Middletown, DE
03 July 2019